FIELDWORK

OTHER BOOKS BY BRUCE JACKSON

Rainbow Freeware (1986)
Law and Disorder: Criminal Justice in America (1984)
Doing Drugs (with Michael Jackson, 1983)
Get the Money and Shoot (1981)
Your Father's Not Coming Home Any More (editor, 1981)
Death Row (with Diane Christian, 1980)
The Programmer (1979)
Killing Time: Life in the Arkansas Penitentiary (1977)
Get Your Ass in the Water and Swim Like Me: Narrative
Poetry from Black Oral Tradition (1974)
In the Life: Versions of the Criminal Experience (1972)
Wake Up Dead Man: Afro-American Worksongs from Texas Prisons (1972)
A Thief's Primer (1969)
The Negro and His Folklore in 19th Century Periodicals (editor, 1967)
Folklore and Society (editor, 1966)

FIELDWORK

Bruce Jackson

UNIVERSITY OF ILLINOIS PRESS
Urbana and Chicago

Portions of "Truth and Voice," in the Appendix, appeared previously in Bruce Jackson and Diane Christian, 1986, *Le quartier de la mort*, 1–5, Paris: Terre Humaine (Librairie Plon). Used by permission.

Portions of "Points of View and Points of Departure," in Part One, appeared previously in Bruce Jackson, 1985, "Things That From a Long Way Off Look Like Flies," *Journal of American Folklore* 98: 131–47. Used by permission.

FIRST PAPERBACK EDITION, 1987
© 1987 by Bruce Jackson
Manufactured in the United States of America
P 12 11 10 9 8

This book is printed on acid-free paper.

Library of Congress Cataloging-in-Publication Data
Jackson, Bruce.
   Fieldwork.

   Bibliography: p.
   Includes index.
     1. Folklore—Field work. 2. Social sciences—
Field work. I. Title.
GR45.5.J33   1987   390'.072   86-16010
ISBN 0-252-01372-7 (paper: alk. paper)
ISBN 978-0-252-01372-0 (paper: alk. paper)

For George Beto

You see what you ought to see.
Euripides
The Bacchae

To see its function is not to explain its existence.
Philip Slater
Pursuit of Loneliness

It is easier to write down the story than to observe the diffuse, complex ways in which it enters into life, or to study its function by the observation of the vast social and cultural realities into which it enters. And this is the reason why we have so many texts and why we know so little. . . .
Bronislaw Malinowski
"The Role of Myth in Life"

Contents

Part Four/Ethics

Acknowledgments

If you're lucky, you have time and money to make mistakes before you get into situations you can't ever repeat and which you never forgive yourself for having botched, and you have friends and teachers who'll help you learn from the mistakes you've been making so the work isn't a total loss. I was lucky.

I began doing fieldwork in 1960 when I was a graduate student in the School of Letters at Indiana University. W. Edson Richmond encouraged me to pursue my interest in folksong, a subject not much in favor at the time in the Indiana University folklore program. Judith McCulloh and Ellen Stekert, then graduate students in folklore, taught me the fundamentals of recording and helped me understand some of my early fieldwork problems. In the summer of 1962, Richard M. Dorson gave me a research assistantship, which permitted me to spend a great deal of time working in the IU Archive of Folk and Primitive Music, where George List set me to work copying MacEdward Leach's collection of ballads done on quarter-inch paper tape and preparing the master tape for the Folkways LP based on Caspar Cronk's field recordings from Nepal (Cronk, 1964). I developed an affection for ballads sung without accompaniment and for Sherpa tunes; I also learned a great deal about the technology of recording and became far more sensitive than I had been to the need for decent field recordings and substantial field documentation.

Several friends and colleagues over the years encouraged me to undertake field projects I might not otherwise have dared, helped me find money with which to do the work, and discussed with me the meaning and value of the pieces of the world I was bringing home. Of these, I especially want to thank Carey McWilliams, B. A. Botkin, Crane Brinton, Harry T. Levin, Wassily Leontief, Robert Creeley, George Beto, John Gagnon, Billy Lee Brammer, Al Hart, John Cohen, William M. Kunstler, Bud Johns, Henri Korn, Margaret Ratner, Gershon Legman, and Pete and Toshi Seeger.

Even at home fieldwork can be expensive. I'll say nothing here about the churlish and shortsighted foundations that rejected my projects over the years, but will with pleasure once again give thanks for the opportunity to work and learn afforded me by the Guggenheim Foundation, Harvard Society of Fellows, National Endowment for the Arts, National Endowment for the Humanities, New York Council for the Humanities, American Philosophical Society, Fund for Investigative Journalism, American Film Institute, Playboy Foundation, Wenner-Gren Foundation for Anthropological Research, Levi Strauss Foundation, Polaroid Foundation, and the Research Foundation of the State University of New York.

Edward D. (Sandy) Ives's *Tape-Recorded Interview* (1980) is, as I note in the Introduction, the best starting place for a novice fieldworker concentrating on taped interview material. Our books differ in the range of jobs we expect our readers to be taking on, the complexity of the questions we expect them to be asking, and the variety of machinery we expect them to be using. Ives, as his title indicates, wrote a manual for individuals using tape recorders to document interviews; I've tried to cover the range of field situations likely to be encountered by folklorists and fieldworkers in several closely associated disciplines. I think we agree on basic principles for doing fieldwork. We've been friends for more than twenty years, we've discussed these matters in the contexts of our own fieldwork and teaching on many occasions, and we've read each other's books. If we're right on the basic issues, those aspects of our separate texts *should* concur. At several points in these pages I quote from or refer to Ives's work; if some other passages are close in spirit to passages written by Ives, that's because part of this book necessarily covers some of the ground covered by his and because in the course of fieldwork we both learned the same logical lessons. Ives read this manuscript in detail and offered many useful suggestions for improving it. He has my thanks for the immediate help and for years of being a pal.

Earlier drafts of the manuscript were read by William A. Wilson, Robert Byington, Christopher LaLonde, and Patricia Gannon, all of whom provided useful suggestions for improvement.

I especially want to thank Ellen Stekert and Judith McCulloh for their extremely cogent and helpful criticism of the manuscript of *Field-*

work, for their advice in various matters relating to folklore theory and practice over the years, and for their very practical and immeasurably useful counsel when I was president of the American Folklore Society and when I become editor of the *Journal of American Folklore*.

Theresa Sears, my editor at the University of Illinois Press, offered advice that significantly improved the texture and tone of the manuscript. Authors' thanks to editors are often pro forma. My gratitude to Terry is real: she has a fine eye and a sensitive ear.

Diane Christian, my working partner in all of my fieldwork since 1972 and collaborator on *Death Row* and four other documentary films, was directly involved in many of the field events described here and in events that provided the grounding for many suggestions offered here. We talked through aspects of the work and the ethical implications of it and discussed them further when Diane read the first and last drafts of this manuscript. I taught Diane how to use the machines but she taught me something far better.

Introduction

This is a book about the logic and machinery of fieldwork. It's a book I long wished someone else would write. I wanted a book I could recommend to students and colleagues that would give them a sense of the kinds of questions asked and problems encountered by folklorists who do fieldwork, the kinds of documenting equipment available, and the principles governing the use of such equipment. When I first realized I would have to write this book myself, I thought I would devote nearly all the space to technical matters, but in the course of doing the work I realized that discussions of field use of equipment are pointless without antecedent and collateral discussions of the ends of such use. So the book is about the logic of fieldwork and how to use fieldwork machines logically and honorably.

Fieldwork isn't an easy book—but useful fieldwork isn't easy. I define "useful fieldwork" as field research from which the researcher learns something and by which valid information is obtained.

I tried to structure the chapters so individuals with varying levels of competence could take from them what was particularly relevant to their situation. *Fieldwork* should be useful to starting students and to experienced professionals who realize they should know more than they do. If the book were used in the context of a class, with an experienced teacher as guide, it could be useful at any level. Some sections may have no meaning or applicability until some fieldwork has been done; skip them now and come back later when they have something to say to you. (There are novels I read as an undergraduate, a graduate student, a teacher, and just for pleasure; the four readings varied enormously, but all were useful in their different ways.) I hope *Fieldwork*

1

will also be useful for reference purposes—to answer specific questions about specific problems.

Fieldwork is principally directed toward workers in folklore, but nearly everything in it can be applied with equal validity to fieldwork in any of the other social sciences or humanities. Workers in those other disciplines don't expect the same kinds of information as folklorists do from fieldwork, and they present their conclusions in different disciplinary vocabularies, but the ethical questions, the human relationships involved, and the technologies utilized are the same. Those matters are not altered by parochial concerns resulting from academic divisions of labor.

Other books deal with segments of the problem. Robert A. Georges and Michael O. Jones's *People Studying People* (1980) is a thoughtful examination of some ethical and interpersonal aspects of social science research. Several authors provide extensive and lucid detail on how to film, how to record sound, and how to photograph (I especially recommend Pincus and Ascher, 1984, and Clifford, 1977). I know of no single book that looks at those crafts in terms of the fieldworker's very specific needs. Kenneth S. Goldstein's *Guide for Field Workers in Folklore* (1964), now more than twenty years old, is a good introduction for someone doing salvage folklore (seeking the remnants of defunct oral traditions in waning communities), but that's not the sort of work many folklorists do now. The best single book for a novice fieldworker concentrating on interview material is Edward D. Ives's *Tape-Recorded Interview* (1980), but interviewing is only one of several strategies available to the collector of folklore.

Most fieldwork manuals or guides are designed either for the absolute novice or the sophisticated professional concerned with a narrow technical or conceptual problem. It's been my experience that both novice and experienced fieldworkers continually encounter new kinds of questions and the options for utilizing new kinds of technology. I see no need for, and some disutility in, treating fieldwork activity as if it were different for one kind of researcher than another. The only differences are in the confidence in focus of the motivating question, amount of time available, and sense of what will be done with the material once the fieldwork is completed. Student fieldworkers know they'll get grades and that the work best be done before the semester ends; professors doing fieldwork know they'll acquire data that may find their way into articles or books and that they need not shut the fieldwork down until their money runs out, sabbatical or vacation is over, or sufficient information is in hand. Those are matters external to the actual work done; they have nothing to do with ethics or technology or methodology.

It's useful for the novice to know how complex things can get. You don't have to *do* it all to learn about the problems and goals of it all. No fieldworker ever uses every available technology or pursues all the potential lines of investigation. But knowing the options and limitations of the technology and considering various methods of investigation will help the researcher know what's possible, what's probable, and what's dreamy. Dreams can be delightful, but success or failure in a field project is real, hence the design should be one that can work in the real world. My hope is that novice fieldworkers will find here suggestions that will make the early work useful and satisfying, and that experienced fieldworkers will find here suggestions for dealing with the more complex problems encountered in their expanding sense of what fieldwork can accomplish.

Few teachers of introductory or advanced folklore or oral history or ethnography courses have time to deal adequately with fieldwork techniques and problems. Students are often expected to do fieldwork, but the teacher doesn't have time to teach them how to do it. The only kind of class in which field techniques are explored in depth is a seminar in fieldwork, and few of those are available. This book is designed to serve anyone who wants to know what fieldwork is about and how to go about doing it.

Fieldwork is about how fieldworkers define their function, how they deal with people they meet in the field, and how they capture for later use media records of what transpired in their presence. My concern is not with the capture of physical objects themselves—pots and baskets and blankets and statues cataloged and brought home for a museum. The collection and documentation of objects, as done by ethnographers or by folklorists specializing in material culture, require skills and concerns in many ways different from those of a folklorist interested in aspects of performance (text, context, or performer), or an oral historian interested in spoken versions of specific factual events, or a sociologist or anthropologist interested in life histories or social histories. Context is critical for all fieldworkers in the human sciences, but it's not critical and it's not defined in the same ways for all of them.

Much of *Fieldwork* deals with specific and practical matters: the difference in filmstocks, how to place a microphone, the comparative advantages of different kinds of machines, how to phrase questions. I hope the book is of practical use in specific situations; I also hope it's of more general use in helping fieldworkers and the users of fieldwork done by others understand the kinds of structures encouraged or discouraged by certain kinds of technology. Every question implies a category of answer, and every machine limits the field of acceptable response. The questions we ask and the machines we use do not merely provide data; they also structure the data we get. The first and immediate purpose of this book is to help people engage in fieldwork intelligently and usefully; the second and long-range purpose is to help people better understand the character and validity of studies based on fieldwork by others.

Fieldwork is not about the analysis of events or objects recorded in the field. There are many models for analysis and there are fashions in the currency of those models as specific and transient as the fashions in literary criticism or automobile manufacture or clothing style. Models for analysis matter in fieldwork insofar as they inform the kind of interrogation done by a fieldworker, and I do try to help fieldworkers be aware of models that might be structuring their vision. It sometimes happens that models seen as useful before the field experience no longer seem adequate during or after the field experience. Doing fieldwork requires continual seeing and continual revising. "The fact that the participant observer constantly redesigns his study as he uncovers new data," write Becker and Geer, "indicates that he engages in analytic activity most of the time that he is in the field. This analysis is often carried on unsystematically, without any consideration of its underlying logical structure or rationale. The observer's 'hunches' and 'insights' are in fact truncated and unformalized acts of analysis" (1960:270–71).

The field data are therefore always antecedent to any analysis and the application of data to any model can never be more valid than the data is itself. "It is impossible," George List used to say to his students, "to overdocument a recording." He was right, for the potential utility of the raw information in any collection is determined by the initial documentation, by the collateral information that tells later users what the data really are. My assumption is that valid data can be used in the service of any valid analytic theory, so long as we know how it was obtained, but that no theory in application can produce useful conclusions if it's based on field information itself distorted or contaminated. The real test of the completeness of a body of field data is not how well it works with whatever model of analysis the collectors hoped to apply before they entered the field, but rather how well it works with models of analysis not even considered relevant or known to the collectors at the time the fieldwork was carried out.

The fieldworker's job is not finished when the fieldwork is over, for something must be done with the material that was gathered. The alternatives are endless. What should be transcribed? what summarized? what merely indexed? what forms should be used? Different institutions and individuals have different archiving styles and utilization plans. This book tells you how to get the information; what you do with it is another conversation entirely. (Ives's *Tape-Recorded Interview* [1980] is written with archiving in mind, and indeed a large portion of his book is devoted to archiving questions and forms, especially pp. 94–122). Some material should be put in an archive, some should be developed into an article or book or film (and perhaps also made available to or archived for persons who might later question how the conclusions were derived or the data obtained); some should form the basis for a class paper, some should be trashed and forgotten. Often, the same body of collectanea will find many different uses as parts of different kinds of discussions. One exciting aspect of this work is realizing you've found things you had no idea would be there and can subsequently do work you couldn't previously have known was there to be done.

I couldn't write (and wouldn't much want to write if I could) an abstract book about fieldwork. The problems and pleasures are too specific for that. This is a personal book about a general subject. Most sections are based on what has or hasn't worked for me or people I know, and the discussions are about why I think some things worked well and other things worked badly. What works for one fieldworker may or may not be equally useful to another, but the mistakes made by one are almost certainly of use to another, and the mistakes should always be useful to the person who made them. "How do we keep from going through these things twice?" asks Bob Dylan. One answer is: Try to figure out what happened the first time and do something or stand somewhere else next time around.

My primary field interest has been how people present and interpret their life situations. I don't believe anybody can ever tell you exactly what happened; people can tell you how they perceive what they think happened. So it's their perceptions and their articulations of those perceptions that fascinate me, and those are the elements from which I fashion most of my books and films. You might have a different goal and it might very well require a different fieldworking style. You might look and you might be more or less gullible than I, more or less naive, more or less knowing—all those things influence the kind and depths of detail you'll get. Even so, we share many of the same questions, have access to the same technologies, and have the same responsibilities to our informants, to other fieldworkers, and to the people who make whatever use of our research.

Learning to do fieldwork is like learning to drive a car: you can be taught the techniques, but each utilization of technique is a new creative moment, one absolutely specific to itself. You may know how to work the levers, buttons, and pedals of your car perfectly, but to get somewhere you must have your own plan of action and you must do the driving and deal with whatever impediments the world puts in your way as you go. You must bring to the task sensitivity and sensibility, factors very much beyond technique and technology. Likewise for fieldwork. "The situations and circumstances in which field observation of human behavior is done are so various that no manual of detailed rules would serve," wrote sociologist Everett C. Hughes. "It is perhaps less clear, but equally true, that the basic problems are the same in all situations. It is the discovery of this likeness inside the shell of variety that is perhaps the greatest and most important step in learning to be an effective and versatile observer" (1960:xii).

We each do fieldwork for our own reasons and we each have our own ways of fulfilling the needs that result from those reasons. As I wrote the technical and practical parts of this book, I realized my perceptions about method and problems were wedded to the kinds of things I was trying to accomplish in my own work. My ideas about fieldwork have been articulated at my desk, but they didn't develop there. So I decided to discuss in this book a number of things that happened to me while I was working on various projects. Those incidents and those learnings are my authority for offering this advice, far more than the books and records that resulted from the research. I worried this might seem more autobiographical than necessary or proper in a book written for workers in the field, but casting the perceptions in the abstract or resorting to the fictive "one" would be disingenuous and probably even silly. This didn't happen in the abstract; fieldwork isn't done in the abstract; you won't do it in the abstract. The personal stories are here simply because they're the stories I know most about, not because Jack Horner is my authorial role model. Knowing my contexts for these suggestions may help you better judge the value and limitations of them—and thereby better understand your own contexts and the value of your own work.

All technical words and terms used in a technical or specialized way are defined when they first appear in the text. Five words should be defined up front.

Collectanea. Folklorists refer to everything nonpersonal and non-contagious brought home from the field as "collectanea." The category includes tapes, notes, pictures, films, drawings—all the things they've labeled and put into pockets or boxes or the trunk of the car. I loathe the sound of the word; it has the rhythm of an annoying and recurrent gastrointestinal disease. I avoid the word whenever I can, but sometimes I can't avoid it and I use it. If I could think of a better word that expressed the same notion I would adopt it; and I serve notice that I welcome suggestions for replacement of "collectanea" in future editions of this book.

Fieldwork. I like Everett C. Hughes's description: "Field work refers, in this volume, to observation of people *in situ;* finding them where they are, staying with them in some role which, while acceptable to them, will allow both intimate observation of certain parts of their behavior, and reporting it in ways useful to social science but not harmful to those observed" (1960:v).

Informant. I use the word "informant" a great deal in this book. I'm not happy with it, but I don't have another word that serves all its functions quite so well. Denotatively, the word means simply "someone who provides information," but connotatively it can be more troublesome. The historian or folklorist or anthropologist or sociologist speaking of his or her "informants" better not do that around individuals who have been or who fear being the subjects of investigations by one government agency or another. During the 1960s the FBI regularly placed informants within civil rights and antiwar organizations; in prison, informants sometimes get themselves killed and their associates get themselves ostracized; in industrial organizations, informants are the people who tell management about employee pilferage and new union organizing. Rosalie Wax, who did fieldwork among interned Japanese Americans during World War II, wrote, "I never used the term 'informant.' It carried the connotation of 'informer.' Instead, informants were called 'the people who talk to me' " (1960b:167). Some folklorists use "respondent," "participant," "interviewee," or "sources"—one term more ungainly and euphemistic and imprecise than the next. Rayna Green recently suggested the word "consultant," but that introduces more confusions than it abolishes.

The son of anthropologist A. L. Kroeber objected to a published reference to his father's informants. "The Boasian anthropology [A. L. Kroeber] practiced was a two-way transaction: the Indians with whom Kroeber and Boas worked extensively—George Hunt, Juan Dolores, Robert Spott—they regarded not as 'informants' but as friends and colleagues. Not until I had grown up and left home did I learn

the technological meaning of 'informant.' Although my father must
have used the word in conversation, I cannot recall him doing so. And
even today the idea of referring to Juan Dolores or Robert Spott as
an 'informant' turns my stomach. There are several appropriate names
for someone who shares with you his knowledge and experience and
dreams, but 'informant' is not one" (Karl Kroeber in Swann, 1983:352).
H. David Brumble III, whose writing had aroused Kroeber's ire, dis-
agreed: "It probably ought to be noted that A. L. and Theodora Kroeber
evidently did not share Karl Kroeber's distaste for the term 'informant.' Theodora Kroeber wrote: 'I myself never saw Kroeber with an
interpreter, since the informants who were also our friends happened
also to be bilingual . . . Juan Dolores [and] Robert Spott' among others.
And A. L. Kroeber could mention 'Robert Spott, who is named as
informant,' just as he so mentioned hundreds of others who provided
'information' " (in Swann, 1983:361).

The fact is, sometimes "informant" does mean an informer in the
vile sense of the word: those who for whatever reason betray people
who believe they are their friends to people they believe are their
enemies. Such informants may do it because they're not what they
seem; they may do it to prevent injury to innocent people; they may
do it for a thousand reasons. And sometimes the word means the
provider of a song, a story, directions along confusing country roads.
In the broadest sense an informant is simply someone who provides
information, as Brumble says; the denotation is unambiguous. In this
book, as everywhere else, you'll have to derive the connotation from
the context.

Performance. In the context of fieldwork, "performance" means any
situation in which one person or group of persons provides information
to the fieldworker. The situation might be a recorded conversation, a
formal interview, the telling of a story or singing of a song or doing
of a dance for the fieldworker alone or for an audience of several
thousand cheering strangers. Informants doing things for a fieldworker—
displaying their art or discussing their lives—are performing for the
fieldworker; informants doing things for and with other people are
performing for those other people, whether or not they consciously
perceive their interactions as performance. This usage has been common long enough in folklore and anthropology and needs no justification here.

Record. As a verb, "record" means to capture and preserve information by any technology available: notes, audiotape, videotape, film,
photograph. The noun is what you have after you've done that verb.

If I'm referring to the objects that are used on phonographs I'll indicate the restrictive usage.

Finally, I should tell you that I've never had what I'd call a perfect field experience—a trip where everything went exactly as I'd planned and where I later thought I'd obtained everything I should've obtained. The first few times I sensed the difference in expectation and achievement I was troubled by it; now it rarely bothers me at all. The reason is this: Fieldwork, if done seriously (seriously, not grimly; you can have fun in the process), is always a real learning event, so you're never quite the same person after it's over. There's no reason you should have exactly the same questions afterward as you had before, because if you've done the work well you won't be the same person when it's done. For most of us that growth is as satisfying and important a part of the enterprise as the book that gets published or the grade that is earned.

Part One/Human Matters

Fieldwork requiring people to study other people at first hand . . . entails much more than merely knowing what to observe and how to record, process, and present it. The fieldworker must explain his or her presence and purpose to others, gain their confidence and cooperation, and develop and maintain mutually acceptable relationships. These requirements create dilemmas, produce confrontations, demand clarifications and compromises, and evoke reflections and introspection that one can neither fully anticipate nor prepare for in advance. Worthwhile projects may fail. Research strategies frequently must be modified or abandoned as researchers and subjects interact. Unexpected opportunities, fruitful leads, and important insights can blossom as fieldwork develops.

Robert A. Georges and
Michael O. Jones
People Studying People

1/Doing Fieldwork

The Hows and Whys of It

Only a lunatic or a person with a great deal of time and a steady income wanders the countryside or cityscape with notebook, camera, and recorder doing fieldwork at random. Collecting whatever comes along without some informing idea probably shouldn't be called fieldwork at all—there should be some other word for it, like "scooping" or "pack-ratting." Fieldwork done sanely is usually done in the service of some specific end; it's planned and deliberate. The work has its pleasures, but it's so often difficult that few fieldworkers do it for amusement only.

Thousands of folklore studies are based on fieldwork; only a few of those studies include commentaries on how and why the fieldwork was done or tell us much about moments the writers found interesting or memorable. I know of no *study* of folklore fieldwork itself, no study in which one folklorist observed the fieldwork techniques of another and used that observation to evaluate the quality and relevance and representativeness of what the first fieldworker brought home. I don't know of any folklorist whose introductory remarks about the collecting tell it all. Some are embarrassed to write so much about themselves; some don't want to tell the truth, some don't know it, and some don't remember it; some never paid enough attention to their own presence to have anything to say about it; some would have so much they'd like to say about themselves there wouldn't be room left for the material found in the field.

What did John A. Lomax do when his informants sang songs he didn't like? What did he say and do when they interspersed in their folksy repertoires songs they learned from the radio or the jukebox? What did Elsie Clews Parsons tell those islanders and Indians she was doing and how did they respond to her presentations of self? Richard M. Dorson published many stories about how he discovered his informants—but he says nothing about how he conducted himself once they were found, what he did in the silences, how he encouraged or discouraged conversation that varied from his predetermined themes. The absent information isn't in my books either; I'm as guilty as everybody else. Nine of my books are based primarily on field research, but in only one is there more than a page or two about the conditions of recording. There's information about the facts of performance—but little about how my work got done, how my tapes were made, how the people I recorded happened to be recorded by me and how the tapes happened to have the content they have. And there's even less about things that didn't work out the way I'd planned or hoped.

Physical scientists often publish their failed experiments. Though not as satisfying as successful ones, certain failures give information that is truly useful. If nothing else, a well-documented failure says, "You don't have to bother with this technique. It doesn't work, at least not in this place or the way I tried it." If you read publications in the humanities and social sciences, you won't learn much about failures, about projects that didn't pan out, about ideas that led to nothing interesting or useful. Folklorists report their successes, not their failures. It would be wonderfully useful to read about field trips that didn't work out: a trip to the Trobriand Islands that resulted in nothing but a rash that didn't go away for two months, a search for an industrial tradition that wasn't there, a week with a family that answered every question in grunts or monosyllables. Those things happen. One of the very rare reports of error in an area close to folklore is Charles Keil's introductory note on why his study of Tiv song and dance worked out differently than he had planned (1979:1–4). Keil's remarks about errors in strategy and inadequacy of preparation are instructive; similar remarks by others doing similar work would also be instructive, but they haven't been forthcoming. ("There'll be plenty of them in my next book," wrote Sandy Ives in a recent letter. The book is "on a poacher. A great idea that didn't work—and serendipity that did.") Some enterprising publisher might start a *Newsletter of Abandoned and Busted Projects*. We might learn where not to go, or at least what routes might not be worth taking, and we might know what accepted methods deserve significant modification. Physical scientists, in publishing their failures, help their brethren more than do workers in the humanities and social sciences.

The literature isn't silent just about failure. It's equally silent about feelings. Other than *Let Us Now Praise Famous Men,* I can think of no extensive report about fieldwork in which the author tells us how he or she really *felt* about things that mattered while in the field. Agee tells us about women for whom he lusted, men he liked or disliked; he writes of the fantasies he conjured in the deep of night and hints at how those imaginings influenced his perceptions in the light of day. We all have emotional responses to the people we meet and the situations we encounter, and those responses influence significantly our own behavior and vision in the field, but rarely do we tell of those things. "It is possible," writes John M. Johnson,

> to review the methodological literature with an eye to discovering how social scientists conceive their actual conduct as scientists, that is, their implied model of competent scientific inquiry. When this is done, two major emphases are unmistakable. First, an implied model of rational scientific decision making consistently emerges in this literature. For example, unlike many of the rest of us, who sometimes do things and then figure out "reasons" for them after the fact, scientists appear always to know what course of action they will elect prior to engaging in any actual conduct. The decision may change, of course, as additional information becomes available, but these alterations of research practice are also made on rational grounds. The second major emphasis is the very strong one on thinking and other cognitive operations by scientific observers. Most of us have an intuitive understanding that our personal feelings are very important ingredients of our everyday practical affairs. There is a vast range of human feelings, and most of us understand the importance of sexual desire, love, hate, resentment, infatuation, exhaustion, and all the others. These are often the prime movers of our daily actions. But the methodological literature contains very few references to the writers' feelings. On the whole, it is impossible to review the literature about methods in the social sciences without reaching the conclusion that "having feelings" is like an incest taboo in sociological research. (1975:146–47)

I never thought much about this sort of thing until I began working on this book. That's when I went back to many collections I'd liked in the hope of finding detailed information about how and why those collections came to be. Except for Ives's books on Lawrence Doyle and Joe Scott (1971, 1978) and the very recent anthology by Tony Larry Whitehead and Mary Ellen Conaway (1986), I rarely found much detail. I went to autobiographical books and essays by collectors I respected in the hope of learning what they'd *felt* about what they were doing and who they were meeting, what they'd learned from attempts that didn't work out. Few of them say anything at all about their feelings as humans for humans; few of them tell anything about attempts that didn't work out. (Such information, Ellen Stekert reminds me, sometimes exists in a researcher's notebooks or dictated tapes, but those notes are even more difficult to cast into publishable form than the usual reports from the field.)

Fieldwork involving other people is one of the most intensively personal kinds of scholarly research I know. Everything about the fieldworker influences the information collected. A scholar studying Melville can bring to the study the quirkiest flukes of personality, but our potential of knowing Melville's work won't be harmed by those flukes at all. The original texts are there for someone less quirky to examine and to set things straight. But quirky fieldworkers—how can we ever evaluate the balance or fairness of their insights? How can we know how much their style of work controlled what we have to examine now?

However much fieldworkers tell us of the contexts in which their information was gathered, can they ever tell us (or themselves know) enough about how their own presence altered or defined the context? A fieldworker doesn't merely observe a context; the fieldworker close enough to observe it becomes part of it.

The paucity of personal information in most folklore studies isn't always a result of people trying to hide anything. Rather, it's a matter of the wonderful power of retrospect: most of us come to believe that our purpose was to do this book in this way. A subtle process happens to collectors when their fieldwork material turns out to be good. (We'll put aside for now a discussion of what "good material" means and implies.) The finished study becomes a statement about that kind of music, that kind of story, those informants, that place in space or time. We—the collectors and editors and analyzers—seem, even to ourselves, relatively unimportant in relation to that material. The motives that got us out into the field may seem in retrospect trivial or whimsical, if we remember them at all. The mistakes we made take a lot of space to describe and explain—why take up space for that? The things we did that were wonderfully smart and perceptive—bragging isn't seemly. So we get the results of fieldwork done and the reconstructions of what perhaps happened during fieldwork and before fieldwork. Almost never do we learn enough about how and why the books were written so we can place the published material into any perspective beyond the studies themselves.

The ends perceived at the beginning of the fieldwork may not be the ends to which the collected material is actually put, just as the uses made of the material may have little to do with the initial intentions of the collectors. That's common enough in this world: the maker of a frying pan wants to make money from its manufacture; the user of a frying pan wants an omelet or wants to whack a burglar over the head. Often, the collecting experience supplies the collectors with reasons for revising their goals and expectations and definitions. If the collectanea is at all reliable and if it's decently presented or preserved, other scholars may come along later to utilize the material in ways the collector didn't foresee and couldn't have foreseen. It's not that the later users are smarter or more insightful than the original collector; rather, they have the benefit of knowing what the collector found. Those later utilizations—new uses by the collector or subsequent uses by others—are possible only if the material collected is acquired, documented, and preserved in ways that make it intelligible and meaningful.

Many teachers of introductory folklore courses require their students to take on a fieldwork project rather than the usual college term paper done in a library. Some student collections find publication in their own right; many more are deposited in regional archives. These collections become part of the data base available for use by other scholars. I consider that a minor and dispensable reason for doing fieldwork: undergraduate classes don't exist so some archive can have its holdings augmented; the classes exist so people can learn things.

The major reason many teachers of folklore have their students do field projects is they believe the only way a student can appreciate the kind of information found in the materials being studied in class is by engaging in the experience that produces such information. Students in college literature classes have already done a lot of writing: all have written class papers, and many have also written stories, poems, diaries, or letters. They may not be good at what they write, but they have a sense of the labor involved. If a teacher assigns them a library research paper, they get some sense of the kind of work done by scholars who do critical or analytic works. Not a profound sense, but some measure of the labor. That's exactly what the fieldwork experience can do for the novice folklore student. It lets the student appreciate how the information is found or ferreted out and how utterances or events in a place become available for analysis and study.

Some folklore instructors insist that their students produce successful field projects—they want the students to know beforehand what they're going to get; they want the students to get what they thought they would find; and they expect the material to be interesting. Others—me included—have other expectations. I've had enough of my own field projects turn out differently than I expected, or not turn out at all, and I know that success can't ever be guaranteed in advance. All one can do is prepare as well as one can, take pleasure in the successes, and try to learn from the failures. I'm happy when my students come up with a good product as a result of their labors, but I'm more interested in having them experience the process itself. If they've designed a reasonable inquiry for themselves, made an honest attempt to pursue their subject, and understood what may have gone wrong, they've done their job and the assignment has served its purpose.

Usually, the neatest reasons for doing fieldwork are clarified only after the fact: we see what we got and develop a rationale for having gotten exactly that. Beforehand, the reasons may be simpler or vaguer or more personal. Those reasons are important, even if they may not be the ones you remember later on.

When you go off on that trip you haven't had the fieldwork experience yet, you haven't seen those things or talked with those people. When you're doing the work you're not just getting bits and pieces of things that go onto your tapes and films and into your notebooks, you're also learning things and seeing new configurations of materials and ideas.

I would probably say that if you finished the field project and got exactly what you'd expected and did with it exactly what you'd planned, that you'd planned a simple-minded project to start with and your fieldwork was superficial and so was your thinking about what you'd seen.

Be ready for surprises and be ready to welcome the unexpected.

The Answers You Give

Fieldworkers in folklore usually give one of three answers when they're asked why they're making all those notes and asking all those questions.

One answer is "I have to do it to get a passing grade in my folklore course." If that's your only reason for doing fieldwork, you may have to come up with something else when you talk to your informants (unless they're Mom, Pop, or Truelove), because if you offer nothing but maintaining your GPA as justification for taking up someone's time, you're going to be insulting them and they shouldn't bother talking to you. "To fulfill the requirements of a course" as the only justification says you're not interested in what they've got to say or in them; they're only a means to an artificial end. If that's the best you can come up with, collect the folklore of toilet walls or something else that doesn't require encounters with real people.

Another answer—more common among folklorists and anthropologists a generation ago than now, but still valid—is to preserve something that might otherwise be lost. This is sometimes called "salvage folklore," about which I'll say more later.

A third answer—probably one of the most common and most genuine, whether or not it's the one most collectors offer—is "I like blues/stories/dances/family history/industrial behavior/whatever." Most folklorists who do fieldwork are sincerely interested in the people and the material they're studying. The people fieldworkers meet are like anyone else: they can tell when someone is honestly interested in what they have to say and they're likely to respond well to such interest; they also can tell when someone isn't interested in what they have to say, and they're likely to respond badly to such disinterest.

It's not just *your* motives in fieldwork that deserve thought. You should also consider the informants' motives for helping you. Be ready with reasonable answers when someone asks, "What are you doing here? Why are you doing this? What's in it for you? What's in it for me?" If you can't think of reasons that make sense from their point of view, get help or rethink what you're doing.

The Phases of Fieldwork

Fieldwork consists of three phases:

Planning—in which you decide what you want to do, why you want to do it, what resources you need to do it, what you hope to do with it, and then consider what research may already have been done on the same subject;

Collecting—in which you gather the information and make your notes and observations about the information, its character, and the collecting events;

Analyzing—which may be nothing more than indexing the field-collected materials for an archive, summarizing them for a term project, or as much as writing a book-length study.

The three phases are necessarily linked. You can't record interviews and music in the field if you haven't previously determined that you need a recorder, tape, and microphones with which to do such recordings and then provided yourself with recorder, tape, and microphones and learned how to use them. You can't know when to quit if you don't know what it was you started out to accomplish. You can't do analysis if your field information doesn't provide sufficient detail for analysis to occur.

So let's take a look at how you get started.

2/Planning

Goals and Resources

Fieldwork is purposive; it's done for a reason. I don't know anyone who does fieldwork just because it's fun. It *can* be fun, and interesting, but so can other things, and many of those other things are more fun and more interesting and require less labor and expense and trouble. If you're going out to do fieldwork, it's because you've got some goal in mind.

Be clear about why you're taking on this responsibility before you define your topic. If you're fulfilling the requirements for a course, you shouldn't be taking on a study that will involve three years of intermittent visitation. The first question you should ask yourself is "Why am I doing this?" Your answer should be specific.

The next question targets your specific goal: "What do I hope to have at the end?" The answers have to do with the forms of information: a term paper, a book, a phonograph record, a film, a summary report, a group of photographs adequate for an exhibition, a group of tapes adequate for deposit in an archive, and so forth. It may well happen that the answers to this question change during or after the fieldwork. The recording you made for a term paper may turn out to be perfect for an NPR documentary; the photographs made for an exhibition may turn out to be the core of a book-length study. That's for later and it's partly based in serendipity, a happy condition for which you never plan. Going out, all you need is some realistic and specific goal.

The third question fills in the middle: "What specific resources do I need to achieve that goal?" The answers involve a series of other

20

questions: What information should you have before going out in the field? What equipment must you have to capture the kind and quality of information you want? What expertise must you have to operate that equipment properly? What level of detail must be recorded? What kinds of details about what kinds of things? What human resources will be required? How much time will it take? How much will it cost? How much fieldwork will be enough? What other help is needed?

The word "specific" appears in each of the three previous paragraphs. Instead of thinking, "I need a recorder, I need some money, and I need to learn something about this stuff," you should determine the kind of recorder you'll need (AC or DC? mono or stereo? cassette or open-reel? sync or non-sync?), how many dollars you must have in your pocket before you leave home and how many more you'll need to complete what you started, and what you need to learn—and then go learn it.

How do you find out what you need to know if you don't know it beforehand? One way is to ask someone who does know. If you're in school, another student or your teacher might be able to help. You might know someone in the community you intend to study and that person might be willing to talk with you even though your plans are still in the formative stage. If you're working on Vietnam war folklore, you might sit down with a Vietnam vet (who may or may not be one of the individuals you intend to interview) and tell that person what you're thinking about doing and ask for suggestions about what to look for and what to look out for. (That's a good question to ask even when you're deep into a project and really think you know what you're doing. "What else should I be asking about?" can be one of the most fruitful questions of all, especially after the informant has gotten to know and perhaps even trust you.) And there's always the library, which will provide you with books and articles about the subject of your study and a range of newspapers that might offer more recent and topical information. If you can't find out *anything* about your topic, you're either onto something terrific and new or you're onto something that doesn't exist at all.

The amount of reading you should do depends on the level at which you're going to work. If you're doing a paper for a class there are practical limitations on the amount of library work you can take on before you begin your class project: you can't devote three months to library research in a four-month semester. If you're working on a project for a Ph.D. thesis or a book, then you should cover *everything* available. If an impossible amount of library work is necessary before you can even begin, you might ask yourself if you should define your subject more narrowly.

Your *subject* is a broad statement about the area of your concern (folklore of this type or occupation or town or person or whatever), but your *topic* is a specific subset of that area of concern, a subset often usefully cast in terms of a simple question. (I take the subject/topic distinction from Titon, 1984:308.) "Occupational Folklore among Machinists" is a subject; "The Function of Occupational Folklore among Machinists in the Greystone Factory" is a topic. I often suggest to students that they put their topic in the form of a question, since the question form helps them think about the resources they need and the work they must do to find the answers they want. For example: "How do the models of behavior taught a rookie policeman in the academy and subsequently by experienced policemen on the job differ?" "What stories do Vietnam vets tell about coming home and what do those stories and the tellers' attitudes toward them mean?" Note that topics and titles aren't the same thing; the finished papers or essays or projects have titles appropriate to whatever they happen to be. The collectanea provide the information for dealing with the topics; the analysis provides the answers to the questions posed in them.

If you're dealing with organizations, your prefield preparations might require you to explain to certain people in those organizations what you're doing and why you're doing it. You might have to get permissions from some of those people and you might hope to get useful leads from others. Useful contact persons and organizational opinion makers aren't always the people with fancy titles. The way you find out about them is by asking: "Who else should I clear this with or who else would it be useful or important to talk to before I start? Who knows this place better than anybody else? Who really decides how outsiders will be treated?"

In the early 1970s I wanted to do a study about police officers in Buffalo. I wrote the commissioner a nice letter asking permission to do the study, and he soon wrote a nice letter back saying he had no objection so long as it was all right with the head of the police union. I tried to contact the head of the police union, but he never took my calls or answered my letters. A newspaper reporter friend told me, "There's no way those cops are going to talk to you without O'Brian saying it's okay." I told him I had done everything I could to have a conversation with the man, but I'd gotten nowhere. My reporter friend said, "Of course not. Don't you see what happened? The commissioner comes off looking cooperative and modern. But he knows damned well that O'Brian would never say such a study was okay." The latter had never cooperated with *any* outsider looking at his "boys." The commissioner, a public official and presumably answerable to the public, had pleasantly agreed to help a scientific study; the union official, answerable only to other members of his union, had continued keeping outsiders out. The commissioner, who no more wanted me poking around than the union leader did, never had to say no.

Failing to give enough thought to introductions can doom a project before it begins. In 1983–84 a large project designed to collect folklore among unemployed steelworkers in upstate New York foundered because the project administrators carefully met with and got permission from steel company executives. They didn't think to discuss the work with officials in the union locals. The fieldworkers just went to work, and they never understood why so few steelworkers talked to them, nor did they ever overcome the initial suspicion, hostility, and resistance. (See Byington, 1978:43–56, for good advice on dealing with this problem.)

Before you go out into the field you should learn all you possibly can about what you're going to be seeing and hearing and doing. If there are books about this area or subject or person, read them. You can't ask intelligent questions about a trade or craft if you don't know what the trade or craft is. You don't have to know everything and you don't even have to seem to know a great deal, but you shouldn't let yourself seem a total ignoramus. Being less knowledgeable than your informants is always acceptable—if you knew more than they did about everything you were discussing, they would be superfluous—but being downright ignorant is inexcusable. Neither should you pretend to be so much an expert you intimidate your informants. "One who has some information and asks for more," writes sociologist Everett C. Hughes, "is perhaps less likely to be refused than one who has no advance information; perhaps the best formula is to have advance knowledge, but to let it show only in the kind of question one asks" (1960:v). If you make a fair search and can't find specific information with which to prepare yourself, or if your topic is such that you couldn't possibly find preliminary information, then you can reasonably ask your informants everything. But if information is commonly available, your total ignorance won't make the kind of impression that gets people talking to you at length.

Your budget estimate should include transportation, meals and lodging (if the work is away from your home), supplies (tape, film, batteries), a reserve in case something breaks down, and any likely expense you can think of. In some places payment of informants is necessary and expected; in others it's an insult. If you'll be taking meals at informants' homes, you might bring gifts of foodstuffs of various kinds; if people will be driving you places they ordinarily wouldn't be going, you might offer to pay for the gas. You should tactfully find out what's appropriate and be ready to act accordingly. You don't want to impose burdens on your hosts, but neither do you want to insult them. The budget also includes such postfield expenses as processing of film and transcribing of tapes (if you're not going to do it yourself). The time budget is as important as the dollar budget: if two weeks in the field will get you what you need, but processing that two weeks' worth of collectanea will take you six months, be sure you've got the six months available.

Tools

It's all right to be amateurish about information you're collecting. Informants *expect* to know more about that material than you do, since that's why you're spending time with them. But it's never all right to be amateurish about the instruments you bring along. Fumbling while loading or focusing the camera or fidgeting with the controls of the tape recorder draws excess attention to those machines, and that's the last thing you want. Most people (and especially those who work with machines or instruments themselves) tend not to think well of people who spend an inordinate amount of time talking about or fussing with the tools of their trade. Think how you'd feel if you were at the dentist's office and he or she kept puttering with the drill, turning it on and off, and then said, "I'll get it right soon, don't you worry." And think how you'd feel about an auto mechanic who worked on your brakes and said, "I haven't done this much but this will probably work." You may love that camera or tape recorder, but your informants rarely share that love. For them, the instruments come between them and you, they're what help make the conversation (if it's conversation you're doing) artificial rather than natural. Your use of the machines should make them as transparent as possible.

Never do fieldwork with equipment you haven't tested beforehand, and never take anyone else's word that the equipment works. Always try out every machine you're going to use so you're sure it works properly and so you can work it efficiently. The field situation is not where you learn how to operate a camera or tape recorder, though it may be where you discover you hadn't learned to operate them as well as you thought you had. Few things make fieldworkers feel more foolish or seem more foolish to an informant than an inability to use the machines they bring with them. Why waste your time finding something to document if you aren't going to be able to document it well? Know how the machine works and know how to get the best it has to offer.

You don't have to be perfect; mistakes happen and they're not necessarily disastrous. Even the best of cinematographers sometimes forgets to stop the lens down after focusing and the best of recordists forgets to check the batteries as often as they should be checked. People are far readier to accept and forgive errors than they are incompetence. Errors may even help relax some informants because they remind them that you're not just a technician, you're a person too. Some mistakes are between you and your notebook (you correct it in silence and continue working without drawing any attention to it), but others—when you miss something so important you feel you have to ask the informant to do or say something a second time—should be handled simply and directly: "I forgot to release the pause button just now. I'm sorry. Do you think you could tell that story again?" Most informants will surprise you with the ease with which they repeat something you thought was spontaneous, but sometimes an informant will feel odd doing something again immediately. If you sense discomfort or awkwardness, you might say, "Let's try that one again later, okay?"

During one of the interviews Diane Christian and I filmed for our documentary about poet Robert Creeley, I happened to be working both the camera and the tape recorder. This isn't a good practice—there are too many knobs and dials to be watched for one person to do both jobs efficiently—but this time it was necessary. Most of my attention as Diane and Bob talked was devoted to the camera, but I glanced over my shoulder at the recorder's level indicators occasionally. Everything seemed fine, but then I noticed that the cassette tape wasn't moving. I had depressed the pause button while I was setting up and I'd forgotten to release it. Nothing said during the previous seven minutes had been recorded. Well-exposed footage of silent talking heads. I stopped the camera and told them what had happened. I began apologizing. "Forget it," Creeley said, "this is real life."

It's not enough to know *how* to use the machine; knowing *what* to do with it is even more important. A recorded conversation with an important informant may not be the best place for your on-the-job training as an interviewer. Some teachers of folklore courses requiring fieldwork insist that their students practice interviews with each other before they ever go out in the field. Ellen Stekert not only requires such an exercise but also has the interviewees then critique the interview event; this collaboration helps interviewers understand the way even friendly informants edit their responses to questions.

The scarcest resource is the recording situation itself; that situation can never be exactly replicated. Use that field time for learning what the field has to teach you, not for learning what you could equally well have learned before you ever left home.

Writing It Down

I encourage novice fieldworkers to spend a good deal of time writing down the answers to the three major questions—Why am I doing this? What do I hope to have at the end? What specific resources do I need to achieve that goal?—and I encourage them to formulate carefully their answers to the question about resources: time, money, machines, skills, access. They often discover that the answers are not consonant. They may see that the resources they need to achieve what they desire are beyond their means, or that the object they expect to produce at the end won't satisfy their reason for undertaking the fieldwork in the first place, or that the hardware they plan to utilize is far more complicated than is necessary. If there's not enough time or money, or if the work needs greater skills than you can present, redefine the project so it makes sense. It's far better to undertake a more modest project that has a good chance of success than it is to undertake a grander project doomed from the start.

Whenever I begin a field trip I still write out in detail my answers to the third question. For me, making the lists puts things into practical perspective. If the project is simple and local, I get by with a few notes. But if the project is distant and lengthy, I start making those lists some time before departure. A few days before I leave I get the equipment together; almost always I think of a few other things I'm likely to need.

If I'm going someplace I don't know well, I like to look at maps of the area. "You'll be surprised," writes Ives, "how much even a cursory knowledge of the lay of the land will help you" (1974:45). The mapwork lets you have some idea where things are when people refer to them, and you know whether you should nod or ask directions if someone says, "You ought to see Joe Farfel. He lives where the thruway meets the loop road out of town." I get whatever the Automobile Association of America has to offer and I use whatever other maps I can find. ("You have more faith in AAA than I have!" Stekert writes. "Use local contacts if possible, and remember that if in a very complex situation, local maps and National Geological Survey maps do quite well.")

Weather Reports

I'm sitting here in my study typing this advice for you. Giving advice is easy; taking it is sometimes not so easy. Even I don't always remember to take my own advice. Sometimes I was lucky and things worked out all right anyway; other times I got into big trouble and had no one to blame but myself. I'll tell you about one such bungled field trip.

Four of us went to San Francisco to make a thirty-minute film about an eighty-year-old fisherman we'd met the year before. He lived on his boat, the *Belle of Dixie*. He was a mine of stories and techniques, one of the last survivors of a kind of fishing life rapidly being replaced by modern technology. (Yes, we were doing salvage folklore. I *said* it sometimes has its place.) We made the trip in late December because the time was easiest for us: everyone in the crew taught in or went to school. I'd spent a year in San Francisco once and remembered late December and early January as a splendid time. We ordered our supplies, packed everything up, and off we went.

We arrived to skies that alternated between threatening to rain and raining; the air was wet and cold. Monday was like that, so were Tuesday, Wednesday, and Thursday. On Friday the sky cleared a little, but our fisherman was himself under the weather. "This is what this time of year is always like here," a friend said. "Whatever possessed you to make a movie about fishing now?" I told him about the splendid December and January I remembered. "A freak year. Don't remember another one like it. You should have called and asked me about the weather. I'd have told you. Anybody would have told you." He was right: I should've called; I should've gone to the library; I should've asked AAA or the weather bureau. But I hadn't thought of checking on the weather.

We did a little filming Saturday, then the weather closed in again. We got some more work done on Sunday and Monday, then it was time to go home. Just about the time we turned in the rental car at the airport the sky cleared totally for the first time. I was depressed but still optimistic: if all the footage turned out all right we had enough for a decent short film.

All the footage didn't turn out all right. I think twelve of the eighteen reels were totally unusable. The camera had developed a problem in the film transport so that the images shuddered constantly. You couldn't look at them without seeing double and getting a headache. But this was my camera and I take maniacal care of my equipment. How could it have happened? The camera had been in my possession constantly since we'd bought it, except for the one day last month I'd lent it to a friend shooting a commercial and he'd brought it back the next night ... and I hadn't used it or tested it since.

We didn't have enough usable footage to make the film. We would have to go back to San Francisco, which is always a pleasure; paying for it isn't. Plane tickets from Buffalo to San Francisco were and are expensive. Film and film processing are expensive. It was two years before we could get back again. This time the weather was perfect (we checked) and the camera worked perfectly (we had it checked out). But there were two other problems: since the sky was now a splendid blue, much of the footage would not intercut with the earlier footage. We perceive color not on the basis of what color an object *is,* but rather on what color an object *reflects.* The same surface reflects different colors or shades if it's illuminated by different colors of incident light. Film (for reasons I'll discuss later on) is far more sensitive to this difference than the eye. Our fisherman's skin looked very different under the blue summer sky than it had looked under the grey winter sky; the water surrounding the *Belle of Dixie* was also a very different color. The other problem was more serious. The fisherman had, in the intervening two years, stopped going out of the harbor at all. He was, he said, too old now for that. He just lived on the boat with his four dogs. (He'd had five the first time we filmed, but one had died in the interim.)

So we made a sixteen-minute film instead of a thirty-minute film. We made a film of a man talking rather than a film of a man doing. We made the film we had to make rather than the film we should've made. All because we hadn't called the weather bureau and hadn't run a test strip of film through the camera.

Now when I'm making a movie in a distant place and we're going to be shooting outdoors, I make it a point to check on the weather. I check on the weather even if we're not going to be making a movie because I don't want to waste space loading up the bags with sweaters if the weather is going to be hot, and I don't want to leave sweaters home and freeze if it's going to be cold. I'm much more responsible about doing my homework since I learned that San Francisco has a winter after all.

3/Collecting

Text and Context

As recently as the 1960s many folklorists were content to pursue and collect items. The text was the thing. "A text, in the parlance of the folklorist," wrote Richard M. Dorson, "represents the basic source, the pure stream, the inviolable document of oral tradition. It comes from the lips of a speaker or singer and is set down with word for word exactness by a collector, using the method of handwritten dictation or mechanical recording. What the state paper is to the historian and creative work to the literary scholar, the oral traditional text is— or should be—to the student of folklore" (1964:1).

No modern professional folklorist would argue Dorson's insistence on the need for acquiring exact texts, but few folklorists now would find a group of texts by themselves an adequate record of a field study. Items of folklore are important, but we can't know what they really are without information about the contexts which give them life. Songs, stories, pots, jokes, recipes: these things are of very limited meaning without information about their places in the world. It might be interesting to compile lists of proverbs known by members of one ethnic group or another, but the meanings of those lists are very different if the proverbs of one group are only bits of words remembered from youth and the proverbs of some other group are rhetorical devices still used regularly. If the latter, the folklorist wants to know how and when they're used, who uses them, and why. How are they imbedded in conversation? It might be interesting to collect jokes told by one ethnic or occupational group about another, but to know the meaning of those jokes we must know how and by whom they're told, how they're re-

ceived, how they come to be told at all. The real folklore fact, to quote
Bronislaw Malinowski on linguistic facts, "is the full utterance within
its context of situation" (1935:11).

Once collected, texts take on a certain legitimacy and can be studied
in a wide variety of ways. They can be discussed with the same kind
of analytic models and techniques we apply, for example, to discussion
of a group of poems. We may change our understanding of a poet's
work after we read a good biography that sets those poems in the
contexts of a poet's life, but the poems nonetheless exist as independent
objects, as groups of words and images, and they can be usefully ana-
lyzed as verbal constructs. Likewise with folklore texts. But textual
analysis is only one of many kinds of analysis that might be made of
folklore materials, and we rarely know in the field what kind of analysis
we or others will attempt later on. Absence of all the other information
cripples the data unnecessarily. A half century ago, folklorists were
happy to come home from the field with a good bunch of words;
folklorists now demand far more.

We can afford our more complex interest because we have technology that permits us to document more complex events. In earlier
years, folklorists had to scribble texts into notebooks or use cumbersome wire or disc recorders (in earlier years they had to use cylinder
recorders). The first portable tape machines became available in the
late 1950s; they were extremely expensive and often hard to find even
when money was available. Now we have inexpensive portable tape
recorders small enough to fit into a jacket pocket and technologically
sophisticated enough to record high fidelity. We have video recorders
small enough to fit into a shoulder bag and capable of making excellent
images in candlelight; some of these video recorders are capable of
recording high fidelity sound in stereo as well. We can afford to pay
attention to and think about contexts because our machines capture
the texts for us. We're freed of the enormous burden that so limited
earlier students of folklore. Folklorists still collect items—we still want
to know what stories people tell, what songs they sing, how they do
whatever it is they do—but we also want to know where those items
live and how and why they matter.

"John Henry"

Not long after I started collecting folklore in 1961 I developed a great
interest in "John Henry." I would ask almost every singer and instru-
mentalist I met if he or she knew "John Henry." If the answer was
yes I was happy; if the performance was good I was delighted. I'd tape

the song and then go on to something else. The queries were always part of some other enterprise; "John Henry" was one of my agenda items, not my collecting program. Getting those versions was like putting pennies in a jar: someday there'd be enough pennies and I'd spend them on something nifty. As things turned out, one day the jar was full but there was nothing of interest the coins would buy.

I recorded more than thirty versions of the song and I found another two dozen versions on records I owned. Joe Hickerson sent me tapes of forty-two performances from the Archive of Folk Song's collection and an equal number from his own extensive record collection. Friends regularly sent me "John Henry" performances from their fieldwork and I continued asking performers if they knew the song. I bet I had more versions of "John Henry" than anybody. On the basis of that assemblage of texts and tunes, it would've been possible to have made comparative statements about those song texts and those musical performances: The Texas versions tend to . . . while the Indiana versions are more likely to . . . in contrast to the Carolina versions, which are. . . . The white versions stress . . . while the black versions are more concerned with. . . .

I had intended to study all the texts and tunes I'd brought together so I could make smart comments on the variations in both, but I'd gathered virtually no information on the variations in the *use* of the song. I was dealing with "John Henry" as if a folksong could have the same kind of independent existence a work of fiction can have. Literary people who studied folklore earlier in this century believed that was possible; most folklorists who study folklore now don't, or they tend to find such studies of limited utility. A work of fiction can be read by anyone who understands its language, but the "language" of a folksong isn't the text only, it's also the context. My charts and tables of text elements and melodic patterns one day seemed to me totally self-contained: they made all kinds of sense, but they seemed to have little meaning.

I didn't know if the versions I'd collected were songs people played and sang or if they'd been dredged up from memory merely because I'd asked for them. I didn't know if the versions Hickerson sent me from the Archive of Folk Song were full songs or if they were all that fit on the discs used by the field collectors. I didn't know what place in anyone's life was played by any of the versions from the phonograph records and the archive because the record notes and the archive files didn't contain any information about the song's place in anyone's life. I didn't know if my inferences about the meaning of what went on in the song, about the varying roles of John Henry, the other human characters, and the steam drill made any sense at all in terms of the people whose songs they were. I was ready to do with all those texts and tunes what literary scholars so often do with the texts at their disposal: put them on my desk or wall and by careful deduction produce my learned conclusions.

One day it occurred to me that the political or psychological or whatever -al inferences to be drawn from those texts in my study might very well have nothing whatsoever to do with anything in the *performers'* world. I was using those texts to illustrate models *I* had beforehand, rather than learning from the singers and musicians what structures *they* had for those tunes and texts and what structures *they* had in which those tunes and texts played a part.

So I abandoned the investigation. There was too much I didn't know, too much I never would know. There are a good number of older and several recent textual analyses that have been truly useful, but I no longer wanted to do a straight textual comparison, and I no longer have much regard for studies that use texts merely to display antecedent theories.

In folklore studies you can demonstrate *any* antecedent theoretical point about texts if you pick the right texts and play with them outside of their contexts. It's like arguing with proverbs: enough texts are around to make any position seem reasonable; winning an argument with proverbs doesn't prove your argument, it merely displays your facility with proverbs. Some scholars even manage to "prove" their point with texts that seem flatly to contradict their point: "These stories I say indicate sexual repression are full of free and happy sexual activity you say? Ah, but you must understand the principle of reaction formation and the principle of symbolic inversion. . . ." In such "analyses" the meaning of texts is determined on the basis of models that themselves may have nothing to do with the texts, so that the texts are read in terms of the models and are assumed to have no meaning independent of those applied models. The texts are presented only to serve the model, to make the model meaningful—or to validate the scholar's private sense of order. For me, the two most egregious examples of this are Miles Mark Fisher's *Negro Slave Songs in the United States* (1963), which with little or no justification imposes on nineteenth-century texts twentieth-century political and social meanings, and Alan Dundes's *Analytic Essays in Folklore* (1981a), a series of essays that finds psychoanalytic "meaning" in groups of folklore items and events, nearly all of which are isolated from performers and conditions of performance. (For an excellent discussion of Dundes's imposition of his own perceptions on texts in isolation, see Stekert, 1986.)

The folklorist's psychological or political responses to the field material may be amusing or even marginally instructive about the mechanics of certain folklorists' thought processes; but if we want to know about the meaning of the folklore, if we want to understand how the folklore functioned in the world, then it's the informants' associations that provide the most useful guidance. If you're concerned with the meaning of the *folklore,* then the people who made it and their context can't be ignored.

For many of the older texts we study, such as most of the ballads in Child's collection or the *Odyssey* and the *Iliad,* nothing *but* texts are available, and those texts have been subject to unknown and generally unknowable editorial tinkering through the years; nonetheless, a wide range of critical inquiries and commentaries are possible and have been extremely instructive. But these texts are literary documents, so it's reasonable for scholars to have applied literary methods to their study. It's not that intelligent analyses of texts alone aren't useful, but texts alone can't tell us very much about things *other than* texts. In folklore studies, texts don't have meanings independent of people.

The problem that developed with my "John Henry" study finally had nothing to do with the texts and recordings; the problem was with me. I began in folklore as someone with primarily literary concerns, so textual questions and textual answers were attractive. Over the years my sense of folklore became more social. Once I understood the terrific resonances that occur when we see folklore in context, simple textual comparisons or reflexive model validations no longer seemed as much fun or as potentially useful as they once had.

What Folklorists Collect

To have made of those captured songs and instrumentals something meaningful, I should have gathered genealogies and contexts. I should have asked such questions as:

—Where and when and from whom did you get that song?

—Did you change it? If so, how?

—Are there other versions you like less or more? What and whose are they and why do you feel the way you do about them?

—What's the song about?

—What else is it about?

—What do you think about that story?

—*Do* you think about that story?

—When would you sing it?

—When do you sing it now?

—If you don't perform the song, do you know it? If you know it,
   why don't you perform it?
Which is to say: in addition to finding out what "John Henry" was, I
should have been trying to find out what "John Henry" meant.

I said above that modern folklorists aren't so much interested in
items as they're interested in items-in-contexts. Contexts are infinite—
every activity humans do may have folklore in or about it—but the
kinds of items are limited. Guides for folklorists tend to vary little in
the sorts of items they suggest fieldworkers seek out. The 1938 guide
for collection of folklore prepared by B. A. Botkin for Federal Writers'
Project workers, for example, includes many kinds of items that would
be suggested today:

> SONGS AND RHYMES: square dance calls, play-party songs of adults,
> game songs and rhymes of children, nursery songs and rhymes, riddles,
> street cries, religious songs, work songs, labor songs, ballads of local char-
> acters and events, love songs, blues
>
> TALES: local anecdotes, jests, and hoaxes; place-names and local leg-
> ends; tall tales and tales of American legendary heroes; animal and just-
> so stories; witch tales and related lore; devil tales and related lore; ghost
> tales and related lore; tales of lost mines, buried treasure, ghost towns,
> and outlaws; fairy and household tales
>
> LINGUISTIC "FLOATING" MATERIAL: localisms and idioms, folk
> and popular similies and metaphors, wisecracks and humorous expres-
> sions, nicknames, coinages and new word formations, curious street and
> shop signs, mottoes and slogans, inscriptions in memory books, trade
> jargon, samples of speech, conversation, sermons and prayers, and local,
> proverbial, and popular sayings
>
> GROUPS, GATHERINGS AND ACTIVITIES: accounts of religious
> gatherings, cults, and sects; accounts of work gangs and camps and oc-
> cupations, processes and customs; accounts of dances, parties, sports,
> pastimes, celebrations, festivals, and other social practices and gatherings;
> accounts of foreign enclaves, colonies, nationality and isolated groups,
> and other "islands" and pockets of culture; interviews with fortune tellers,
> mind readers, witch doctors, herb doctors, and healers; interviews with
> old-time street musicians and singers, with lists and specimens of their
> repertoires; interviews with local poets and story-tellers ... and beliefs
> and customs (luck signs, omens, taboos, and miscellaneous superstitions;
> weather and crop lore; cures and remedies; love, courtship, and marriage
> lore; birth, death and burial lore).
>
> (pp. 14–16)

Botkin urged the collectors to examine the world in which the folklore was found, thus anticipating attitudes that wouldn't become commonplace among American folklorists for more than three decades:

"Although in most cases it is impossible to establish the origin of a piece of folklore, we want to know as much as possible about its source, history, and use, in relation to the past and present experience of the people who keep it alive. This information enables us to understand the function and meaning which folklore has for those who use it and so enhances its interest and significance for others. Just as a folk song or folk tale cannot be said to have a real existence apart from its singing or telling, so in all folklore collections the foreground, or lore, must constantly be related to the background, or life" (1938:5).

Peter Bartis's guide for fieldworkers written forty-one years later (1979) and published by the American Folklife Center echoes many of Botkin's suggestions and concerns. Bartis's two-page list of what might be collected includes verbal genres (legends, personal experience stories, proverbs, riddles, toasts, mnemonic rhymes, nursery and game rhymes, family histories, dialect, sermons, etc.); music and songs, dances, games and play; artifacts (houses and barns and other buildings, tools, construction styles); foodways (food preparation, recipes, canning and curing, traditional meals); crafts and trades; folk art and medicine; custom, belief and ritual, family traditions, religious observations, ethnic traditions, rites of passage; seasonal and calendar events, feast days, political and civic celebrations, etc. (1979:5–6). He suggests a wide range of collateral information that should also, when possible, be obtained:

1. name and address
2. place and date of birth and rearing
3. family information
    size of family
    ethnic heritage
    language spoken at home by siblings, parents, grandparents
4. first-generation immigrants
    who immigrated and when
    circumstances of immigration
    reasons for immigration
    activities in old world
5. education, apprenticeship, and training experience
6. occupational experience
7. migrational experience and travel in the U.S.
8. church membership
9. membership in organizations other than religious
10. special interests, skills, hobbies, and interesting possessions
11. important events during life (civic and personal)
12. repertoire of folklore and traditional materials
13. informant's commentary on performance

when, where, and how was it learned and performed?

how does he classify or understand the folklore and customs?

14. photograph of person or event
15. description of person visited including:
    circumstances of interview
    character of informant
    contact with mass media and modern world
    disposition of collector

(1979:15–16)

Bartis's list assumes an interview collecting situation. Sometimes interviews are impossible or the range of questions you can ask might be restricted or inappropriate. We'll see later that interviews are just one of several collecting strategies available to the folklorist. Most of the material in Michael J. Bell's *World from Brown's Lounge* (1983), which deals with verbal and social folklife in a neighborhood bar, is based on conversations and events Bell recorded in the bar. The people in the bar knew he was observing and sometimes recording, but only rarely were they doing things specifically because he was there, and many times what they said to him or enacted for him was done or enacted because he was one of the people in the bar, not because he was working on a book about life in the bar. I'll say more later about the differences in the two kinds of work, but for now keep in mind that you can learn a great deal about an event or a place just by sitting down in one spot and paying attention to what's going on. You can often learn more from what happens to be said and done in your presence than you can from what's said or done in response to your questions or requests.

William Sturtevant, writing for fieldworkers sending archaeological objects back to a museum or sending back information about such objects, suggests a range of kinds of information the collector of objects should provide: ethnic group of users, name of artifact in local language and in English, use of the object, history of the object (where, from whom, and date obtained, where made, age), condition, component materials, typicality, etc. If time permits, the object collector should also acquire the names of the component parts, the materials used, how the object is classified, who or what group owns the object and the class of objects, the purposes to which it is put, and the results of its use. When, where, and how often is the object used? How is it used and what other objects are used in conjunction with it? How is it stored? How is it made and what tools and raw materials are needed? How is the manufacture done and by whom? Where do they do it?

What is the meaning of the object? Are there aesthetic values, symbols, myths, folklore traditions, stories of origin and ownership, changes in form or style or use? (1977:31–34)

Even in whatever rural areas are left, few people sit around anymore and play old-time tunes on the banjo, and few tell traditional tales of the kinds found in tale-type indexes: the television is on, the tape deck is playing, radio is universal, the same Top Forty hits play across the country. Folklorists, as any folk group, have adapted to the opportunities provided by changing demographies and technologies. Early folklorists were principally interested in traditions found among people who weren't literate. But as education has become nearly universal and the centers of population have become urban and suburban, there's been an enormous expansion of things to study: the folklore of politics and politicians, of homemakers and warmakers and steelworkers, of subway graffiti artists, of computer hackers. As Ben Botkin predicted almost fifty years ago, the city has become a more various and more engaging field than those rural areas that for so long occupied American scholars of traditional ways.

The lists of things to look for and questions to ask prepared by Botkin, Bartis, and Sturtevant can seem overwhelming, but there's a sense to them. They don't have to be memorized once you get the idea of what they're about, and they're equally useful in rural areas and in busy cities. They can be summarized in two simpler and more general questions: What sorts of things do people do? What sense do those things make to the people doing them?

Salvage Folklore

"I had responded . . . to the sense of urgency that had been conveyed to me by Professor Boas and Ruth Benedict," wrote Margaret Mead. "Even in remote parts of the world ways of life about which nothing was known were vanishing before the onslaught of modern civilization. The work of recording these unknown ways of life had to be done now—*now*—or they would be lost forever. Other things could wait, but not this most urgent task" (1972:137; also cited in Georges and Jones, 1980:24).

It's *always* too late to capture such things. Aspects of culture being changed can never be seen by the visitor for or as what they were. We can learn things of value by trying to discover what's been lost, but the knowledge is never more than partial—exactly as all historical inquiries can never give us knowledge that is more than partial. The world of our forebears will never be ours. Learning what we can about their world might let us know them better, but we can never know them for what they were before our sense of change and loss moved us to begin looking for what was no longer commonly available.

"Locating informants only begins the battle," wrote Richard M. Dorson. "Now face to face with a member of the 'folk,' the collector proceeds to the task of extricating the lore." Dorson suggested an approach that at once identifies the collector and tells the potential informant what is wanted: " 'They tell me you know a lot of old tales, the kind people used to tell before radio and television came along. I'm trying to write them down before they get lost, and I wonder if you would help me. I'm a professor from the state college, and I'm interested in any kind of story that doesn't come from a book' " (1964:9). That kind of question may have been reasonable to ask in the early 1960s, but few people are still alive who remember what kinds of stories were told before radio, and television has been a major force in American life for more than thirty years. Dorson himself moved on to a more active notion of folklore in later years. His last field project (1981) is a collection of industrial folklore from northern Indiana.

Salvage folklore work can be valuable, but only if the collector understands the place the information collected plays in the lives of the people supplying the information. "I tell you this stuff," a woman in Massachusetts said to Diane Christian, "because I can remember it if I'm asked. But it has nothing to do with the life I live now." That it has *nothing* to do with the life lived now isn't likely: new attitudes are based on old attitudes, on the attitudes they replace or enhance; new technologies are adopted or adapted because current technologies seem inadequate in comparison. The new is valued because of how it compares with the old; the old, for many reasons and in many ways, influences the new, but whether it's present in the new is another question entirely. Land-based animal life on this planet occurred only after a long period of aquatic life and an interim period of amphibian life. Scientists can better understand the development of certain organs in meadowlarks and humans if they're aware of those ancient aquatic and amphibian phases, but little in meadowlark or human behavior can be *explained* by a wet reference. (Little, not nothing. In February 1984 a young boy in Chicago was underwater for nearly thirty minutes. He lived, doctors said, because something triggered a vestigial survival mechanism they called the "mammalian diving response.")

The heart of the salvage folklore operation is to rescue from oblivion some art or artifact or piece of knowledge. That's a perfectly legitimate reason for doing fieldwork: those songs or stories or legends or folkways or folk arts are part of our heritage, part of what made our world what it's become, and they should be preserved for exactly the same reasons works of literature or sculpture or letters of prominent persons or old city maps should be preserved. Knowing such facts helps us understand cultural adaptation and change. The reason few folklorists do salvage folklore nowadays isn't because they've all decided such preservation is useless; rather it's because the definitions of folklore and the folk process have expanded in ways that permit folklorists to deal with modern life and with traditions, processes, and styles that are very much alive. Twenty years ago, Kenneth S. Goldstein wrote, "The Western folklorist must dig for his treasures, covered over as they are by the products of modern mass communications media and mass production methods which have contributed to the destruction of traditional ways of living" (1964:175–76). Modern folklorists find traditional ways of living within the technological world of modern life, and much of what they find is part of the fabric of life rather than something covered by it.

Salvage folklore is always collected in radically different contexts than the ones in which it was formerly learned and performed. The stories remembered now are not necessarily representative of the stories told then. Personal anecdotes are always revised in the remembering and in the telling: the story of what the first years in America were like or stories of Prohibition or the war (any war) are told from the point of view of someone living now, someone who's had all the experiences between the memorable event and the recounting of it for you and your tape recorder. Most people are more likely to remember good things than bad; and the "good old days" get better the farther away from them one is. Salvage folklore materials give a collector bits and pieces about a world of another time or a life in another place; those same materials give a collector a great deal of information about the attitudes of people living in this time and this place.

Watching, Listening, and Asking Questions

Many student projects in undergraduate folklore classes are salvage folklore operations. That's because older family members are often a resource easily accessible to young people without funds or time for more extensive fieldwork. Getting people to talk about what they did or what happened to them years ago or how things were years ago can seem far easier than looking at their lives now and trying to decide what is and isn't folkloric about the parts of those lives. Family salvage folklore can be interesting and can provide much valuable information, but many other collecting options are open even in the restrictive context of an academic term.

All families have active traditions, though these are sometimes difficult for students to see as folklore because, as one said in a recent class, "You're talking about our everyday life." Exactly the point: folklore is very much the stuff of everyday life. The stories told at dinner about friends or acquaintances, the ways holidays are celebrated and injuries are treated, the organization of jobs within the household, attitudes toward and ways of dealing with the IRS and city hall—these are as much folklore as reports of exactly the same kinds of events and behaviors by a grandparent. (See Zeitlin, Kotkin, and Baker, 1982, for extensive discussion of ordinary family folklore.)

Many students collect personal narratives having to do with classes, teachers, sex incidents, drinking, working, and family relations. Some document dorm and classroom building graffiti. Some study folklore of occupations related to jobs they've had. Students who live in or near cities probably have an easier time of it than students in rural areas, but folklore performance is so common a part of everyday life that the material for study is available anywhere. Students who define their projects in terms of producing a lot of items identifiable as folklore often have trouble getting what they want; finding fifteen pages' worth of proverbs or stories can take a long time. Students who understand that everyone has folklore, that most people have folklore of several kinds, and that what's valuable is understanding folklore in its living context, have little difficulty finding projects that are instructive and useful.

It's unlikely you'll *ever* collect all the collateral information that could be adduced about an item or a situation, but you should be aware of the range and categories of questions you might ask. If you overhear a joke or story told, you might in your notes write up all the aspects of the situation you can discern: Where and when and by whom was the story or joke told? What prompted the joke- or storytelling? How did the listeners respond? How did the teller respond to the listeners' responses? What did the storyteller or others do subsequently? What were you doing there? What was the nature of your relationship to the people present? How representative do you think the story, performance, and response were? What were they representative of?

Those are questions you can try to answer simply on the basis of your own observations. Interviews might give you other information. If, say, you later engaged the storyteller in conversation, you might ask where the story was learned and when and from whom. How closely does this telling compare with what the teller thinks was the original? Does the teller vary it for different audiences or situations? What variations for which audiences and which situations? Has the teller heard other people tell that story or stories like it? Why does he or she like to tell it?

"Even the most willing and cooperative informant," wrote Richard M. Dorson (1964:14), "cannot pour forth a stream of lore the way one turns on a spigot or uncorks a bottle. Items of tradition lie beneath the surface of the mind, some buried deep in the subconscious, and both narrator and listener must strain to coax them up." Few American folklorists would have found cause to disagree with Dorson when he wrote that more than twenty years ago. But the intervening decades have seen significant changes in the ways American folklore field-workers define their task.

Interviews and set-ups are efficient: in a short period of time informants might deliver themselves of and say more about items of folkloric interest than they would in a great deal of normal time. But a price is paid for that efficiency: the context in which the information is gathered is altered. Interviews or set-ups (where you get people to perform for your recorder at a time or in a way they would not be performing otherwise) can provide valuable information, but it's not the *same* information you would obtain if you recorded the same persons in a natural context, if they were performing the songs or stories or instrumentals in their own way and at their own time. Recordings and notes made in each of those situations may provide the "same" songs, but they don't provide the same information.

Folklorists often distinguish between folklore in active tradition and folklore in passive tradition, and they distinguish between informants who are active bearers of tradition and informants who are passive bearers of tradition. Since publication in 1974 of Dell Hymes's seminal article "Breakthrough into Performance," they also distinguish between material that's reported and material that's performed (reprinted in Hymes, 1981:79–141). The differences have to do with the circumstances in which utterances occur. If you want to discover items, it doesn't matter whether your informant is an active or passive tradition bearer, but if you want to know about the place and significance of the items you're finding, then the difference is important. If I know several stories about my family's first years in this country but would never in the course of normal life tell those stories, I'd be a passive bearer of that family tradition. I might tell you those stories if you asked, but only because they're part of your agenda, not because they're part of mine. Some passive bearers of tradition can tell you a great deal about items or conditions of performance, though they might never have performed such items themselves. Collecting from the active bearers is more attractive because they produce the best items; collecting from passive bearers can be enormously important because they can produce extensive information about the place of those items (see Stekert, 1965). Someone talking about a story offers you very different words and intonations than someone actually telling or performing the story.

Staying Open

I've always liked Joel Chandler Harris's article "An Accidental Author" (1886). Harris insisted, and I have no reason to disbelieve him, that when he started with what became the Uncle Remus stories he had no idea where it was all going to go. It just seemed like a good idea at the time and he followed his own lead. I've been telling you about the necessity for careful planning, the need to know what you're doing. The difficult thing sometimes isn't so much finding topics worth looking at but seeing what's right in front of you. It's like when you look for your car in the airport parking lot: your mind doesn't register or store information on the cars that don't fit the image of the car you're seeking. Sometimes fieldwork projects come out of nowhere, or they turn out to be half done before you're conscious of beginning them.

Maybe a better way to say this is, if you've decided exactly what you're going to get then there's no real need to go out there looking. You have a reason for collecting, you decide what you should do to get the information you want, perhaps you have a plan for what you'll do with whatever you get. But even in a well-planned project you never know what you'll find until you get out there and begin looking. And not until you've seen something in the world can you begin telling others what you've seen or explaining to them what you've understood.

Finding Informants

There are nearly as many ways of making contacts with informants as there are collectors and collection projects. Once you understand how central to everyday life folklore is, you begin to see that nearly anyone you meet could be an informant for a folklore collection, and you see that most people could be informants for several different folklore collections. Starting the work is often difficult, primarily because you're doing something new or because you're talking with someone you haven't talked with before, or you're talking with someone you know well about subjects you haven't previously discussed and you're assuming a role you haven't previously assumed. Most people doing fieldwork for the first time are nervous about it, and many people who've done fieldwork but are starting a new fieldwork project are equally nervous. It's natural and it's nothing to worry about. Almost always the nervousness disappears very soon after the work begins. The best way to deal with the jitters is to get to work.

Students doing fieldwork for a class suffer a more restrictive time constraint than professional folklorists or graduate students doing field-work for a thesis: the former must complete their fieldwork and get it written up before the semester is over. So they often use as informants the people closest to them—fellow students or family members. Many students in folklore classes, as I noted earlier, do salvage folklore collecting: they get from relatives or friends of relatives old-world stories or folkways or survivals of such things here. That's probably the easiest kind of collecting to do because it requires little observation and because the collector need make few decisions about what to record. Many other students, and most professionals, deal with a different notion of folklore. Instead of looking for survivals of an age dead or dying, they seek folklore that matters in present-day life—folklore of the normal and present rather than folklore of the arcane and past. Sometimes the choice is made on the basis of time: if a project gets underway early in the term there can be time for a more complex investigation. And sometimes the choice is made on the basis of an information source being available: the topic is chosen because of ready access to a person or situation of folkloric interest.

When Edward D. Ives did research for his three studies of ballad writers (1964, 1971, 1978), he often asked newspapers in the regions he intended to work in to publish his letters asking for help. "In writing about Larry Gorman and Joe Scott, since the 'community' was actually all of Maine and the Maritime Provinces of Canada, I published such letters in practically every daily and weekly newspaper in the area, and I received dozens of responses. In writing about Lawrence Doyle, I only published a letter in the Charlottetown (P.E.I.) *Guardian,* and here again I got excellent results" (1980:34). Similar letters written to general newspapers in large cities may also prove fruitful. Ellen Stekert, for example, got numerous responses to her *New York Times* query for information about Malvina Reynolds. Most large cities also have ethnic language newspapers catering to specific readerships, as well as trade, union, and interest group newsletters of various kinds. These are often fine sources of help. One student of mine decided to do a paper on UFOs. He had a part-time job as host on a late-night radio talk show in Buffalo, so one night he said he'd be interested in hearing from anyone who'd seen UFOs or who knew stories about UFO sightings. He was still getting calls about UFOs two weeks later, even on nights he began the program with a firm declaration that he'd be taking calls only about the plans for a new downtown stadium or the demand by some lakeshore residents for early removal of the Niagara River ice boom.

Folklore informants can be found anywhere, in any occupation. But some occupations are often closed and hostile to outsiders. Most people can't just walk up to a doctor or lawyer or police officer or crook and ask for folklore and get it. Even people in far less paranoid occupations want to know who you are and why you're asking questions and what'll happen to the information you get. Contacts are sometimes necessary to get the work started. A contact can be anyone who helps you say hello comfortably to the first few people you want to say hello to. After that introduction, things usually move along on their own. It's important to be sure that your contact will make starting conversations easier for you; some people can make introductions, but their own reputation or position is such that the people introduced will mistrust anyone they recommend. If you use the wrong person you can wind up further back than if you'd started cold and on your own. The 1983–84 New York study of steelworkers I mentioned earlier foundered because the project workers had their initial introductions from management and not from anyone in the steelworkers' union. By the time the group's leader understood her mistake it was too late to save the project.

Contacts may bring you and other people together and help get you started; more often they'll say, "You should see Joe. Tell him I sent you." Unless there's no way to reach Joe other than walking up to his door, I always call or write first. I know how much I hate it when someone appears at *my* door and demands some of my time; I want the option of saying yes or no without awkwardness, and if my answer is yes, I want to be able to pick the time most convenient for *me*. Ives writes that some fieldworkers tell him they don't like writing letters because it gives people more of a chance to reject the request. But, he points out, "You would normally write an opening letter to a retired general or actress you wished to talk to; why not offer the same courtesy to a laboring man or a farm wife?" (1980:37). Whatever kind of contact you have for meeting people, think about how you'd receive someone under the circumstances you're presenting. If the approach would get your hackles up, if you'd find it intrusive or pushy, take a more polite and considerate path.

The contacts need not be informants themselves, nor must the contacts always understand fully what you're doing and why. When Harry Hyatt, the clergyman who did the amazing five-volume study on conjuration and folk medicine (1970–78), arrived in a strange town, he'd often hire a taxi driver to take him around black neighborhoods and tell him what was what. Hyatt said that once he met one or two good informants they would invariably lead him to others. He was perfectly comfortable doing fieldwork in places where he knew no one and making his own contacts through people he happened to meet along the way.

"Sometimes," Richard M. Dorson wrote, "even a point-blank approach will do the trick, if no other means are available and one's nerve is strong. Wandering around the tumbledown Negro settlement of New Bethel in Michigan, without leads or contacts, I saw a fleshy, somber woman standing in the doorway of the last house on the path, and called out, 'Do you know any old stories?' Sarah Hall said yes and invited me in. So I met the storytelling mother of three storytelling daughters, who was also the hoodooed ex-wife of still another narrator" (1964:7–8). Dorson wrote elsewhere of several times starting conversations with strangers at bars and on the street (1967:19–47).

Hyatt and Dorson were doing what door-to-door salespeople call "cold canvassing." Some of us are very good at it, others are terrible. I'm one of the terrible ones; as I said, I've never been comfortable strolling up to strangers and asking them questions. If you have that kind of easy sociability and the kind of personal style that gets strangers to trust you right off the bat, you'll do very well with the cold canvassing technique; if not, you'd best start with people you know or find people who can introduce you to the people you need to know.

The people identified as the most representative or best performers or most interesting conversationalists by your contacts might be none of those things. Sometimes you're led to people who present what your contacts think will provide you the best image of the place or the institution or group. You have to think about the conversations you're having and be aware of other possibilities. While working in the Solomon Islands in the 1960s and 1970s, Elli Köngäs-Maranda "was very frustrated by *knowing* that several young people, and especially frustrated by knowing that several of these young people were girls, mastered myths, but that the specialists, recognized and respected males, pre-empted my time. It also never was quite clear if and what offense would have been taken if I chose my informants rather than my informants me" (n.d.:198). Take all the help you can get, but remember to help yourself as well. However you start, you'll find that the work gets easier and easier because your connections and leads multiply exponentially.

Folklore fieldwork isn't always a matter of serendipity. You can't count on finding good providers or on having someone who'll lead you to what you want and need. Sometimes you have to dig, and sometimes you get a lot of rejections from people who don't want to talk about what you want to talk about or who just don't want to talk to *you*. That happens. Don't take it personally (not too personally, anyway). Go find someone else.

Striking It Lucky and Striking Out

Sometimes informants just walk up and say hello. In 1964 I'd spent a week in Saltville, Virginia, visiting a musician named Hobart Smith and recording some members of his family. Early on the day I was leaving I brought my car to the service station to have some work done. While the car was in the bay and the mechanic was fiddling with the carburetor, a Saltville police car slowly cruised by several times then pulled into the station and stopped just behind my car. The policeman got out, looked at me, looked at my Massachusetts license plates, said hi to the mechanic, then walked slowly around my car. I hadn't done anything wrong, I wasn't on the lam, I was just a citizen visiting a town in southwestern Virginia, but I felt extremely uncomfortable anyway. The cop had an enormous pistol, and he wore mirrored sunglasses; I'd seen a lot of movies.

"What's that on the back seat of your car?" he asked me.

"A tape recorder."

"Not that."

"Oh. You mean the guitar. It's a twelve-string guitar."

John Gallagher, one of Hobart's cousins, had given me the guitar the day before. Someone had given him the guitar in 1917, John said, and he didn't need it anymore because he now had a bright red Gibson six, which was much easier to play since he'd gotten arthritis, and anyway, the neck on the twelve was a little warped and there was that hole in the side from the time someone had hit his brother over the head with it. I'd told John the guitar was a treasure and I couldn't afford to pay him what it was worth. "I didn't say I was selling it to you," John said, "I said I was giving it to you." I made faint protestations but was delighted with the gift. I had the guitar on the back seat because I didn't want it to suffer further damage in the heat of the trunk. And now this cop with mirrored sunglasses and an enormous pistol was investigating my guitar.

"I've never seen a twelve-string guitar," he said.

"There aren't many of them."

"That's what I thought," he said. "How do you play it?"

"Same way you play any other guitar only you have to press harder and it's a bitch to tune."

"I bet," he said. "Can I try it?"

"If I can take your picture while you're trying it."

"It's a deal," he said, laughing.

I got the guitar and he played it, not at all badly considering the warp of the neck and the hole in the side. I took his picture; we had a long conversation about instruments and what Nashville was doing to what he called "real music." He said his family got together regularly and played real music. His dad played everything, he played fiddle and banjo, his brothers played banjo and guitar. "You should come out and visit. Everybody's going to be at my dad's house for Sunday dinner this evening. Why don't you join us?"

I groaned. I had to leave Saltville now if I was to be on time for my Tuesday morning appointment in Huntsville, Texas, with George Beto, director of the Texas Department of Corrections. This was to be the beginning of my fieldwork in the Texas prisons, I had never met Beto, and I didn't want to call and delay the meeting. If I couldn't connect with him I wouldn't be able to get started. "I can't," I said. "I'm leaving now. I'm on my way to Texas. I wish I could stay. I really do."

"You coming back?" the policeman asked. I said I probably would be back, but I didn't know when. "When you come back, you call me. You come on out and visit us. My dad lives in Lodi." He told me his name—Ron Holmes—and he wrote his telephone number in my note-book.

A year later I visited Saltville again, doing more work with Hobart Smith's family. I called Ron Holmes. "I heard you were back," he said. "If you didn't call I was going to come find you. You coming out for Sunday dinner?" I said I was, and I did, and it was a delightful day, one I still remember with pleasure. His dad was, as he'd said, a splendid musician, and so was his brother, and in time I was able to record some fine tunes and stories over there in Lodi.

What happened on the rest of that first field trip illustrates as well as anything else the way contacts lead into other contacts and then you find you've got your own network going.

At nine A.M. two days after the conversation in the Saltville garage, I was in Huntsville, explaining to George Beto what I wanted to do and why. We had already exchanged letters and he'd written that he'd do whatever he could to help. We talked for perhaps thirty minutes, then he suggested I begin my work at Ramsey Unit. "You can go anyplace you want in TDC," Beto said, "but I think you'll find what you need at Ramsey. You should visit Ellis, too." I assumed he was sending me to his prettiest prisons, but since he said I could go wherever I wanted I was sure I'd be able to find the people I really wanted to meet eventually. As it turned out, Ramsey wasn't anything like the prettiest prison in Texas; Ramsey was hot and tough—and a perfect place for doing the work I wanted to do.

Before I left his office, Beto telephoned Sidney Lanier, warden of Ramsey Unit in Brazoria County. "I'm sending someone down to you, warden," he said. "He may have some strange requests. Give him whatever he wants." Beto and the warden chatted for a few minutes about prison business, then Beto hung up the phone and said to me, "I expect Warden Lanier will take care of you."

Years later I asked Beto why he so freely gave me run of the place. He said he had great respect for the Society of Fellows, the research group at Harvard that sponsored my work, and he was interested in what I'd find, because "How do we know what we're doing wrong in these places if we don't let outsiders in to tell us?" There are lessons here. First, try to have for your base an agency or organization or purpose that's seen as legitimate by the people you're asking for access or help. Don't lie, but don't hesitate to use whatever credits you've got, and think about finding sponsorship from organizations whose names might help. Second, remember that people give help—as contacts or as informants—because they have reasons of their own.

"Dr. Beto said to give you whatever you want," Warden Sidney Lanier said when I arrived at Ramsey a few hours later. "What do you want?"

"I'd like to work inside without any guards around, talk to whomever I want, go wherever I want."

"That's easy enough. Anything else?"

"No. I'll find the people to talk to."

"Fine. But how about I give you somebody to show you where everybody's at?" Lanier told Johnny Jackson, an inmate trusty, to take me back to the tanks. He sent word to the guards in the halls that I'd be around and to let me go where I wanted. He looked out the window. "That blue car yours?" I said it was. "I'll tell the field major when he comes in tonight. Nobody will bother you if you drive around the farm. If they don't recognize the car they get excited sometimes." I had a brief panicky vision from those movies I'd seen. I hoped the guards got the description right: this was the first new car I'd ever owned. "Mr. Jackson will tell you what he wants," the warden said to Johnny Jackson. "Fix him up."

Jackson was a "building tender." I didn't know it at the time—but I learned quickly enough—that building tenders, long-term convict trusties, were the intermediaries in the Texas prison world. They did much of the day-to-day management for the guards, and they provided an institutionalized channel for information to go in two directions. The guards could pass the word on anything through the BTs in minutes, and an inmate who had a problem or who wanted to inform on someone else without becoming The Man's snitch could snitch through the BT and tell himself his honor was intact. Some building tenders maintained a higher degree of order in the areas they controlled than had guards in any prisons I'd previously visited; others were thugs who ruled by the same brutal techniques that had helped get them locked up in the first place.

Jackson asked me what I was looking for. "Those old-time convict worksongs."

"River songs," he said.

"What?"

"We don't call them 'convict worksongs' down here. We call them 'river songs'."

"Why?"

"All the farms are on the river."

Indeed, all the Texas prisons where external work was done at that time were located on the rich bottomlands of the Brazos and Trinity rivers. Jackson told me where to start, who to talk to, who to listen for, what to watch out for. He said he knew many river songs himself and later recording sessions proved him a fine song-leader with a broad repertoire. On that first Monday he introduced me to people, he walked me around the building, he told me he'd be nearby in case I needed help. I said he didn't have to do that, I'd be all right. "Sure," he said. For several days he was always nearby anyway. At first I worried that he was snooping for the warden, but there was no way to get rid of him without being offensive. Then I realized that he wasn't snooping (well, he may have been, but that wasn't what he was doing primarily), he was protecting. The warden had told him to take care of me, and if anything untoward had happened, Jackson would have failed in his assignment. One day he decided I was handling myself appropriately and that the other convicts were comfortable about what I was doing. Thereafter I saw him only when I asked someone to find him for me.

After I started recording, other names kept popping up. People would suggest other people; they would tell me who I could or couldn't trust, who was a reliable talker, who was a bullshit artist. Some of the reports about reliability conflicted with one another, but that was fine with me. I recorded things other than worksongs. I taped a lot of interviews. I watched the rhythms of life in the prison. That led me to other inmates.

Several Two Camp singers told me about a man named Chinaman, who they said was the best song-leader they'd ever heard in the Brazos bottoms. I asked where Chinaman might be found now. "He died," I was told. "A long time ago. He died." Back on One Camp, I asked Johnny Jackson about Chinaman. "They told me he died," Jackson said. "He got out and he died."

The next week I moved to Ellis Unit located on the Trinity River near Huntsville. The warden at Ellis, Carl Luther McAdams (referred to by all convicts and most guards as "The Bear" or "Beartracks," though never within his earshot), had already discussed me and my interests with Sid Lanier. The first thing McAdams said to me was, "If you want to record those old river songs you better start with ole Chinaman. He knows more of them than anybody."

"Chinaman? They told me he was dead."

"Somebody didn't tell him, I guess. He sure don't know it yet."

I had started the work in Texas with some ideas about what I wanted to find, but my priorities changed as the people I met there taught me what to look for and said what they thought was important. They taught me about other people who could continue my education. That's happened to me several times since, and it's happened to most serious fieldworkers I know. When it happens it's always a delight because instead of you digging for bits and pieces of useful information you find yourself realizing there are more *kinds* of useful information there than you could've imagined earlier, and there are more people willing to help you find it than you can possibly manage.

Even experienced folklore collectors sometimes blunder and miss fine opportunities. I've been telling you about times when things worked out nicely for me. I'll tell you about a time I missed a chance to learn from an informant who started the conversation herself.

I was reading one morning in my study in Adams House at Harvard. The tape recorder was playing a Gaelic song. I no longer remember why I happened to be listening to that particular tape. The cleaning lady let herself in and began working in the other two rooms. Then I realized she was standing just behind me, not moving and not saying anything.

"I didn't know you knew Gaelic," she said.

"I don't."

"Then why are you listening to this?"

"I like it."

"Do you know what the words mean?"

"No."

She sang with the tape and when the song was over she translated it for me. She asked if I was going to the Scottish picnic. I asked what she was talking about. "Every year they have it down in Brockton. People come from all over. They have piping and drumming contests. This Saturday down in Brockton." She looked at her watch, said she had to get back to work, and left.

On Saturday a friend and I drove to Brockton. I lugged along a portable recorder and a camera. My friend said, "You're getting compulsive about this stuff." I said that it might be a fine opportunity to record something interesting. The *day* was interesting, but it would have been just as interesting if I hadn't felt the need to go poking around with my instruments, if I'd just enjoyed it the way the rest of the tourists did. I made some tapes of bagpipers and drummers and took a few photographs of people in kilts and got one nice picture of Edward Brooke, a candidate for what would be his first term in the U.S. Senate, posing in a tam-o'-shanter and standing next to a red-faced burly man with bagpipes. There was a better picture of the candidate in the Sunday papers, and I had tapes and records of pipers and drummers already. Since I didn't record any conversation, the tapes I made weren't of much use. I was functioning at the kind of epidermal level you use when you're doing journalism, when you're after facts rather than meanings. On the drive back to Boston I told my friend about the cleaning lady. I said I was going to spend some time soon talking with her.

I planned to do it, I really did. But the time was never quite right. The spring was a busy one, I was away for a while doing fieldwork someplace exotic, a book was being finished, things consumed the hours. Then one day a stranger came to clean the office. I asked where the regular cleaning woman was. "Retired," the man said. "Went back up to Canada someplace."

4/Points of View and Points of Departure

The Problem with Facts

I use the word "informant" in this book to refer to the person who provides the fieldworker information—the storyteller, the singer, the musician, the craftsperson, the artist, the technician, the source of autobiographical reflection, the person who knowingly helps the fieldworker collect data and those who happen to be where the fieldworker is looking at the moment information is being taken down. But the final informant of any fieldwork study, the person who does the most informing of all, isn't some relative or farmer or corporate executive or neighbor or hangers-on at a corner bar or residents of a street or city. Rather, the final informant is the fieldworker, the person who offers the information not just to one person who seems worthy of a measure of trust but rather to the world at large: "Here's what I saw and what I thought about it. You can trust what I say."

Well, maybe we can and maybe we can't. No one collects everything that might be collected, and no one publishes every fact recorded and every observation made. A fieldwork collection, therefore, can never, without a great deal of independent information, be assumed to be representative of what was out there to be collected. Fieldwork collections, published or unpublished, should rather be seen as reflecting what individual collectors found, preserved, and selected, based on their ideas of what folklore was, what folklore information could be used for, and what recording technology was at hand. This applies equally well to an academic who's been collecting folklore materials for thirty years and to an undergraduate student taking an introductory folklore class.

For both the experienced and the novice collector, the most difficult question to answer is not "What folklore should I get?" but rather "What assumptions about the nature of folklore do I hold and what intentions for the use of collectanea do I hold?" No one can answer such questions fully. Those underlying assumptions are so basic an aspect of our intellectual attire they're nearly invisible. (Ruth Benedict said that the film doesn't see the lens through which it looks). But at least you can remind yourself that you do have structuring ideas and try to be aware of ways in which they might influence your fieldworking perceptions. ("Yes," writes Ives, "you can try. But you always fail in different ways." Sure you fail, but failure properly achieved, as I several times note in these pages, can be a faithful instructor.)

Fieldworkers, just as informants, have points of view and limitations of vision. The world is a great mass of facts, and the only times we confront the world with no useful organizing ideas at all are times of immense confusion and disorientation. Medical friends tell me that the first question asked most often by people who have been unconscious is "Where am I?" People who have been in automobile accidents ask that question, as do surgery patients coming out of anaesthesia and people who have fainted. Without a sense of place the world is a confusing mass of unconnected points of information. We read facts in terms of our understanding of the facts' context: the "meaning" of a man on a surgical table is different if we know that surgical table is in a hospital operating room, on a soap opera set, or in a museum diorama. Our inference about the "meaning" of a smile depends on the context in which the smile occurs. We deal with objects and events in terms of our sense of the boundaries of objects and events. At dinner, we eat the food on our plate but not, normally, the food on the plate of the person next to us. Our sense of boundaries influences how we negotiate conversations. If the person sitting to our right says to the person sitting to his or her right "I love you," we do not, normally, respond "And *I* love *you*." All of us are encyclopedias of codes about boundaries of things that apply to us and things that don't. We have codes for our social behavior, our occupational behavior, and our intellectual behavior. Our ideas of what is and isn't folklore, what is and isn't meaningful, are dependent on our ideas of where things belong and where things are, where things begin and where things end.

When does an event start and when does it end? Does a formal dinner begin when you receive the invitation, when you change from street clothes into what you'll wear for the dinner, when you arrive at the house where the dinner will occur, or when you lift your fork? Does it end after dessert, when you go out the host's door, when you reach your door, when you pay the baby-sitter, when you change into comfortable clothes, when you get up at three A.M. for an Alka-Seltzer, when you weigh yourself the next morning and swear never, never will you do that again? You can describe the dinner well enough in any of those time frames, within any of those temporal contexts, but you can't make the same sense of it. Our sense of useful boundaries fixes what will be our sense of useful information. The facts of the world are at once unambiguously objective and pervasively subjective. "We understand other people and their expressions," writes Edward M. Bruner, "on the basis of our own experience and self-understanding" (1986:6).

If our goal in collecting songs is to get tunes and texts, the material that matters begins when the music starts and ends when the music stops. If our sense of boundary is the performance event, our information collecting begins before the first song and ends after the last song. If our sense of boundary is the place the music occupies in the performers' lives, then our collecting must include enough information on those lives for us to be able to locate the music within it.

I'll argue in the second part of this book that the machines we elect to use influence the kinds of information we get; the models we carry have the same effect. Not all methodologies can handle all kinds of questions; methodologies structure questions yet unformulated. Our models control the information we bring home from the field, the information we elect to analyze, the analyses we think deserving of publication and offering to others. Scholars often pretend that their systems of classification are derived from the raw facts of their research and that their theoretical models are in turn derived from their analysis of the systems. In fact, the process works quite the other way around: we have our models, and from them we derive our systems of classification. That's why the systems of classification always make such perfect sense. And it's why the facts we find fit our systems of classification so well: the system tells us what bits of the world *are* facts and what bits are inconsequential fluff or clutter. The difference between "meaningful" and "meaningless" in any analytic context has to do only with whether and how something fits the analytic structure— with whether or not the analytic structure has a way to use the information.

"Francis Bacon," write Edgerton and Langness, "champion of the inductive method in science, was wrong in his belief that if a scientist were merely to collect all the facts, these facts would somehow speak for themselves. Social and cultural facts require some kind of interpretation before one can even know which ones to look for out of the infinite number possible. To make the interpretation requires a frame of reference or a point of view. As the philosopher Abraham Kaplan (1964:132–33) put it, 'After the moment of the observer's birth, no observation can be undertaken in all innocence. We always know something already, and this knowledge is intimately involved in what we come to know next, whether by observation or any other way' " (1974:12). The facts are always out there; the variables are our needs, our uses, and whatever colors and organizes our perceptions of the facts.

The Scientific Method

Folklore studies lean either toward the humanities (and the kinds of studies done by humanities scholars focusing on textual structure, history, comparisons, etc.) or toward the social sciences (and the kinds of studies social scientists do: the function of items in culture, the behavior of people performing items, etc.). A few folklorists (e.g., Goldstein, 1964:15–16) have been entranced with a model drawn from the physical sciences—the "scientific method," which is attractive, which promises a kind of certitude, but which I think is finally useless for folklore and folklife studies and, by extension, for productive fieldwork. It might be reassuring if it could be shown that folklore information profited from the kind of manipulation central to the scientific method, but I know of no such evidence. No folklorist who has argued for a scientific model of folklore studies has ever done more than *assert* a connection. (The argument over whether a field's materials are subject to kinds of analyses used in the physical sciences rages fiercely in fields like sociology and psychology. The argument there isn't so much whether data and analysis can be replicated, for in gross ways they can, but rather whether the results are as unambiguously meaningful as are results in the physical sciences. Cf. Johnson 1975:16.)

The scientific method consists of developing a hypothesis, collecting data in a replicable way (the report of research done includes sufficient information for another researcher to carry out exactly the same experiment), analyzing the data in a replicable way (the report of analysis includes sufficient information for another researcher to carry out the same analysis), and proceeding to a conclusion. The reason for the replicability is so other scientists can check the data and the computations.

Experiments don't reveal what we didn't think we knew previously; they confirm models rather than generate them. Hypothesis is central to the scientific method, not because it leads to a better or more efficient understanding of the world, but because it ensures that the experiment will be performed in terms of the science we have already determined to be "true." The experiment then proves or disproves the hypothesis, but always in terms of the model we had going in.

The heart of scientific inquiry is not getting answers to questions; rather, it's in knowing what questions to ask and how to ask them. In science, once the question is posed the answer is structured. Physics, Martin Heidegger observed, "requests nature to manifest itself in terms of predictable forces, it sets up the experiment precisely for the sole purpose of asking whether and how nature follows the scheme preconceived by science" (in Prigogine and Stengers, 1984:33). Experimental science, as Nobel laureate Ilya Prigogine and Isabelle Stengers wrote, is "the art of choosing situations that are hypothetically governed by the law under investigation and staging them to give clear, experimental answers. For each experiment certain principles are presupposed and thus cannot be established by that experiment" (1984:88).

The scientific method is useless in humanistic studies exactly because of its structural purity. It takes us only where we thought we were in the first place, speaking with the voice of the first and last lines of T. S. Eliot's "East Coker": *In my beginning is my end* and *In my end is my beginning.*

The facts of the humanities aren't the same kinds of things as the facts of physical scientists. The former are the products of human intelligence and imagination; they're idiosyncratic; they're made up: a poem, a painting, a symphony, a joke, a jumping jack. Being made up doesn't make those things less true or valid or useful, but we know we must deal with them differently than we do with a sparrow, a cloud, a boulder, or a subatomic particle emitted from a nucleus. We use a different rhetoric and have different expectations when we set out to describe or understand what seem to be the natural histories of facts collected by folklorists and other humanists.

There is another, equally important difference in the ways scientists and humanists work. The world of the physical scientist is perfectly located in the foreground; the world of the humanistic scholar is ever deepening in time and space and range and complexity. In the physical sciences, new work occurs beyond the edge of all previous work; it builds on the most immediate step and can safely ignore everything else. One correct insight in science can render forever useless all previous insights in its line. Not so in the humanities, where there's none of the linearity of the physical sciences; the past, for the humanities scholar, remains forever present. And that past, as Stanley Cavell has observed, "may at any time come to life, not merely as the recovery of certain neglected problems within the field but as a recovery of the field's originating, or preserving, authority" (1983:185n). Our job never gets simpler, for we need to know it all, and more is being put on the table all the time. If the behavior of the physical scientist is best characterized by the experimental method, the behavior of the humanist is probably best exemplified by Wallace Stevens's "Thirteen Ways of Looking at a Blackbird."

Folkloric inquiry never has the kind of certitude and simplicity to which physical science aspires. Science tends to be complicated in getting there; the conclusions of science tend to be uncomplex. The humanities offer us complex conclusions that immediately force us along to more complex inquiries. No folklorist presumes to conduct the kind of inquiry that would reduce the analysis of a myth recitation to the unambiguous certitude a physicist expects from the analysis of a physical process. The humanities reveal to us the complexity of human experience and give us intellectual tools that help us take comfort in that complexity; the sciences reveal to us the simple relationships that describe the most complex sequences of events and interactions. The two are not the same kind of thinking, nor are they the same kind of quest.

The scientific method is useful only for investigations that are absolutely replicable. Chemists can do spectrographic analyses of tiny bits of material, then check themselves or have their work checked by other chemists a dozen times. If the material sampled is homogeneous, if the process is followed exactly each time, and if the equipment functions correctly each time, the results will be exactly the same each time, whether they are produced by an American or Russian or Israeli or Italian chemist. Not approximately or nearly or more-or-less. Exactly the same.

That never happens in a folklore field study because nothing of importance is ever exactly the same. The researcher and the informant are changed by, among other things, each of their previous encounters. Folklore fieldwork is personal work. It isn't neutral and it isn't objective. It's too much subject to such factors as the unique chemistry between people at a specific moment in time, by the presence or absence of indigestion that day, by a slight memory of someone who had exactly that color eyes, by the response to the fabric and hue of the shirt one of you happens to be wearing, to a faint odor there below the edge of consciousness. And those are the simple factors influencing what goes on. The ideas about the material and the world are far more deeply hidden, far more pervasive in their influence.

Seeing What's There

"If we consider," wrote Elli Köngäs-Maranda, "as I am increasingly inclined to do, folklore as the *communication of meanings in small-group interactions by the use of conventional, shared, and therefore understood and expected, expressions,* then we must become very aware of the collector's role in shaping what is collected. For if he is not acceptable as audience, he will not get his work done; and if he is, as folklorists easily are, then he influences the phenomenon he is observing. This contamination is inevitable in all human sciences . . ." (n.d.:197).

The folklore field situation is never fully created and controlled by the folklorist; we're not like chemists studying bits of matter or biologists studying cells. The folklorist studying normal behaviors is an intruding and disruptive force or element. The task isn't so much one of controlling what goes on as *not* contaminating it any more than absolutely necessary. Köngäs-Maranda described a fieldworker who went to such an extreme to avoid influencing the situation that his results were irreparably compromised: "I once knew a graduate anthropology student at Harvard who had spent two years in a Papago village in the South-West of the U.S. During the two years, he boasted, he had been sitting in the village plaza, under a tree, watching the life of the people. This he had done, he said, in order not to influence what was happening. One wonders: first, how much information did he carry back, since, if I understood him right, his purism included not taking notes; second, what the Papago thought of his presence there, under the tree, day in and out. This must have been even more mystifying than the presence of a stranger who at least explains what he is doing and then tries to do it. Both disturb, but at least one makes sense" (n.d.:205).

Most fieldworkers have an interest rather than a question: "I'm interested in worksongs . . . Armenians . . . my mother's side of the family . . . what remains of Finnish customs in this neighborhood . . . how factory workers communicate in this noisy shop. . . ." The actual questions to be asked of the material often aren't apparent until the fieldwork is well underway. And the most important learnings from the field experience aren't apparent until long after the fieldwork is over. You can, of course, narrow things so you get only what you knew you were after from the beginning. You can say (and some collectors have),

"Don't tell me those stories about the Irishman, I'm after real Negro stories, you know, the ones about animals." You'll get your animal stories, but you'll have no idea how they figure in the tellers' repertoires or even what those repertoires really are. All you'll have are responses to your preset demands, not what you could have gotten from being flexible, from an ability to see what's happening and to follow leads you hadn't suspected would be there. Fieldwork requires constant attention and the willingness to continually modify your design as your sense of the possibilities change. Physical scientists modify their technique if the technique fails to result in the end they seek; they rarely decide in the middle of the research process that the goal is less important than the information itself.

That doesn't mean folklore fieldwork can be done with no starting ideas at all. "Collecting initiated without careful problem statement," writes Goldstein, "is usually arbitrary, unorganized, perfunctory, and wasteful. The time a collector spends in the field is rarely long enough even without such waste" (1964:17). If you're too vague you won't know how to prepare; if you're too specific you lock yourself down before you get out of the house. So by all means have a good idea of what you hope to find and prepare yourself to uncover that sort of information. But when you get out there, be prepared to dump your plan if something better comes along or if what you learn in the field teaches you that you didn't understand earlier what you would better have been looking for.

Folklorists call "shotgun collecting" that work done with no particular subject in mind: "I'll go out and get whatever they've got and later on I'll find some order in it or impose some order on it." The other kind of collecting doesn't have a name. It's more specific: a ballad, a single informant's repertory, the trajectory of a tale or technique, the folklore in a specific place or particular to a certain profession, and so on. If there were world enough and time, shotgun collecting would present no problem. But there is rarely enough time to do anything fully, so folklorists, like most fieldworkers, limit their focus fairly early on in the work, often before they even leave home. Just be prepared to dump your plan entirely if something really fine presents itself.

In the field, *seeing* can be the most difficult task of all. What is most obvious may not be what is most representative; what is most obvious is often what is most unordinary. We look at everything within our field of vision, but we don't *see* everything we look at. We see what our mind tells us is for some reason meaningful or important. Our eyes focus on the plane we think is important; our mind records the information it thinks is important. Seeing the commonplace requires great and continuing effort. Asked to describe dinner at someone's house, we're not likely to mention that next to the plate with the steak were a knife and fork; we *know* a knife and fork are part of any dinner array. We would notice the absence of such instruments, or alternative instruments such as chopsticks. A fieldworker is "more likely to report on phenomena which are different from those of his own society or subculture than he is to report on phenomena common to both. When the participant observer spends an extended period of time in a foreign culture ... those elements of the culture which first seemed notable because they were alien may later acquire a more homey quality. His increased familiarity with the culture alters him as an instrument" (Webb et al., 1966:114).

Describe an ordinary dinner at your house as you would describe it to a friend who asked what you had for dinner last night. Then try to describe the same meal as it might be described by an Inuit ethnologist whose frame of reference was meals served north of the Arctic circle. It suddenly becomes necessary to say what animal the "steak" came from and to note that it was served cooked and that it was served on certain kinds of plates and eaten with certain kinds of utensils and that various people seemed to have different roles in the preparation and serving of the meal. . . .

Different questions of the field require different field strategies. Some field investigations take years of repeat visits to the same places and the same people. Others can be wonderfully done in a day, a weekend, a week. Some field questions require all the technical devices now available: videotapes, film (for record and for frame-by-frame motion study), audiotapes, a range of microphones, 35mm cameras with various lenses; others require nothing more than you paying careful attention to what you see and hear and remembering those things long enough to write them down in your notebook. Some field studies require that you ask a lot of questions or even have formal interviews; others require that you make yourself as small and quiet as possible and just watch what's going on.

We see what we value, what we know how to see, what we train ourselves to look for. The machines never capture anything we don't tell them to capture, and the hardest things of all to see are the things we knew were there all the time.

Part Two/Doing It

The anthropologist is a human instrument studying other human beings and their societies. Although he has developed techniques that give him considerable objectivity, it is an illusion for him to think he can remove his personality from his work and become a faceless robot or a machinelike recorder of human events. It is important to accept that this human instrument is as much a product of biological, psychological, and social conditioning as are the people he studies.

Hortense Powdermaker
Stranger and Friend

Every anthropological fieldworker would readily acknowledge that the accepted genres of anthropological expression—our fieldnotes, diaries, lectures, and professional publications—do not capture the richness or the complexity of our lived experience in the field. There are inevitable gaps between reality, experience, and expressions, and the tension among them constitutes a key problematic in the anthropology of experience.

Edward M. Bruner
The Anthropology of Experience

5/Fieldworker Roles

Folklorists, as all other field researchers, are observers.

Observation is when you're outside what's going on and watching other people do it, or you're watching what other people have done. This might cover anything from what you observe from a good seat at a political convention or ball game to your photographs of graffiti to mating behavior you note in the park across the street from your house to conversations taking place next to you at the kitchen table.

Participant-observation means you're somehow involved in the events going on, you're inside them. You might, like Bruce Nickerson (1983), study factory work by taking a job in a factory; or, like William Foote Whyte (1943), you might take up residence within the community you want to study. You might go drinking or fishing or picnicking or campaigning with the people whose folklore concerns you.

"The term 'participant observation,' " write Becker and Geer, "covers several kinds of research activity. The researcher may be a member of the group he studies; he may pose as a member of the group, though in fact he is not; or he may join the group in the role of one who is there to observe. . . . In general, the participant observer gathers data by participating in the daily life of the group or organization that he studies. He watches the people he is studying to see what situations they ordinarily meet and how they behave in them. He talks with other participants and discovers their interpretations of the events he has observed" (1960:268–69).

Participant-observation provides folklorists great access; it also presents difficult ethical questions. If you're studying the folkways of police, what happens if you see a police officer take a bribe or overlook a crime or brutalize a suspect? If you're studying the folklife of a teen gang or rock musicians or professional athletes, what happens if you see a drug transaction take place or if you overhear plans to harm an informer? If you're working in a factory to get your information, what are your responsibilities to your fellow workers who think you're there simply because you need a job and who wouldn't talk the same way if they knew who you really were and what you really were doing? If you're studying a family, what happens when one spouse reveals to you that he or she is having an affair? What happens if one spouse wants to have an affair with you? What do you do, in sum, when, because of the trust you've developed or secrets you've kept, you learn things that can hurt people? Each variation of the participant-observer role requires some measure of trust—in exchange for which the fieldworker is given greater access to what goes on than outsiders are given; in exchange for which the fieldworker has responsibilities more complex than those of the complete outsider.

Scholars in several social science fields do fieldwork, but the different ends of the studies may require that different kinds of information be collected. Folklore fieldwork and oral history fieldwork, for example, differ in several important ways. The student of history is largely dependent on documents—on letters, diaries, official and private records, and on public and private statements of individuals involved in events that for some reason are of historical interest. The student of folklore is primarily dependent on performances—on stories or gestures or techniques as found in practice or as later described or performed by people who know about them. The oral historian is seeking information about an event or a person, about something in the past; folklorists are also interested in getting reports of past folklore events or about folklore performers, but they're equally concerned with documenting the actual performers and events and performances. For the historian, the content of the statement is what matters most; for the folklorist, the content matters but so does the statement itself.

The student of oral history, then, can do quite well with a tape recorder and someone to talk into the microphone. Tape recorders are important for folklorists, but not just for recording talk; they're also useful for recording performances of various kinds, ranging from formal performance in a formal setting (on a stage, in a church, at a celebration) to an interview in which those things are discussed and performed as exempla. Since folklorists are interested in the doing of something as much as they're interested in people talking about doing something, they're also likely to use in their work still and motion picture cameras and videotape recorders.

Anthropologists generally take fieldwork to involve a long-term and often residential commitment:

> Fieldwork is not just a single method but a varied set of procedures. The core of fieldwork is *participant-observation*. As participant-observer, the anthropologist lives intimately as a member of the society he has chosen to study. He shares in the people's day-to-day activities, watches as they eat, fight and dance, listens to their commonplace and exciting conversations, and slowly begins to live and understand life as they do. But he also remains detached from their life, at least to some degree. He is not living among another people to enjoy their way of life. He is there to understand it and then to report his understanding to others. Complete involvement, then, is incompatible with the anthropologist's primary goals, but complete detachment is incompatible with fieldwork. Successful fieldwork requires a balance between the two, a balancing act which is every bit as difficult as it sounds.
>
> The kind of understanding that arises from being a participant-observer takes time. Anthropologists count on spending a substantial period in the field; most go for at least a year if possible, and many stay longer or return for a second visit. In the small societies that anthropologists have typically studied, the natural unit of time is a year. Throughout man's history, nature and the seasons have been closely tied to economic life and through that to man's social rounds. Groups form and disperse, activities change. There are times of hunger and want balanced by times of feasting, celebrating, and plenty. A stay of at least a year is usually required for the anthropologist to acquire an understanding of the range of behaviors and customs in a strange society. (Edgerton and Langness, 1974:2–3)

Folklorists, on the other hand, do not usually work in primitive societies where the entire life cycle is determined by the calendar. In industrial society (even agriculture in modern societies is industrial), the cycles of production have less to do with the weather than with interest and inflation rates and with government land management policies; for families with young children, the school year is more important than the solar year. Folklorists, moreover, rarely attempt to understand whole communities, and rarely do they attempt to discover and analyze the set of symbolic forms by which whole communities function; rather, they study individuals or genres or processes. Folklorists and anthropologists are not usually interested in the same types of materials. The kinds of questions folklorists attempt to answer do not usually demand the total immersion required by many anthropological inquiries. Folklorists can do fieldwork evenings or on weekends; they can also do it full time for a week or month or year. They are more flexible in options than anthropologists and more ranging in concern than oral historians.

Most folklore fieldwork involves both observation and interviewing.
Both are tools; each has its own advantages and disadvantages. Interviewing is often the fastest way to get information; it isn't necessarily
the best. To learn about someone's personal history, the interview is
perhaps the best technique; to learn about how people relate to one
another in a work or play environment, the interview is probably the
least useful. There's a difference between the folklore people know and
the folklore they do; interviews will produce the former, not necessarily
the latter. "Observation," write Becker and Geer, "is not always a
feasible alternative and is considerably more expensive and time-consuming than interviewing is. It provides, however, firsthand reports
of events and actions and much fuller coverage of an organization's
activities, giving direct knowledge of matters that, from interviewing,
we could know about only by hearsay. Whether or not one should use
observation in any particular study depends on the resources available
and the character of the problem one is attempting to solve" (1960:268).

Interviewing changes whatever is going on. "Interviews and questionnaires," wrote Webb and his colleagues, "intrude as a foreign element into the social setting they would describe, they create as well
as measure attitudes, they elicit atypical roles and responses, they are
limited to those who are accessible and will cooperate, and the responses
obtained are produced in part by dimensions of individual differences
irrelevant to the topic at hand" (1966:1). Fieldworkers must be aware
how their intrusion influences the information provided to them if
they're to make sense of that information.

Probably the greatest portion of folklore information is provided in
situations set up by the collector: the folklorist asks groups or individuals
to perform or to talk. Even if the collector has been doing extensive
observation of normal folklife, interviews are often necessary to obtain
the information needed to understand what has been observed and to
learn the performers' attitudes toward their own actions. "It has often
been charged," writes D. K. Wilgus,

> that the American folk music collector has chosen to record folk music—
> other than that in domestic tradition—"out of context." In truth, material
> is always collected "in context," but the context has often been that of
> the interview rather than the "natural context." The interview context is
> not one that I shall be heretical enough to say should be preferred, but
> one which I shall say is necessary. Of course the interview context has
> been enforced upon fieldworkers by their own beliefs that the traditions
> they are investigating are at the last dying and can be salvaged only in
> this way. But the interview context is necessary even in a tradition rec-
> ognized as vibrant. Let us assume that by the most sophisticated means

a traditional music performance is recorded in its natural context—be it a work song, a curing song, a frolic tune. The interview technique is still necessary for significant contextual information.

... It should be pointed out that the folk music collector, like the proverb collector, cannot wait around until the event takes place. Quite often it is a solo performance for the individual's benefit or part of a structured/familial relationship. The investigator cannot follow the performer driving home the cows, waiting for a spontaneous burst of song. ... One may well record in the highly structured context of an Appalachian fiddle context or a Bavarian wedding, but these situations must always be supplemented by in-depth interviews of the performers. And the collector of folk music is more fortunate than investigators of some other genres in that traditional music performances tend toward the "fixed text" side of the scale. The collector of anecdotes had better catch his bird on the wing, for the request to repeat the story may well result in an inferior production—the listener has already "got the point." A musical performance, on the other hand, may well improve in a later repetition—certainly it is less likely to deteriorate. (1983:373–74)

Fieldworkers are always working in contexts of their own devising, whether as hidden observers or asking individuals to perform. There is, as Wilgus points out, nothing inherently wrong with this, so long as the fieldworker understands the nature of the devised context, knows how it limits whatever information is provided and how it influences the behaviors of the informants. Fieldworkers deal with real people in real situations, and they must, therefore, understand the ways their presence influences what's going on. They must be sensitive to the kinds of relationships they develop with the people who may agree to perform for them, and they must understand that the rhetorical form called "the interview" is different from ordinary discourse in critical ways.

6/Rapport

Friends and Strangers

Rapport isn't something you develop like a photographic plate. It comes and goes: you can lose it in a moment and in a like amount of time with another person achieve it to an astounding degree. Merely having rapport is no guarantee you'll be able to record anything. Sometimes the individuals with whom you have the greatest rapport are those with whom it's most difficult to have real interviews—close friends. That's because the role of interviewer puts you outside the role of friend and makes for a situation more unnatural than that between a near-stranger and a person willing to talk about something that matters.

Cynde Kibler, a student in my spring 1983 undergraduate folklore class at SUNY Buffalo, wrote at the end of a paper about folklore she had collected from a Ukranian friend: "Varslaw's heritage is a natural part of his everyday life, and I see it and know it just as I know other characteristics in the personalities of my other friends. But when I turned on the tape, he became an American talking about the traditions of Ukranians (in a very reserved way), and I become a stupid 'reporter.' I had wanted to ask questions that would bring out the 'Ukranian' aspects of Varslaw's personality, but all I managed to get was sort of a documentary on his life. Neither one of us were ourselves, and I'm disappointed by that."

The danger in fieldwork of the fieldworker turning the person whose life is being studied into an object is obvious; less obvious, but just as much a danger, is that the person studied will do the same thing. I can't tell you how to avoid the problem, because every time the tape recorder goes on and questions are asked the relationships in the room

68

change. As Ives astutely points out (1980:49), the tape recorder becomes the third person at the table; it doesn't talk, but it's very much a part of the dynamic.

I once thought of doing a book of interviews with some friends who were well known for various reasons: one is a civil rights attorney, one a poet, one a filmmaker, one a novelist, one a musician, one an actor. . . . I had some theme that would tie it all together, but now I suspect the real theme was these were all interesting and successful people and we were pals, so it would be a collection of interviews easy to do, the work would give us an excuse for hanging out for a while, the book would be worth reading and likely to find a good publisher.

I never did the book. I tried the interviewing with one or two friends, and while it wasn't quite a disaster, neither was it much of anything else. The work was curiously unpleasant: we were suddenly in roles that were completely unnatural, roles that violated the friendship we had spent so long building. We were dealing with one another as objects. I had the same problem Cynde Kibler had and it beat me too.

Kenneth S. Goldstein calls the curious advantage strangers have in certain information-collecting situations "stranger value." "The collector who comes from afar and will disappear again," he writes, "will be able to collect materials and information which might not be divulged to one who has a long-term residence in the same area" (1964:64; see also pp. 71, 161, 162). Ives, sixteen years later, discusses "stranger value" in the context of his own interviewing experience.

> [It] means that none of these assumptions [about things already known] exist between people who don't know each other, and sometimes people will say things to strangers that they would feel awkward or silly saying to a member of the family. It's a kind of paradox, but people frequently find that being interviewed by a close friend or relative is an odd and not entirely pleasant experience, while they will feel quite at ease with a stranger under the same circumstances. The paradox is less obvious if you are asking for specific items like stories or songs than if you are after more general cultural information, but it is still there. I would far prefer to interview a stranger, myself, but there are plenty of examples of successful interviewing of close relatives and friends. (1980:38)

There is another danger in working with friends: they're less likely than other people to tell us things we might not like to hear—they may not tell us that a third party we like is unreliable or that there's something seriously wrong with our project itself. Rosalie Wax writes:

> Inexperienced field workers sometimes err in regarding the statements of friendly informants whom they like as more truthful or more valuable than those of offensive or less engaging individuals. In point of fact, the

latter may give more significant information, since informants, like other humans, tend to conceal unpleasantness from those they like and, conversely, delight in telling the bitter truth to those they dislike. On this question of rapport one can therefore offer the not particularly helpful suggestion that a person with sufficient insight may in a few hours learn more from one informant, be he friendly or hostile, than a person lacking insight will learn in months, even though the truth be presented to him daily written in letters of fire. (1960a:91)

It's always more pleasant working with people we like, but when doing fieldwork it's more important to spend time with someone who can provide information that matters.

Stranger value isn't something you get to keep, by the way. If your relationship with an informant continues over a period of time, you're less and less a stranger and you sense more and more the unspoken restrictions on the kinds of questions that can be comfortably asked. And sometimes, Ellen Stekert points out, there's "a boomerang effect the next trip—the 'I told too much' syndrome." The lesson here is that fieldwork is a dynamic enterprise: each encounter is different from the one before and the one that follows. Collectors, therefore, can never afford to go into collecting sessions without giving careful thought to the structure of the relationships between themselves and the informants, without giving as much thought to the informants' reasons for talking as for their own reasons for listening.

Why People Talk to You

It's possible to do folklore research without rapport. I know someone who did a study of folklore themes in soap operas and someone else who did a study of graffiti. But if you're in face-to-face situations with human beings who are telling you things or who are expected to do things to help you in your work, then rapport matters.

Every human being is different and every combination of human beings is different. You may meet Charlie and immediately have rapport; your best friend may meet Charlie and immediate and irreparable enmity might manifest itself. Rapport is connected with respect and affection, but it can exist among people who don't respect one another and who have little affection for one another. Rapport is critical to doing fieldwork, but it's the only aspect of the entire enterprise I find so mysterious that I can only talk around it, not about it directly. And I don't know of anyone who can tell you how to make rapport happen. Anyone who has done any fieldwork, anyone who has any common sense, can tell you things certain to kill it: make inappropriate sexual advances, joke about people when you don't have license to make jokes, sneer at their religion, be the only one to get drunk or get drunk incompetently, be caught lying, and all those things that screw up any normal relationship and that you shouldn't have to be told to avoid anyway.

As Ives points out, no one agrees to be a fieldworker's informant unless that person finds something in it for himself or herself (1980:40–41). True altruists are so rare in this world that you should not plan on encountering them. Some reasons for helping are obvious and are just what they seem: Uncle Conrad likes you and wants you to succeed in life so he sings for you the old songs that for whatever reason are of interest to you now; Mr. Bargarian agrees with you that the preservation of Armenian legends is one of the world's most pressing needs so he tells you every one he knows and introduces you to the good storytellers of his acquaintance; Officer Tom has been waiting for years for someone to ask him what it's been like being a cop in this city. . . .

Sometimes money is a factor. Some collectors pay informants whether the informants ask for it or not; some informants won't do anything without pay. There are various reasons for paying or for not paying. Andrew Giarelli, doing research about narrative among the Cheyenne (1984), learned that the value of the transfer of a narrative is diminished if no payment is made and that payment is required whatever degree of friendliness exists between teller and listener. Sometimes you may be taking time when your informant would be earning needed money; you might not be asked for payment, but offering to replace what's been lost would not be insulting. Sometimes paying can be dangerous because you might encourage the generation of a great deal of phony information or you might create expectations among other performers you won't be able to fulfill. Part depends on your situation: if you've got a lot of money, share it; if you're broke, let people know it and don't be embarrassed about it. (Ellen Stekert reminds me that a claim of poverty, whether true or not, may not be believed if there's a great class difference between the collector and the informant. The meaning of "I'm really broke" is not the same to someone with an annual income under $10,000 and someone who can afford to go to college or graduate school and spend time asking people questions. Ellen is right. My advice would be to tell the truth about your situation, if it seems appropriate, but don't make a big deal out of the information. Nothing convinces of its opposite so much as an inappropriately excessive denial.)

Sometimes the reasons people talk to you aren't so obvious. I've never known an informant to say, "It's been swell recording for you. I was bored to tears these past few weeks and had nothing to do and your visit this weekend gave me a way to pass the time." Neither have I met one who said, "No one has asked me my opinion about anything ever and I've been willing to give you all these stories and opinions out of sheer frustration." But those are legitimate reasons and they're not uncommon. Don't knock them if you realize that's what's been going on. Folklore is often used to pass the time so it's not surprising that talking about folklore (which is a kind of folklore itself) serves the same function.

Fieldworkers want to know, Rosalie Wax writes, how to get informants to talk and how to know when they're providing reliable information.

> ... The field worker may get what he wants more efficiently by stating these questions differently, namely by asking himself (and subsequently answering) the questions: "Why should anybody in this group bother to talk to me? Why should this man take time out from his work, gambling, or pleasant loafing to answer my questions?" I suggest that as the field worker discovers the correct answers he will improve not only his technique in obtaining information but also his ability to evaluate it. I suggest, moreover, that the correct answers to these questions will tend to show that whether an informant likes, hates, or just doesn't give a hoot about the field worker, he will talk because he and the field worker are making an exchange, are consciously or unconsciously giving each other something they both desire or need. (1960a:91–92)

Stories

I said the whole business of rapport was mysterious to me, and it is. It's like Thomas Aquinas's line about the beautiful: *quod vigum placet,* "that which when seen pleases." Rapport matters in fieldwork; it matters in other kinds of human activity as well. The best and most detailed report I know about establishing rapport can be found in Jean Malaurie's great field study, *The Last Kings of Thule* (1982). Here are some stories about times it happened and times it didn't.

Diane and I met a fellow who asked us if we knew Norman Mailer. I asked why he asked that question. "You're writers and you're from that part of the country," he said. I said I'd met Mailer once.

"You friends?" the man asked.

"No. I told you, I just met him once. Do *you* know him?"

"Yes," he said. "He used to come to our office a lot when he was working on that book about Gary Gilmore. Do you think he's got a sense of humor? Mailer, I mean."

"I don't know him well enough," I said.

"No," Diane said.

"Neither do I," the man said. "The first day he came into our office, he came in there and he said, 'My name is Norman Mailer. You probably never heard of me. I'm a very well-known writer and I'm from New York and I'm here to do a book on Gary Gilmore.' I told him I hadn't ever heard of him but we'd help him out anyway."

"Had you heard of him?" Diane asked.

"Sure," the man said. "I'd read three or four of his books. *Naked and the Dead.* I liked that. Still think it's his best. *Marilyn*—I thought that was cheap stuff. And I'd read some others."

"Did you ever tell him what you thought of his books?"

"Never told him I'd read any. None of us did. If he wanted to think we didn't know about books, well, let him think what he wants."

The man and his colleagues were mildly annoyed at Mailer's assumption that they were country bumpkins, but they were far too polite to tell him that. They were not, however, too polite to take revenge.

Mailer frequently stopped by their office for information, so they worked out a code with the receptionist. When Mailer arrived, she would buzz them and say, "Mr. Mailer is here." Then she would tell Mailer, "They're all in conference just now, Mr. Mailer. But if you'll have a seat they'll be with you in a few minutes."

"How long did you keep him waiting?" Diane asked.

"Twenty minutes. It was always twenty minutes, exactly twenty minutes, between when she told him that and when she told him it was okay to go in now."

"Why twenty minutes?" Diane asked.

"Because that was the signal for the start of our morning coffee break. Twenty minutes was all we were allowed for coffee break."

"Did he ever catch on?" I asked.

"No," the man said. "He never even knew we were funny."

New Yorkers who haven't spent much time elsewhere in the land never get to learn that a major strain in American folk humor is characterized by its silence. If you don't get the joke, people may not tell you a joke happened. Your missing it just makes it better for them because now there are two things to laugh about.

* * * * *

Charles Keil was doing research in Tivland. He realized that stories told to him in an interview situation were shorter and less well told than stories told in natural situations, so he sponsored a storytelling session. Performers were invited, Keil provided refreshments and announced a prize for the best teller. He expected twenty or thirty people, but more than a hundred came, so he quickly ran out of beer. There weren't enough seats. But the stories started anyway.

> Everyone seemed to be having a good time, but soon the stories dwindled and thunder was heard rolling in the distance, and when the departing guests discovered that the anthropologist had provided only a duck for a prize, the scene became chaotic. Everyone had expected at least a goat or beast of sufficient size to give at least a piece of meat to all participants and a bigger portion to the best. Under the circumstances, local elders whom I had counted on to assist in the judging were reluctant to appear connected to the fiasco, much less offer an opinion. It began to rain, and I found myself in a reception hut, surrounded by a chorus of eloquently angry Tiv. Expert storytellers had become equally proud of their skills at invective, and no one was eager to walk home in the rain carrying a duck or part of a duck. Finally, some hours later, I was left holding the duck, a mercifully quiet Muscovy. (1979:59)

*　*　*　*　*

In the spring of 1966, two years after I began doing field research on black convict worksongs in Texas prisons, Pete Seeger called and asked if I knew of any decent films about the songs. I said I didn't. "Let's make one then," Pete said. "That tradition won't be around much longer and it's an important part of our heritage."

"Fine," I said. "But I don't know where we'll get the money."

"I'll pay for it," Pete said. "There isn't time to go looking for grants." (He was right: within a year the Texas prison work gangs were integrated and the songs were gone forever.)

A few weeks later, Pete, his wife Toshi, and his son Dan met me at Ellis Unit, not far from Huntsville. They arrived not just with film equipment but also with Pete's complement of longneck banjo and six- and twelve-string guitars. I asked what he intended to do with the guitars. "They're going to sing for us," he said, "so I'll sing for them."

"I don't think that's necessary, Pete," I said. "Not necessary at all." What I was thinking was: This is quite crazy. Ellis was the Texas prison for multiple recidivists, the men doing the most time because they'd been in for serious crimes more times than the rest of the state's prisoners; it was the prison for the inmates who had been in the most fights or who had killed other prisoners or escaped from the other places. Pete's songs were fine for folk festivals and concerts in cities, where people knew and liked him and his songs, but this was *Ellis.*

"No, Pete," I said again, "I don't think you have to worry about reciprocating."

We began filming. On the second or third day Pete said, "Did you set up that concert yet?"

"You still want to do that, huh?"

"He's serious," Toshi said.

I spoke with the warden. He shrugged. (The shrug said, "You people are already running around my prison, I thought that was bizarre enough, but what difference will it make.") The warden said, "He really wants to do this?" I nodded. "You told him about this place?" I nodded again. "Okay. Tomorrow night in the gym."

The next night at seven o'clock approximately one thousand of Ellis's convicts were seated in the prison gym. I expected one of two things: hoots and jeers, which would be annoying, or stony silence, which would be worse. This wasn't, as I said, Newport or a college campus.

Within five minutes most of the convicts there were singing along and within ten minutes so were the guards and their supervisors and the assistant warden. After Pete's last encore the men cheered and yelled for ten minutes. It was for real; this was not a crowd that patronized anybody. It was one of the best concerts I ever heard and saw.

That's not why I'm telling you this. The reason for the story is what happened the following week, after Pete, Toshi, and Dan had gone back to New York.

A convict I had seen around many times during my visits the past two years was in a group of men coming out of one of the cellblocks on the way to the evening meal. He motioned for me to come closer. "Come to the cellblock after dinner. I want to talk to you."

An hour later I went back to the block and found him waiting near the bars facing the prison's long central corridor.

"I want to know why you never recorded me singing any of them river songs," he said.

"I've been coming here for two years," I said. "You knew what I was doing. You never said you knew any of them."

"That," he said, "was before I knew you was a friend of Pete Seeger's."

* * * * *

While on a research expedition to New Guinea in the early 1960s, physiologist Jared Diamond woke one night to see his chief porter

leaning over him. The porter held a fair-sized boulder. The boulder
was positioned directly above Diamond's face.

"What do you think you're doing?" Diamond said.

The other porters, who were gathered in a circle to watch the chief
porter drop the boulder on Diamond's face, began laughing. "Boss
catch him, boss catch him," they chanted. The chief porter dropped
the boulder to the ground and backed off in acute embarrassment.

When Diamond told me this story I said, "So you got no sleep for
the rest of the expedition."

"Oh, no, quite the contrary. After that I slept very well. There was
nothing to worry about, you see. He and I understood one another
and we both knew it would be extremely bad manners for him to try
to drop another boulder on my head and so did everyone else."

* * * * *

Immediately after a traditional singer who had known and recorded
for Ellen Stekert for a long time heard her sing "The Wife of Usher's
Well," he decided he wouldn't sing for her anymore. The song was in
the man's repertoire (he had learned it from his mother), but he decided
Stekert sang it the "right" way and he didn't. "Lady," the man said,
"if I could sing like that I'd not want to hear anyone sing; I'd just go
up on a mountaintop and sing all day." It took Stekert "a long time
to reconvince him that we just sang differently—that we each had songs
to offer joy to the other."

* * * * *

I first visited Cummins Prison in Arkansas in the summer of 1971.
My second visit was almost exactly a year later. Late in the first full
day of that second visit, I was sitting at the back of one of the dormitories talking with five or six convicts. The conversation went very
well. People were telling me a lot. I was surprised, since it takes a while
to establish that kind of rapport.

Later, I was alone near the barred wall at the front of the tank and
one of the men from the group walked to where I was standing. "You
were probably wondering why they were talking to you like that," he
said.

"I was," I said.

"I told them you were all right," he said.

"Thanks for the help. But what makes you think I'm all right?"

"I know you. I've read two of your books." I felt myself going red.
"Embarrassing when somebody knows you and you don't know him,
isn't it?" I allowed that it was. "Well," he said, "there's more. I watched

you work. I was at Ellis when you were talking to the guys there five years ago. I told these guys here, 'This guy was at Ellis and some fools told him *every*thing and no shit ever came down. He's okay.' That's why they talked to you."

"I don't remember you from Ellis," I said.

"No reason you should. I never went near you. I didn't know whether you was all right or not."

* * * * *

My favorite story about the ability to establish rapport involves my mother, who was at the time in nurse's training and was doing an internship in a mental hospital. One night she found herself locked in a short narrow corridor with a very large woman named Sadie. Sadie was in the hospital because she had strangled two people who just happened to be nearby when she got angry. "She was *always* angry," my mother said. "I backed up to the door leading to the corridor where everybody else was and it was locked. I couldn't turn around to see if anybody was there because I couldn't turn my back to Sadie. The only other way out was the opposite end of the corridor and Sadie was between me and that door and Sadie was big. There was no way to get around Sadie. Sadie just came toward me so slowly. She had her hands out in front of her and she put her fingers around my throat. It was like one of those movies where it goes into slow-motion. Only, it was slow and fast at the same time, if you know what I mean."

I said I knew what she meant. Since she was here telling me the story it was obvious she had survived the incident. She didn't say anything at that point. (In later years I realized that was a technique a lot of good storytellers have: they hit the climax and then go on hold so you have to ask for the denoument.) "So what *happened?* Did you use some judo or karate you learned in nurse's training?"

"They don't teach you karate in nurse's training. Don't be silly. You're trained not to get yourself locked in corridors with people who strangle people. If you do that, you don't need karate. Nurses aren't supposed to be using karate on patients anyway."

"So what did you do?"

"I said, 'Sadie, you want to kiss me. How nice.' Sadie stopped right where she was. She just stood there for a long time, with her fingers right where they had been. And then she smiled and she said, 'That's right,' and she kissed me. Then she turned around and went back to her room."

* * * * *

I lifted my mother's technique. I used it at Bridgewater Hospital for the Criminally Insane (where Frederick Wiseman made *Titicut Follies*) in a day room where construction was going on. A large man in inmate's clothes watched me take the cellophane off then light a cigar. He stuck out his hand for the cellophane. I handed it to him. He took it and dropped it on the floor, then said, "You through with that butt yet?"

"It's not a butt yet," I said.

"Looks like a butt to me."

I walked away, heading toward the doorway at the far end of the room. (I would have given him a cigar if I'd had two, but it was the only one I had with me and I'd been holding off smoking it all morning. I should say that the rationalization now seems silly and selfish.) Perhaps fifty patients milled about. Near the middle of the room some carpentry work had been going on. The carpenters were not around, but their tools were. The large man, who was walking alongside me and watching me smoke the cigar, saw where I was looking.

"Wouldn't it be something," he said, "if one of these nuts picked up that axe and wacked you over the head with it."

I hadn't noticed the axe until that moment. My expression must have changed because the man smiled broadly.

"It would sure be something," he said.

"None of them would do that," I said.

"Why not?" he said, still smiling.

"Because you wouldn't let them," I said.

He frowned suddenly, then smiled. "Right you are," he said. "Right you are." He waved and walked away.

7/Interviewing

The Problem of Conversation

The worst interview tape I ever heard was handed in as part of a term project in an undergraduate folklore class by the son of a New York police detective. The student couldn't get home to do his interview, so he wrote out his questions and mailed them to his brother, who had agreed to interview their father for him. The brother, then a New York policeman himself, read off the written questions in a clear, decisive voice:

"Question! Why did you join the police department?"

"I joined the police department because I wanted to be in public service and because police work looked like a good career."

"Question! Was the force different when you first joined?"

"Yes, it was."

"Question! What is the most difficult part of being a policeman?"

"The most difficult part of being a policeman is dealing with the public."

I don't know which was worse, having so many questions demanding a yes or no answer and thereby cutting off any discussion before it got started or the brother's "Question!" at the beginning of each cycle. As one might expect, the father responded like a cop on the witness stand; the answers were short and unambiguous or vague and empty. I didn't learn much about that father and son listening to the interview tapes except that the father was expert at responding to questions with a minimum of information and words. I'm certain they did not at any other time exchange those "Dragnet" lines when they were sitting around the house talking about work.

Having a conversation about a part of life and interviewing someone about a part of life are not the same kinds of event; they're not even the same kinds of discourse. "You are gathering, and the informant providing, information to be processed and stored," writes Ives, "and while you should certainly work to keep things relaxed and friendly, you are *not* simply 'having a nice chat' " (1980:50). The student who got his brother to make the tape understood there was a difference, but he went all the way to the silliness extreme in trying to avoid conversation and produce what he thought was a useful interview. He produced a parody instead, something that was neither interview nor conversation.

The best interviewers somehow make the difference between conversation and interview as unobtrusive as possible: the interviewer and Charlie discuss how and why Charlie learned those stories, but Charlie remains Charlie rather than some other person in the distant past Charlie is reconstructing for the recorder. Interview and conversation go on simultaneously, and the interviewee becomes more interested in the conversation with the interviewer than concerned about the image being projected for the abstract and distant and later listener.

Insofar as possible, it's best to act naturally in the collecting situation. I don't mean you shouldn't adapt to the situation. We all make adaptations all the time. I automatically adopt different styles and levels of discourse when talking to one of my classes, to a police officer who insists I was exceeding the speed limit, to an auditorium full of strangers, to my family at home, to my mother, to someone who owes me money, to someone I owe money. You do the same thing. None of those styles is necessarily dishonest or phony; most of them are what seem appropriate for the situations in which they emerge. We slip into those vocabularies and postures naturally: we don't think, "I'm going to adopt my family vocabulary and linguistic style now," we just do it, the same way we move the right foot from accelerator to brake when the taillights of the car ahead go on. Linguists call that kind of behavior "code-switching." Interviewers engage in code-switching and so do people being interviewed. Both adopt whatever mode they think appropriate for whatever they think the thing called "interview" is.

The reason I suggest acting as naturally as possible when doing fieldwork is this: if you present contrived poses and postures and personalities to people who don't know you very well, they'll decide you're a phony and the flow of information will dry up; and if you act that way in front of people who *do* know you very well, they'll decide you're coming unglued and they'll be distracted. Note that I didn't say that you should *be* natural. Doing what comes naturally when you're doing fieldwork can wreck the enterprise.

Until very recently, I did all my own tape transcriptions. At first I didn't have the money to hire someone else to do the work, then when I did have the money I found northern typists made too many mistakes transcribing southern conversations. I cursed and muttered and spent a lot of time at the typewriter. Afterward, I was happy for the labor because I learned a great deal listening to those tapes line by line, again and again. The most important thing I learned was that I talked too much. An informant would say something that would make me think of something and I would talk about it and then the informant would say something and I would say something—we were having conversations. Each time, each of us would redirect the conversation in reaction to what the other had just said. That's fine if you're hanging out, but if you're trying to get a lot of information in a limited field time, it's extremely inefficient. After a while, I found the amount of time on the tapes filled with my voice grew less and less. My recent interview tapes have a question now and then, but that's about it. Many times when someone gets to what he or she thinks is the end of something and I don't, there'll be a long silence when I don't ask any question at all; almost always the interviewee will fill the silence by a longer explanation, with more details, with aspects I hadn't thought to ask about. In earlier years I would have filled all those silences and not let the interviewee provide the absent information. I would have asked questions, announcing what I thought we should talk about now.

In a field collecting situation you're not a conversational participant. Whatever your reasons for being there, whatever your reasons for getting that information, the simple experience of participating in a conversation is *not* one of them. You're there to get information you don't already have. You want to know what the other person or persons think about certain things; you want to hear things from their repertoires. A contract has been made, sometimes tacitly. The informant has decided to help *you*. Not a university, not a collection project, not an archive, not any other abstraction. You, the person sitting there and setting up the recorder or opening the notebook or aiming the camera. The informant has his or her reasons for talking and you're justifying those reasons.

Everything you do while in the collection situation signals the informants: the expressions on your face, the questions you ask, the attention you pay to your recording machine. You're constantly cueing them about what matters to you and what doesn't.

You, alas, usually don't *know* what really matters; if you did you probably could have stayed home. So your problem is to keep the information flowing as freely as possible, to remain deeply enough involved in the discussion to let your informants inform you, but distant enough so they'll deliver more than what you came there thinking you'd find. The point is for you to learn what they know and you don't, so you should as much as possible let them lead the conversation. Every time you take it away from them, you cut the threads. (My favorite instance of interviewers not knowing something existed and not knowing to ask questions about it until the informant happened to mention it in passing is Alexander Butterfield's aside to the House Watergate investigators about the White House taping system. That aside led to Nixon's resignation.)

Look and act interested. After all, you're the one who asked for this meeting. If you're bored and can't hide it, do something else for a little while. Don't fiddle with the machinery unless there's a good reason for fiddling. Don't doodle meaningless, complex figures. Don't stare at your shoes or the ceiling. Don't clean your nails or look at your appointment calendar. And don't overaccentuate things, at least not without a reason. Every time you say, "Hold on a second, I want to be sure I get *this*," you're telling the speaker exactly what you think is valuable and, by exclusion, what you think isn't valuable. It's fine for you to focus the conversation, reasonable to direct the sequence of subjects, appropriate to get more detail about what matters to you most. You may want to let people know that what they're saying is truly useful to your project—both because people like to know when they're doing well and because people who feel they're on the right track may decide to be even more expansive. But be aware that every time you put out a roadsign or traffic light you may be pursuing your concerns rather than discovering the informant's structures.

Journalistic interviewers such as Oriana Falacci or Mike Wallace can be so fractious they get people to blurt out revealing things they would never otherwise say. I don't know any folkloristic or ethnographic or anthropological interviewer for whom that confrontational style is productive. Our goal isn't to get people to reveal themselves so we can nail them to the wall; rather, it's to let them reveal themselves so we can better see what the world looks like through their eyes. The people who do our kind of interviewing best become nearly transparent in their art.

Fear of Machines

A friend in Kentucky called to tell me how the rural poor were being exploited by the politicans who had taken control of the Poverty Program resources in Pike County. Organizers had been arrested on a trumped-up charge of sedition, windows had been shot out, a house had been dynamited. Unemployed coal miners were doing heavy sabotage, and across the county line a photographer had been murdered. Willie Morris at *Harper's* assigned the article and promised me a minimum, which meant I had enough money for the trip.

One cold and misty afternoon a few weeks later, I was at the Pikeville Holiday Inn for an interview with Tom Ratliff, the Pike County prosecutor. Ratliff had an official office someplace else; the Holiday Inn office was where he conducted his private business. I'd been told that he was a slick fellow who expected to run for governor soon, and I'd been warned that he'd be especially suspicious of me because I was from the North and had a beard. At that time in Pikeville there was a lot of talk about outsiders with beards who were communists. I left my tape recorder and camera in the car because I didn't want to spook Ratliff any more than was necessary. His secretary announced me and ushered me in. He stood up and we introduced ourselves, then he waved his hand at a chair across the desk from his own. I took out my notebook and pen, but before I could sit down Ratliff said, "How come you don't have a tape recorder?"

"I have one in the car."

"Well go get it. I don't trust somebody who writes things down. You never get it all when you're writing it down. Get the tape recorder. That way, if you don't get what I say right it's your decision and you can't say it was a mistake."

"Yes, sir," I said. The interview was splendid. Ratliff said just what he wanted to say and it was better than anything I might have made up for him if I were the kind of reporter who did things like that, which I wasn't.

What Ratliff reminded me was this: Someone who is willing to talk to you *wants* you to get it right. There's no reason to worry about the machine.

I don't think I've ever had a problem with anyone being really nervous about the recorder. People may sometimes be nervous about the interview itself; assuaging that is a different problem, one that usually takes care of itself. (It's similar to the fear some people have about public speaking: absolute terror before it starts and for the first few minutes, then it disappears entirely as the audience begins to respond and the speaker gets more involved in the performance than in anticipating it.) But as long as the fieldworker doesn't mystify the instruments, the informants won't be spooked by them. Informants may sometimes say, "Turn that off for a minute, this is just between

me and you." That's no different from someone saying in regular conversation, "Now this is just between the two of us, don't tell anyone
else about it." Tape recorders are so common now and people are so
used to seeing them and owning them that they no longer need discussion or explanation or justification. Twenty years ago, tape recorders were less an everyday thing, and that's the only reason older
discussions of fieldwork treat the need for dealing with informant fear
of the machine (cf. Whyte, 1960:366).

Some informants may be willing to perform certain materials for
friends and relatives and even for a collector, but they may not be
willing to perform them, or perform them in the same way, before a
tape recorder. Dennis Tedlock recounts a time when a narrator told
singularly different versions of a story at sessions with and without a
tape recorder:

> Here we were, with a Zuni audience that included the narrator's daugh-
> ter-in-law and children of both sexes, and the narrator was telling all. The
> audience at the recording session had been a strictly adult male one, so
> there was no doubt that the crucial factor in Andrew's earlier censorship
> had been neither his own nor his immediate audience's prudishness.
> Rather, Andrew had been mindful of the larger audience that might lie
> somewhere on the other side of that tape-recorder, an audience that might
> include the kinds of Anglo-Americans he had met up with in the gov-
> ernment boarding schools, back in the days when Indian students were
> treated to mandatory Sunday-school attendance, corporal punishment,
> and even confinement in on-campus jail cells. Here, then, was a reminder
> that however much the mythographer may try to normalize a performance
> by gathering a native audience and by building rapport at the level of
> personal interaction, the presence of a tape-recorder and the eventual goal
> of publication raise larger questions of what might be called interethnic
> rapport. (1983:292)

The problem wasn't that the narrator feared the machine; rather, he
was censoring himself because he was sensitive to the different audiences that would be found by his voice in that room and Tedlock's
tape in the world. That's a different situation entirely—one that most
informants don't worry about as much as they should. Diane Christian,
when she was doing the interviews that formed the major portion of
our book on death row in Texas (Jackson and Christian, 1981), several
times cautioned informants about being too specific about crimes they
hadn't been convicted of or, in some cases, not even accused of.

There used to be a professor at SUNY Buffalo who, whenever he
introduced a motion in faculty meetings, would always list *all* the
arguments that might be brought against it, then he would give his

one or two reasons for the motion and sit down. The problem was, he was smarter and better informed than most of the people in the room, so he was far better at thinking up reasons against his own motions than anyone who might have opposed them. He went to battle against himself, and the odds were never even because he thought he had to justify the motion from one position only, yet he would list all the opposing points he thought might exist. If he had just introduced his motions, said why they were important, and shut up, most of them would have passed. As it was, the con arguments he provided often convinced even those of us who supported him in the beginning that we'd better vote no on this one. The message: Be ready for trouble but don't look for it, and above all don't stoke it up yourself.

I've had a few friends and students who've had terrible times with nervous informants. I used to think they were just unlucky, then I noticed that some people *always* have a terrible time with nervous informants and other people never do. It doesn't seem likely that the laws of probability attack some fieldworkers with vicious consistency and then with benign consistency leave others alone.

A couple visited us one time with their two-year-old daughter. The wife was an attorney, a good one I was told; the husband was a photographer who specialized in inanimate objects. He held the child while his wife told us about her new job. After a while, he put the baby on the floor and she crawled about the rug. Our dog wandered into the room, looked around, noticed the baby, and padded over to investigate. The husband looked suddenly at his wife; the wife stiffened and went very pale. "It's okay," I said, "he likes ki--." Before I got to finish the word "kids" the attorney let out a shriek that brought Diane running in from the next room, sent the dog tearing down the corridor with his ears pinned back and his tail between his legs, and got me looking around to see what horrible thing had come into her field of vision. She leapt from her chair, scooped the baby from the floor, and held her high above her head. "Baby is *afraid* of dogs!" she shrieked. About then, "Baby" began crying hysterically. The lawyer handed her to the photographer, who rocked her to tranquility, which took a good ten minutes. "Baby is afraid of dogs," the lawyer said again, her voice calmer but still strained. "She really is. I don't know why."

Well, *we* knew why.

It's the same thing with your microphone and tape recorder. You go around letting people know *you* think there's something to be afraid of or nervous about and they'll be afraid or nervous. They'll think you know something they don't know—maybe something they *ought* to know. If there are reasons why your informant should be skittish about going on tape and you know them and the informant doesn't, then you're honor-bound to bring those up. It's fine to say, "Your ex-wife works in our archive and she may listen to this tape even though we mark it 'restricted, no public use for ten years.' " But it's not fine to say, "A lot of people are terrified about being recorded, but I think there's nothing for you to worry about, really, it's all right, don't worry, there's no reason not to put this on tape, at least no reason I can think of now."

Just go ahead and *do* it.

Except for the times you feel you shouldn't. Sometimes something tells you not to record. I think it's a good idea to follow those instincts. I remember times with friends when interesting things were being said, so I hauled out a machine to immortalize the moment and found that I'd suddenly stepped outside the circle and become an observer rather than a participant and that everything had changed in an unpleasant way. I once wrecked a friend's dinner party when I started recording a fascinating monologue by a man who had a short time before been released from Cuba's Isle of Pines Prison. He had spent a year there after his capture at the Bay of Pigs, and my friend Umberto, rather weirdly now that I think about it, thought we should have a lot to talk about.

About thirty minutes into the man's monologue I decided the stories were so good and my memory so bad that the only way I'd remember any of this would be if it were on tape. I brooded a while about whether or not the machine would interfere with anything and in that time a few more terrific stories disappeared in the holes of failed memory. So I went to my apartment next door and got a recorder. About twenty minutes later the man noticed the recorder and mike, both of which were directly in front of him, and went quite crazy. He pointed a finger at me and screamed, "Spy! You're a goddamned spy!" "A spy for who?" Umberto asked him. "Who cares?" the man said. "You can't just be a spy without spying for someone," Umberto said. "What difference does it make?" the man said. "He's a spy." "Why should anyone spy on you?" Umberto's wife said. "You were working for the CIA when you went to the Bay of Pigs and Castro had you for the last year. What's to find out?" The man didn't like that one bit. He pounded the table and yelled in colloquial Spanish, which I couldn't understand at all but it must have been something interesting because Umberto looked quite startled and whispered to me, "He doesn't really mean that." Umberto then valiantly tried to serve dessert, a flan he'd learned how to make in his native Colombia, but only one person at the far end of the table was up to it.

After that I became less likely to wreck nice times. I tend to be more interested in my relationships than in my tapes. Real life is full of stories and sometimes stepping out of real life to document other people doing it isn't the smart, decent, useful, or even satisfying thing to do.

Having a recorder going all the time doesn't solve the problem either, because you have to change reels or tapes, or you're aware of the potential need for changing reels or tapes, and that means you never fully participate in the action of the room because you're watching the clock. People sense that; if you're at all sensitive, you'll sense it too. What do you do in those circumstances? Lean back and forget it. Have a good time. Tell yourself to remember as much as you can and be sure to make notes later. Sometimes it's okay just to be a person.

Everything I've said about tape recorders applies equally well to photography. If you know that your pictures won't be used for anything that will hurt people, if you believe you aren't exploiting them or taking pictures that will embarrass them or compromise them, then there's no reason at all not to take whatever pictures are appropriate to the work you're doing. Cameras are far more commonplace than they used to be, but I find that cameras interfere with an immediate relationship even more than tape recorders do, because to use a camera you must break off normal eye contact and place this box with a cyclops-eye between you and the person you're talking to. Even so, if you act as if it's something reasonable and natural to do (if you *believe* it's something reasonable and natural to do), you'll rarely have any problems. "People are far more used to being photographed than being recorded," writes Ives. "I've found video sometimes less intrusive than tape." The great American photographer Walker Evans once said,

> I'm often asked by students how a photographer gets over the fear and uneasiness in many people about facing a camera, and I just say that any sensitive man is bothered by a thing like that unless the motive is so strong and the belief in what he's doing is so strong it doesn't matter. The important thing is to do the picture. And I advise people who are bothered by this to cure it by saying to themselves, what I'm doing is harmless to these people really, and there's no malevolence in it and there's no deception in it, and it is done in a great tradition, examples of which are Daumier and Goya. Daumier's *Third Class Carriage* is a kind of snapshot of some actual people sitting in a railway carriage in France in eighteen something. (1982:125)

Leave the recorder or camera at home or in the car or in the box or bag if you think the machine will alter the situation in ways you don't want or if you think it will cause harm. But don't suppress the machine because you assume people will automatically take fright when they see it. The fright is most often transmitted by you, not the inanimate box.

The Silent Participant

I said people aren't likely to be nervous because of the recorder if you don't make them nervous; I didn't say the recorder left the situation the same, because it doesn't. In William Foote Whyte's term, it makes the event "formal" and may lead informants "to talk more 'for the record' . . ." (1960:366). I've noticed many informants code-switch when the recorder goes on: they become less likely to chatter idly and more likely to explain things in detail. That means many of them have a sense of some audience beyond that microphone. I don't think this is as artificial as it might seem. The interview *is* an artificial construct, whether or not it's recorded. If your goal is to acquire as much information about a subject as possible, there's no harm in having your informants try to cast their presentations in ways that provide as much detail as possible. If you're recording a normal conversation between people (say, family members or friends at a bar) and the presence of the recorder changes the character of the conversation, then you have a problem that must be reckoned with. But if the only effect of the recorder in your interview is that it gets your informant to provide more detail than would otherwise be provided—thank that machine and keep on working with it.

When the machines are introduced can be more disruptive than whether they are introduced. Introducing the machine at a later stage of the study makes a statement of some kind (what depends on the circumstances) about some change in the value of the information or relationship that the researcher assumes has taken place. I often have my machines visible early on though I may not actually use them for some time. If I'm starting work in an institution, for example, I may walk around for a day or two having conversations and getting the feel of the place before I take a photograph or tape an interview, but I'll almost always have my Leica M-4 with me the entire time. That gets people used to seeing me with machines and it means they're not surprised when I begin using them at some later point.

Folklorists, unlike sociologists and unlike most anthropologists, are just as interested in the specific form of the utterance as they are in the abstractable content of the utterance. It's true that the recorder has people talking to it as much as the interviewer, but that may make them more likely to perform rather than to report, which can be to the folklorists' advantage.

Sometimes starting the tape recorder is a good way to make the shift from normal conversational discourse to interview discourse. It can let your informant know that you're doing business now, that you're no longer chatting idly. "When I am ready to begin the interview," writes Ives,

> I pick up the mike and say something like, "Well, let's get started." Then I speak directly into the mike, not looking at the informant at all, while I say, "This is Friday, September 29, 1980, and I am up in Argyle, Maine in the home of [*Now I look at the informant*] Ernest Kennedy, and we're going to be talking about the days when he was a river-driver. My name is Sandy Ives and this is tape 80.3." Then I put the mike back in its place, sit back and relax, and continue, "O.K., now that's taken care of. Now. . . ." That is to say, I involve myself with the machine to begin with, then I involve the informant, and the interview is suddenly underway. I try to do it all in an offhand, diffident way. At the same time, I have made it unmistakably clear that the interview has begun. (1980:51)

Ives's technique nicely separates the interview from the conversation immediately preceding it. An interview is *not* a normal conversation; the rules are different and so are the expectations. A Brownian random motion that might be perfectly acceptable in conversation might not be at all appropriate or useful in an interview about a specific subject or group of subjects. The interview may demand a measure of detail not necessary or appropriate to a conversation about the same subjects. The statement starting the interview off is like the words at the beginning of a ritual that separate ritual time from regular time and that distinguish ritual behavior from quotidian behavior.

The interview situation permits you, the interviewer, to ask far more questions about far more subjects and in far greater detail than would be permissible or reasonable in conversation. Once in the interview mode, most informants understand that a greater measure of detail may be necessary, so they don't automatically think you're stupid if you ask for a step-by-step explanation of a process or if you ask the names of things or a lot of other questions. Very often people will shift their eyes from you to the microphone when those questions are asked, as if to say, "I know Edna here understands this, but this explanation is for you people out there in tape-land." Some individuals who are interviewed frequently become very good at this kind of shift. Whenever he is interviewed for print media, for example, civil rights attorney William M. Kunstler spells every name without breaking his conversational flow: "The judge in the case, Judge Rickover—that's r-i-c-k-o-v-e-r—said to me, 'Are you accusing the government of. . . .' "

Control

For the interview to work, both you and your informants must continue to get what you want and need. You want to find out something specific; you want them to give you information that will lead you on to other things that matter that you don't yet know about; you want their perception of events or facts or people, you need *something* to hand to your professor. There are other reasons for you to be there and it's possible that many or even all of them are operative at once. Some of that information can be extracted with questions you had in mind or in your notebook when you arrived at the door, but more often a good informant will lead you to questions you didn't know beforehand you should or would be asking.

The informants, as I said earlier, have agreed to be interviewed by you because they like you and want to help, because they owe you a favor, because they think the information you collect and transmit will do them some good, because they think the information you collect and pass along will help someone or some cause they want helped, because they are bored and therefore happy for the opportunity to talk to someone not noticeably bored by their rambling, because you are paying them for their time and talk—or for other reasons buried so deep in the mind neither of you will ever know what they were. By the time you sit down to talk, the decision to help you has been made. They want to give you what you want and what you need, at least insofar as giving you those things is consonant with their own wants and needs. But if you don't handle yourself carefully, you can miss the most important information they have to give you.

I once worked on a film with a director who was desperately anxious to have everyone think he was hip to what was going on. He wanted them to accept him as if he were an insider. Even if he'd been successful he would've been disastrous to the project—you don't talk the same way or about the same things to insiders and outsiders. But he *wasn't* an insider and everyone knew it. When we were interviewing cops, he told cop stories he'd gotten from his cousin the detective; when we were interviewing gangsters, he told gangster stories he'd gotten from his cousin the gangster; when we interviewed a bartender, he told bartender stories he'd gotten from his cousin the bartender. It never ended. After he finished jabbering and establishing himself, the interviews were almost always dreadful.

It's really okay to be what you are. That's the role you know best, the one in which you'll impress your interviewee as being the most honest. People don't expect you to know everything about their subject; if you did, you wouldn't need them. Most people are happy to know you're interested. Nothing kills an interview faster than an informant's realization that you've been faking your interest so far.

It's good to let them know you're interested—but it may not be good to let them know too much about the specifics of your interest. If, for example, you respond enthusiastically to certain kinds of things and not enthusiastically at all to others, the informant learns quickly what to express and what to suppress. The informant's decisions won't always be right, since you yourself won't know until later what you're really going to find useful and important. You go into a field situation with certain background information and certain questions; but you learn from the field situation more background information and you learn to ask questions you didn't previously think to ask.

Your task is to keep the informant informing without you imposing so much direction on the performance that you foreclose the possibility or likelihood of getting new information. You needn't and shouldn't be a phony about what you want and what you're doing, but you have to impose some measure of self-control on your actions and reactions so the informant can feel safe in offering information and won't cripple the study by preediting in the direction your interests seem already headed.

Never turn off the tape recorder when you're doing an interview. Every time you turn the tape recorder on or off you're giving the informant an instruction about what you think is valuable and you force a reconsideration by the informant of what should be considered valuable and what should be considered useless. Every time you turn the recorder off you're saying, "What you're talking about now doesn't strike me as being important or interesting." Even if what's being said *is* unimportant and boring, you don't want to communicate that message so clearly. It's far better to waste a little tape or to redirect the conversation by a question or a comment than to make the exclamation mark statement by pushing that button.

I don't mean *absolutely* never turn the machine off. If everyone leaves the room you can turn the machine off, or if the informant asks you to turn it off you should do it. Otherwise, there are few reasons for stopping the recorder before you're done with the session. Tape is cheap. If you don't like what you've got, you can use the tape again. The recording opportunity is difficult to achieve and impossible to repeat.

The first time I did fieldwork I started and stopped the tape recorder a lot. Then I realized that every time I turned off the recorder I was also turning off the informant, and often by the time I turned the machine back on the informant was so far into what he or she was talking about that I missed the beginning. If I asked for a recap, the spontaneity was lost; if I didn't, the information was lost. When I'm recording sound now, interviews and discussions especially, I just let the machine run. With a cassette recorder, turning the tape over or putting in a new one takes only a few seconds, so it's easy enough to keep the interview going without puttering with the machine. (One bit of putter you should always remember with a cassette after you flip it over is to fast-forward it a moment before going into record again so you get past the five seconds of leader.) The great advantage of a tape recorder over a pen and paper for recording interviews is the tape recorder lets you maintain eye contact with your informants and it doesn't let them know what parts of what they're saying seem to you more important than others. But the machine can only free your eyes and help you keep from influencing content if you leave it alone.

There's another reason for keeping your hands off the machine as much as you can: even informants who are nervous about being interviewed generally relax after you've been talking for a few minutes, but they won't be able to relax if you keep reminding them about what may have made them nervous in the first place. Don't look at the tape in despair in the middle of a long story. You're already committed to the story, you might as well get the end, and it might surprise you.

You don't want to keep looking at your watch, either, and for the same reason. But if you're in a room with a clock you can position yourself so you can sometimes check it without seeming to be fretting about the time. It's good to have a tape recorder that shuts itself off when the tape runs out—with one of those, you'll hear the click when the control buttons pop up. If you're in doubt about whether there'll be enough tape for the next item or sequence of items or the next phase of conversation, turn the tape over or put on a new tape before the side has run completely out.

A Thief's Primer

I spent a few weeks in July 1964 doing interviews and recording work-songs at Ramsey state prison farm in Texas, a few miles from the country towns of Brazoria and Rosharon. It was a Gulf Coast summer—massively hot and muggy. Most of my time during the days was spent recording convict worksongs in the live oak groves along the

Brazos bottoms and in the cottonfields closer to the old whitewashed brick building that held Two Camp's 800 convicts. The only room within Ramsey Two Camp that had air conditioning was the prison dentist's office. The free-world dentist was never there, but the convict assistant was. I talked with him a few times about slang. He told me nickname stories, defined words, suggested people who might be worth a conversation. I took to going up there for breaks and to hide from the weather in the worst part of the afternoon. At first, my rationale was that I was getting background on stories told me by other convicts, then after a while I really *was* getting background on stories told by other convicts. I sat in the dentist's chair and drank instant coffee. I put the tape recorder on the instrument tray and let it run while we talked. Sam answered my questions and commented on the interviews I'd been doing. He talked about his own prison experiences and later on about his work as a check-forger and safecracker. The recorder kept on running. The next few times I made field trips to the prison, I did more interviews with him. A few years later, he wrote that he was being paroled. I arranged to be there to pick him up. We visited his old haunts in Houston and San Antonio and Nuevo Laredo. All of this resulted in *A Thief's Primer* (1969), a book I hadn't planned on writing when I began my Texas research. It's about safecracking, check-writing, and Texas professional crime. Sam very much led me into the conversations that formed the substance of that book.

The raw transcriptions of those tapes themselves did not become the book; they became the *basis* for the book. After I realized that a subject was there that was worth specific attention, I had to develop a research strategy for managing that subject. One must determine what seems to matter, then ask further questions about those things; one must also come to some sort of conclusion about what's true and what's not. That's not because one publishes only verifiable facts—articulations of facts and perceptions of the past are, as I say in the conclusion to this book, facts themselves—but so one has some idea what logic the material demands. The decisions seem to make sense in retrospect, but at the moment they're largely intuitive. It's the tolerance for ambiguity characteristic of the humanities scholar that makes complex fieldwork possible, not the desperate need for certitude of the scientist.

I spent more time with Sam discussing what seemed to me themes of importance. As long as Sam was commenting on my conversations with other people, there was no need to explore with others Sam's statements as they related to Sam's career and the kind of career Sam said he'd had. But once Sam's career became the subject, then Sam could no longer be the only informant. I interviewed other people about specific aspects and general themes that had come up in the conversations with Sam, and those interviews helped form the basis for future questions and discussions with Sam. We re-covered ground we had passed over quickly in earlier meetings.

I worked on the transcripts and edited what I thought was the story in them. You might have found another story in there, just as different sculptors might find different figures in the same block of stone. One story isn't necessarily more valid than any other (though neither are all equally valid), but the writer's job, at a minimum, is to find one that does no injustice to any fact he or she knows. Anyway, that's how I work once I get a great mass of recorded spoken material.

With Sam's story my sensibility of things wasn't enough. He provided so much technical information that I wanted comments by experts. So I gave copies of the portions of the interviews I planned to use in the book to several experts: police, lawyers, other safecrackers and check-writers. Their comments became part of the book, for they were able to gloss Sam's statements with an authority I couldn't claim.

What happened, then, was conversation with an informant opened an area of investigation I hadn't planned. That area had its own set of questions that demanded development of a new fieldworking and analytic strategy, which in turn became a new project that grew alongside the first like branches from a common trunk.

Don't be afraid to follow an informant's lead. You can always come back to your main subject, but you may get lucky and come upon a story or genre you didn't even know was there. If you're working on folktales and the informant begins a long digression on truck tires, you might want to engage in a little subtle redirection—but not until you're sure the person isn't going to tell you interesting trucking stories.

If you keep your mouth shut whenever possible, if you listen rather than lecture, if you don't load the conversation, if you follow their lead, you get taken places you didn't know were there. If the places are dead ends or boring or irrelevant, you can always steer the conversation back to where you hoped it would be going, and you can do it directly: "But before we talk more about the truck tires, I'd like to hear a little more about the time you were on the ice floe. Just how did you get off of it and what happened to the two fishermen and the dog?" People might be a little insulted if you change the topic entirely in favor of something that interests them not at all, but if you're just returning to the main topic of the day, that's usually accepted easily. You can always ask questions about what you think matters.

Asking Questions

In the right context you can ask anything; if you misperceive the context, the wrong question may close things down entirely. Before you ask personal questions—sex, politics, family relationships, money, crime, religion—be sure that your relationship with the informant licenses such questions from you and that the recording situation (who else is nearby or who else might hear the tape) doesn't restrict the answers.

Remember the notion of stranger value: outsiders can often ask questions insiders can't. Some kinds of things are discussed freely before people perceived as representatives of an institution or agency, but not at all with people who are known and appreciated as individuals; researchers doing sex studies are regularly told, "I've never told this to anyone. . . ." Some things we don't like to discuss with people we know because the preexisting intimacy makes the new revelation embarrassing—the revelation says, "I'm not who or what you thought I was." Other things are hard to discuss because we assume that insiders know parts of the answers already, so basic questions asked by them immediately produce an artificial response. But if you're honestly naive, you can ask simple questions about basic things (the best kind), and sometimes you may even be excused asking tactless or inappropriate questions.

Every question makes a statement, and some questions make multiple statements. A question tells what you're interested in, which is fair enough, but it may also reveal answers you're assuming, which isn't at all useful. Other than "Do you want the change in quarters or dimes?" there aren't many neutral questions.

The questions that tell you least about the interviewee's categories are questions that can be answered with a simple yes or no. Most of the time, that yes or no is a full sentence, and the last thing you want in an interview designed to elicit information is a bunch of one-word sentences. Questions with yes-or-no answers don't give the informant a chance to give you the collateral information that makes facts meaningful. Many times slight rephrasing of a question puts it in a form that demands a discussion rather than a word. Instead of "Did you like what she said?" ask "What did you think about what she said?" Instead of "Did you always want to be a potter?" ask "How did you become a potter?" Instead of "Have you heard other versions of this song?" ask "What other versions of this song have you heard?" The differences are not minor. Putting the question in a way that elicits discussion rather than a single word gives the subject a chance to talk, and it indicates that you value the response.

How a thing is said is part of *what* is being said. The same word or line or story can have very different meanings if it's uttered rapidly or slowly, or if it's told at the instigation of someone else or on one's own. The best way to collect stories is when stories are being told by people who normally tell them to the people who are the usual audiences for those stories. But the best way isn't necessarily the most efficient way; fieldworkers often ask questions designed to elicit discussion or performances of items. You do what you can to make those responses as free and easy as possible and to make those performances as natural as possible.

Part of the task is being sensitive to the rhythms of utterance. Native New Yorkers, for example, rarely have notable pauses in their conversations; when pauses occur, other speakers usually leap in. Native Americans frequently have pauses; leaping in is rude. Furthermore, the order in which facts are presented is a fact itself, and often one of great importance; we understand different things from the order of facts if the order comes from the order of an interviewer's question sheet or if it comes from the informant's natural flow of associations. The goal of an interview might be as much to get the performer's style of saying what is to be said and the performer's ordering of matters as it is to get the facts the performer has. I find it best, therefore, to ask as few specific questions as I can. I'd much rather have someone ramble for a while than I would plunge in myself and impose my order on the conversation.

Interviewers talk of two kinds of interview style. *Directive interviews* involve specific questions posed by the researcher; the interviewee's comments are welcome only insofar as they are part of the answers to those specific questions. *Nondirective interviews* are totally open: the researcher listens, the subject talks. The term "nondirective interview" comes to us, says William Foote Whyte, from the therapeutic style that had patients expressing themselves about whatever they wished for the ear of a listener who was interested and sympathetic. "Whatever its merits for therapy, a genuinely non-directive interviewing approach simply is not appropriate for research. Far from putting informants at their ease, it actually seems to stir anxieties" (1960:352). Whyte notes a number of similarities and differences in what therapists and researchers expect from their interviews:

> Like the therapist, the research interviewer listens more than he talks, and listens with a sympathetic and lively interest. He finds it helpful occasionally to rephrase and reflect back to the informant what he seems to be expressing and to summarize the remarks as a check on understanding.

The interviewer avoids giving advice and passing moral judgment on responses. He accepts statements that violate his own ethical, political, or other standards without showing his disapproval in any way. Generally he does not argue with the informant, although there may be justification for stimulating an argument as a prod to determine how the informant will react. This, however, should be a part of a conscious plan and not be done simply because the interviewer disagrees with the informant and cannot contain himself on the point.

The therapist is told not to interrupt. For the researcher the advice should be: Don't interrupt *accidentally*. In normal social intercourse a person interrupts because he is impatient and needs to express himself. This is no justification for interruption in a research interview. However, some people will talk forever if they are not checked. Since they seldom pause for breath, anything that anyone else says to them is necessarily an interruption. Such people circle the same topic with an infinite capacity for repeating themselves. The interviewer who waits patiently for new material will hear only variations on the same theme. (1960:353)

Folklore interviews tend to be a mixture of the two styles. Fieldworkers have specific things they want to know about (objects, processes, stories, beliefs, whatever), but they want to know about those things as they function and have meaning in the informants' world. The fieldworker *wants* the informant's opinions, biases, attitudes, beliefs, phrasings. The investigation should be as objective as possible, but the information gathered is more useful the more subjective it is.

Often the most interesting responses are produced by *follow-up questions*—questions you ask after you get the first answer. The follow-up question interrogates the response itself: someone tells you what was done, the follow-up asks why it was done, or why it was done that way, or when and how often and by whom it was done; someone tells a story, the follow-up asks what the teller thinks the story was about, and whether the teller believes it, and whether the teller heard it any other time. Anything to expand the dimension of the response and help you better understand what's being said. Many informants respond with only part of what they know—because they don't want to bore you, because they don't know how much detail you really want or need, because they don't know how much of what they just said you really understood. The follow-up question lets them tell you more of what they want to tell you.

Prosthetics . . .

Most things are hard to talk about in the abstract. You can sit at a table talking about carving with a carver and you may get good information about technical procedures and aesthetic concerns, but you'll probably get much more specific technical detail and more extensive aesthetic remarks if you're talking in the presence of the physical objects involved—the tools and the things carved by that artist and by others doing similar things. (You can take photographs of the objects later on so you have visuals to go along with your audiotapes.) While the conversation is in process you can point to things that you don't understand or things you'd like to hear more about: "But why did you make this long deep cut here?" and "What is the purpose of this double-sided knife?" Talking in terms of specific objects lets you discover if you need to ask about things that are so obvious to the informant he or she felt no need to mention them but that are of vital importance if an outsider is to understand them.

Some novice interviewers are embarrassed about asking questions they think they can answer; they fear that the informant will think them naive or foolish. I've found that when informants understand (as most do quickly) that it's *their* perceptions that matter to me and the potential users of the discussion, few mind digressions into the obvious. In most interview situations two people grope toward areas of shared concern. The interviewer has categories of information he or she wants filled but doesn't know what portions of that information the interviewee has; the interviewer knows nothing about things the interviewee knows but which haven't been identified as categories. The interviewee wants to help and is usually trying to find out what the interviewer really wants to know and trying to decide what's worth telling.

Physical objects can provide part of the meeting ground, but only if you make your questions as specific as possible; otherwise, later on you might not have any idea what your informant is talking about. "Why is this cut like this?" is less helpful than "Why is this cut crosswise to the grain when all the others are with it?" Interviews are talking events (unless you're doing them on video, which is not commonly the case), but the things to which the interviews refer may be physical facts. Incorporate those physical facts whenever possible, for they'll help you ask intelligent questions and they'll help the informant provide specific information.

Sociologist Douglas Harper shows interviewees photographs he's taken of them and then asks them to comment on the objects and actions in the photographs and to discuss whether the photographic depiction captures the event or object properly. Many subjects come up in the conversations about the pictures that hadn't come up in previous interviews. Folklorists can extend Harper's device: sit down with an informant and go through a family photograph album or some-one else's album. Go through the tools in a shop and ask what each one is for and where it was obtained. Anything that comes to mind. Such a device won't always work and the technique isn't always appropriate, but it can introduce you to areas you knew nothing about and can ease enormously the task of the informant who's trying to help you understand what's going on. (See Ives, 1980:74–79, for an extended discussion of similar techniques.)

I know of an instance where the family album technique was a disaster because the fellow using it hadn't bothered to think through what his interrogation meant to his informant. The informant was his mother, who at the time was in her early seventies. Archie taught folklore and literature. He read the very nice book on family folklore by Steven J. Zeitlin, Amy J. Kotkin, and Holly Cutting Baker (1982) and decided it was about time he struck close to home. He had been hearing his mother tell stories for years about this or that cousin, about what it was like when they lived in one town or another. So Archie invited his mother to his house (his first mistake—the conversation would've been better at her kitchen table) and hauled out the family albums. He set up his tape recorder, carefully placed the microphone so it would get both their voices, poured his mother a cup of tea and himself a cup of coffee. He yelled at the kids to turn the TV set off. He started at the beginning of the first album, pointing at a picture of a young woman he knew was his mother and a young man he didn't know at all.

"Who's that?" he asked.

"Me on the left. He was a friend of mine." Long silence. Archie waited for her to go on with one of her stories. She went on with the silence.

"What was his name?"

"Charles." More silence.

"And where was this picture taken?"

"At the beach. You can see it's at the beach."

"And what about this picture? That's a great car."

"Yes, it's a nice car."

"Where was the picture taken?"

"Where we lived in Pittsburgh."

And so it went for nearly an hour. Archie didn't even bother starting on the second album.

"Nothing," he said to me later, "absolutely nothing. Every question I asked she answered with a monosyllable or with a single line. Not one story. I mean, she's always telling stories about her family. Why not when I finally ask for them? Why not when I've got the tape recorder going?"

Archie's wife spoke up for the first time. "*Because* it's the first time you asked her to do it, idiot. Didn't you think she'd wonder why you were suddenly interested in stories that always bored you before? She probably decided you thought she was old and was going to die soon and you just wanted the tape for a family souvenir or something."

"I thought she'd be happy I was interested."

"You depressed the hell out of her is what you did."

Use whatever will help you get the information you need, but never forget you're working with human beings who have feelings and who think about the questions you ask and how you ask them.

. . . *and Prosthetic Damage*

We trust our machines. They relieve us of labors and they do things we can't do. That's wonderful. But there are two great dangers for the fieldworker who uses machines and they're exactly the same as the danger for the users of any machines: we tend to define our work in terms of what our machines can do, and we tend to relax our attention when we know the machine is on the job. Both tendencies can be costly; both should be guarded against. The only defense is vigilance: pay attention to what you're doing and why you're doing it, and pay attention to what's going on around you just as if the machines weren't there.

Almost every fieldworker I know who has done a lot of taped interviews has had the experience of realizing he or she had no idea of what was said in the past minute or five minutes. If I have to *remember* a conversation, I pay very close attention to everything my interlocutor says, I make mnemonic keys as we're going along, or I try to jot down key words and phrases so I can call it back later. If I know the tape is doing the remembering (far better than I could), I relax. I might think about the nail that seems to be working its way through my boot. I might think about the rest of the day's work. I might think about what he just reminded me of. I can . . . oh, damn: he's looking at me and waiting for an answer. An answer to what? You can feel pretty stupid when you're interviewing someone and you have to ask, "What was that you just said?" And the feeling is justified.

Not only does the machine let you miss some of what goes on in front of you, it tends to let you get by committing far less to memory than you otherwise would. And it's the same with images. If you're photographing a lot, there's a tendency not to jot down or even *see* details. The negative's got it all. Alas, too many times the negative doesn't have it all, and sometimes the negative doesn't have anything.

Force yourself to pay attention to what's going on and make as many notes as you can manage and make those notes as good as you possibly can. Whenever you have the time and quiet, make notes about what has happened, about what has worked and what hasn't, about how you got to a certain house and who was whose cousin, about your impressions of the day's encounters. In the note making you often realize questions you should be asking. Better to have that realization when you have three more days in the field than after you're back home when you can only kick yourself because you realize there are crippling holes in your data. If you can't come this way again easily, use your machines for whatever help they can give you, but don't ever depend upon them entirely.

Rules

Every field situation has its own rhetoric of interaction, and none of the rules is invariable. But here are some rules you shouldn't break unless you've got a very good reason:

1. Don't be so tight-lipped the interviewee thinks you're an idiot, and don't be so loquacious the interviewee can't get a word in edgewise.

2. Don't show off so much you seem more fool than researcher, and don't be so greedy for information you forget the informant is a person with feelings that must be respected. Be as normal as you can—but always remember why you're there.

3. Talk as little as possible and keep your talk as empty of content and opinion as possible.

4. Don't ask questions that can be answered with a simple yes or no unless you have a very good reason for asking such conversation-stoppers.

5. If you do ask yes-or-no questions, follow them up with questions that will put the answers into some kind of perspective: "But why did you do it?" "How did you feel about it?" "Why did you think it was true?" "What did it mean?"

6. Ask follow-up questions whenever you can, even if your previous question elicited a ten-minute narrative: "What do other people think about it?" "How do other people do it?" "Did it happen another time?" "What do you think about it now?"

7. If the informant tries to steer the conversation, go along for the ride.

8. Never turn the recorder off during an interview unless you're alone in the room or you've been asked to turn the recorder off.

9. Use whatever you can to help the informant provide as much detail as possible.

10. Use whatever machines will help you, but remember who's the boss: don't let the machines let you get lazy.

Experience helps more than anything. Go out and do interviews, come back home and listen to them carefully, and don't be surprised at the fits of embarrassment and depression that almost all honest field-workers go through when they hear themselves walking over an interviewee about to give an expanded answer, or when they hear themselves explaining to the interviewee what the interviewee "really" means before the interviewee gets to say it. Then go out and do it again.

8/Ordinary Talk

Fieldworkers in folklore, sociology, history, anthropology, and several disciplines employ interviewing techniques because they're efficient. The interview focuses the conversation and provides license for extraordinary questions and responses. It's like meeting your doctor in a supermarket the day after your annual physical. Yesterday you disrobed without question or embarrassment when told, "Take your clothes off." The same line uttered today, somewhere between canned goods and paper products, would probably strike you as inappropriate—and if you responded as you did in the examination room, your behavior would surely strike most other shoppers as inappropriate, albeit interesting. Examination contexts—and an interview is one of these—have special rules. Interviewer and interviewee know that the interview is not ordinary talk, so it's possible for the interviewer to pose questions he or she would not ordinarily ask, and it's equally possible for the interviewee to respond at far greater length than would ordinarily be assumed or expected.

There is a trade-off for the interview's efficiency, however, and it matters more in folklore studies than in the other fields I listed above. The formulation and performance of an item of verbal folklore uttered in an interview situation rarely is—and can never be assumed to be—identical to its formulation and performance in ordinary life. Much folklore is situational: it's performed in specific situations and the nature of the performance is often linked to various aspects of those situations. A joke or personal anecdote told in response to an interviewer's request may or may not have the same verbal content as that narrative told in an ordinary social situation; and it will surely have a different meaning.

103

Collecting stories or other conversational folklore genres outside an interview situation is difficult and time-consuming. Someone who, on request, might recite a dozen stories in a single sitting, might, in ordinary conversation, never have occasion to tell any of those stories at all. When engaging in fieldwork, therefore, it's useful to consider the kinds of information you can get simply by being there and the kinds of information you must elicit. Both types of information gathering are valid, so long as you realize they don't provide the same kinds of information.

If, for example, you're studying the folklore of fire fighters, you'll get a great deal of information about their work and life by sitting in the firehouse kitchen between calls and asking questions. But if you want to know how the fire fighters express their concerns to one another and how they actually tell stories to one another, or if you want to study the structure of the stories told, you'd do far better keeping your mouth shut and letting them talk to each other.

I'm presently studying storytelling in ordinary life, and it seems to be the most difficult field-based study I've ever done. I've recorded thousands of stories over the years, but very few of my earlier tapes are at all useful for this study. I want to know how people utter and perceive the cues and announce that a story is about to be told, and what rules of narrative seem to be operative and whether those rules differ from the rules implied when a story is being told formally (as in an interview situation). Unobtrusive recording instruments help, but I don't record people in secret, so there's always the matter of introducing the recorder and then getting people to forget about it. That can be done, but it takes time. The mechanical and ethical questions and problems involved in this kind of project differ from those involved in a project based on focused and obvious interviews. If the project works, it should produce results unobtainable by interviews.

Interviewing, as I said earlier, is just one of the strategies folklorists use to gather data. If your time is limited or if the facts are of a kind that can be discovered only by an interview, then it's an efficient and reasonable mode. But keep in mind that the interview provides only a certain kind of information, so if your concern is with how folklore is actually performed and used, then you should be using noninterview information-gathering strategies as well.

Part Three/Mechancial Matters

Stored in the rear of the car were two army cots and bedding, a cooking outfit, provisions, a change of clothing, an infinite number of "etceteras" which will manage to encumber any traveler. Later, as a crown to our discomfort, we also carried a 350-pound recording machine—a cumbersome pile of wire and iron and steel—built into the rear of the Ford, two batteries weighing seventy-five pounds each, a microphone, a complicated machine of delicate adjustments, coils of wire, numerous gadgets, besides scores of blank aluminum and celluloid disks, and, finally, a multitude of extra parts, the purpose and place for which neither Alan nor I had the faintest glimmer of an idea.

> John A. Lomax
> *Adventures of a Ballad Hunter*

It is always possible to clothe the nudity of a primitive tale in the drapery of modern paraphrase, should our conventionality see fit to demand it; but it is impossible ever to reconstruct the original frame, the living body, if at its first presentation we have only its encasings and swathings.

> A. L. Kroeber
> "Cheyenne Tales"

9/Minds and Machines

The Dark Side of the Eye

Walker Evans was more than just our finest documentary photographer. There is far more in his works than the lucid recording of a time and place and thing or person. Nonetheless, the records of time and place and person in his photographs are a part of our national imagination; it's impossible for many of us to think about America of the 1930s without having in our mind's eye Evans's images of those years.

Evans disliked questions about machines, about the tools of the trade. "People are always asking me," he said to Diane Christian and me not long before his death, " 'What kind of camera did you use? What lens did you use?' " He shook his head in annoyance at bunched-up memories of all those questions.

"And what do you tell them?" Diane asked him.

"I say, 'It's *here,* not in the camera.' " When Evans said "here" he pointed to his eye. "If it's not here, the camera won't do it for you. If it is here, what you have in your hands doesn't matter that much."

I've thought many times about what Evans said that day—especially when I know I've missed something important while doing fieldwork, times when I haven't seen something I should have seen or heard something I should have heard because I was so busy dealing with my machine or ratifying an idea I had beforehand.

When you work with machines you've got to remember who's in charge and why you're both there. You've got to keep your eyes open, and that includes the dark side of the eye, the side that talks with the brain.

107

What Machines Do for You and to You

The machines available to the fieldworker now are a delight. In a decade, the weight and cost of portable sound and video recorders have dropped by a factor of ten and there's been a spectacular improvement in the quality of recordings those machines produce and the ease with which those machines can be operated. Audio recorders weighing less than two pounds and smaller than this book produce recordings of higher quality than were available a decade ago with anything but the most expensive and bulky equipment. Modern 35mm cameras automatically set their own focus, aperture, and shutter speed. Portable video cameras using digital technology record clear images in candlelight, along with high fidelity stereo sound. We can capture more information and capture it more accurately than ever before.

What must be kept in mind is this: the machines and their products are allowed on the premises only because they're in the service of something else. For fieldworkers, no recording or strip of film or videotape is an end in itself; the machines and their products are never more than tools to capture information which in turn will add to our knowledge and increase our understanding.

In this and the next few chapters I explore the advantages and disadvantages of various devices and suggest ways of using them and pitfalls to avoid. The technical descriptions are meant to help the fieldworker answer questions that may occur; they are not meant to teach the fieldworker everything that should be known about a mode of documentation or even a particular aspect of technology. If some sections are more technical than is appropriate for what you're doing, follow your instincts and ignore what doesn't seem to fit. If you later realize you needed that information after all, the pages will be here waiting for you.

Don't be terrified by the mass of things to learn and the range of dangers to avoid. Nobody learns it all at once, and in fieldwork we learn most of what we know on the job, largely by making mistakes. There's nothing wrong with making mistakes, so long as you understand why you made them and what they cost you. An enormous portion of the advice I offer you in these chapters results from good mistakes I made in the field. (A good mistake is one that teaches you enough so you understand better what you're doing.)

Few people can use all of the available documenting modes and instruments well, and no one can use them all at once. Trying to document in too many media at once is like going on a hike with 200 pounds of supplies and equipment in your backpack: you may have everything you might need, but you won't last long in the company of the rational travelers. In fieldwork, less is sometimes more. Far better to decide in advance the form of documentation most appropriate to your needs and skills and limit yourself to that and do it well than come home with inadequate notes, inadequate recordings, and inadequate photographs. You'll never get everything anyway.

Your goal is to acquire a certain kind and a certain amount of information. Every machine you use to help fulfill your goal requires attention and care; and there comes a point when the machines are getting more of both than they're returning in time or labor saved or in information preserved. Every machine limits your mobility and defines your options. Know what your needs really are and never use more technology than you need. It's possible, for example, to make recordings of wonderful fidelity if you pay careful attention to the room ambience, mike placement, and equipment quality. But you may have no need or use for wonderful fidelity; you may need only a recording in which a voice is intelligible. Increasing demands of fidelity require not only greater cost but more attention, which means they increase the risks of error and loss. If you know your recordings will never be used for records or broadcast, there's little reason to fret about making broadcast-quality tapes. Just because the machines are able to deliver a certain level of performance is no reason you have to extract that level of performance from them. You're the boss; take what you want and need and let the rest go. (That's *not* a license for slovenliness: an unnecessarily poor recording lets too much go.)

Sometimes the work leads you into the use of other instruments. I began using a camera in my early Texas prison fieldwork to help me remember what things looked like when I got back to Cambridge and began putting things down on paper. By the time I did my book on convict worksongs, *Wake Up Dead Man,* I realized the book would profit from images, so some were included. A few years later, I decided many of the things I wanted to say about prison life might be better said in photographs than words, so I did a book, *Killing Time,* in which the dominant statement was visual. The photographs there were primary and independent images, not illustrations of the text, which was designed to be a collateral statement. While doing that work, I had to get serious about photography and learn how to use the instruments. I never worried about the awesome amount of photographic information I didn't have because, like everyone else, I learned what I needed to learn in small increments, as each fieldwork problem presented itself. The same thing happened when I decided there were things that could best be said in film. Never was my goal to become a master of any medium; that's a different game entirely. The technologies were then and remain for me now just tools.

Almost all the good fieldworkers I know developed their technological expertise in exactly the same way: step by step and in the context of specific projects. The goals were always practical. But it doesn't stop there: once you learn a technology you begin to define projects in terms of it. If you know how to make films and you want to document a tradition, you're more likely to consider making a film of that tradition than you would be if you knew nothing about making films. Nonetheless, the goal remains the documentation and explication of the tradition, not the film. When the film or photograph or recording becomes its own end, the fieldworker is in trouble. I'll say more about this later.

Folklorists doing fieldwork document two kinds of situation. One consists of folklore in its natural context (a festival, a ritual, a musical performance, work going on); the other consists of folklore performed or discussed within the context of the collection event. In the collection event normal life is suspended so the documentation can go on. The informant, instead of watching television or reading the paper or playing poker, talks to you and your tape recorder; the room, instead of being lighted by natural light and table lamps is lighted by the lamps you have placed specially for photographing persons or objects. Many of the suggestions will apply equally well to either kind of situation: what I say about mike placement in an interview applies also to mike placement in a noninterview recording situation. Sometimes the suggestions will not apply equally well: the kind of lighting you can impose when you're photographing artifacts with someone's permission and cooperation is different than the kind of lighting you use when you're photographing a public event in which you're merely one observer among many. I assume the differences in these situations will be obvious and you'll be able to decide what applies and what doesn't.

No machine will get all the information you want or need. Every recording device has inherent limitations that are inextricably coupled with its advantages. Whenever you select one method of information gathering and preservation over another, you simultaneously exclude certain kinds and classes of information. If you keep yourself aware of this, you can take precautions to fill in the lacunae; if you forget, you'll find yourself selecting information-gathering situations on the basis of your machine's abilities rather than on the situation's contents.

The Law of Inverse Attention

The more complex and comprehensive the data-gathering equipment, the less likely is the operator to understand the event while it's going on. That may seem contradictory, but it isn't. The machine operator defines the world in terms of the machine's needs. The more things the machine is doing, the more machine-questions one must deal with. Even though the camera may be fully automated, the handling of it isn't; it has to be steered into situations where its automation is useful. The more complex the equipment you use, the more attention that equipment demands and requires, and the more attention your equipment gets from you, the less attention you can devote to your informant.

The data-collection technology that gives the collector the best opportunity to observe what's going on, the best chance to understand the broad interrelation of things and events, the greatest physical mobility, and the least cost, is probably a sharp eye and a good memory. Next is paper and pen. All machines must be corrected or altered to operate in changing physical conditions; pen and paper work anywhere—some ballpoints even write underwater and in free fall. Pen and paper, generally, bring back the least amount of detail, but that doesn't mean the detail they bring back is the least important or the least useful. I've seen beautiful field videotapes that were useless as folkloric or ethnographic records. Every recording device limits the mobility of the collector in some way, but the pen and paper limit you least of all (since you can work in any situation except total darkness, and even there it can work if you don't try to get too many words on a page); sound movie cameras limit you most of all.

Pen and paper give you the most mobility and are least likely to cripple you because of mechanical breakdown (if the pencil breaks you cut a new tip, if the pen runs out of ink and the notes are critical you can tap a vein), but they're not very good instruments for doing interviews. "An interviewer who takes notes," wrote William Foote Whyte,

> cannot give full attention to the informant. Physical movements, gestures, and facial expressions give clues not to be found in the words themselves, and some of those fleeting non-verbal cues will be missed while the interviewer is writing.
>
> Furthermore, a good interviewer cannot be passive. At all times he must reflect upon what is being said, ask himself what each statement means and how he can best encourage the informant to clarify a certain point or give detail on an item only hinted at. He must be ready at the conclusion of each informant statement to raise a question or make a statement to develop the account further on the items most pertinent and appropriate for the interview at this stage. The interviewer who is busy taking notes cannot be as alert at picking up productive leads as the

interviewer who is paying full attention to the informant. Note-taking is likely to interfere with the flow of the interview in another way. The interviewer is always a little behind the informant in his note-taking. (1960:367)

The problems Whyte described are compounded with film or video instruments. As I noted earlier, all mechanical devices used to record field information can produce *field amnesia:* we just don't pay as careful attention as we would if we had to *remember* everything. We know it's on the tape, so we let our attention drift. That can be useful (we can afford to notice other things going on at the same time if we don't have to be writing madly, and we can maintain eye-contact the way people in normal conversations do), but it can also be deadly, because we may fail to hear nuance and detail and therefore fail to ask appropriate follow-up questions.

There's a more serious problem: one tends to define field situations in terms of the instruments available. The fieldworker with a camera looks for a nicely lighted scene, for fine images. Sound doesn't seem so important when you're walking through the house with a Nikon or Canon dangling from a broad strap around your neck. The fieldworker with a tape recorder looks for the things the tape recorder can capture: conversations, songs, instrumentals. The posture of the performer, the position of the hands, the arrangement of furniture in the room, the expressions on faces—these don't seem so important. "To what extent," asks Ives, "does a particular artist *consciously* reshape his material, and to what extent is his *perception* of that material shaped by the traditions of the medium in which he has chosen to work?" (1980:405–6). We might paraphase that for the scholar: To what extent does the scholar gather the material needed, and to what extent is one's perception of need shaped by the instruments available?

Whatever machine you use, stay alert to the world around you, to parts of the world that have nothing to do with your machine. That's not as easy or as automatic as you might think. I know combat photographers who so concentrated on what they were filming they forgot everything else. It was as if the only possible direction danger could take was the direction in which their lens was pointed, and they were sure they'd see that in time to duck. The world doesn't work so neatly. Objects impinge from 360° in the vertical and horizontal planes.

Once I was recording in the Brazos bottoms on Ramsey prison farm. Convicts were chopping live oaks and clearing brush. I put my tape recorder and microphone on a log and began taking photographs. I was having trouble getting one particular tree to stay in focus; at first the focus was set too far and then it was set to near, then the tree was clear in the viewfinder for a moment, and then it was out of focus again. At the edge of perception I sensed a change in the workers' voices. Then I realized that the difference was they were shouting, "Watch out, watch out there!" I took the camera from my eye to see who was the fool they were shouting at and I saw they were all looking and waving at me. The tree that wouldn't stay in focus rocked away one last time and then rocked straight toward the spot where I stood. I got out of the way a moment before the upper branches of the tree crashed on the tape recorder. I was so worried about losing the machine—I didn't have another with me, I had little money, and I was 1,800 miles from home—it was a good five minutes before I thought about the close call. As it turned out the recorder held up fine; branches had hit either side of it, but it hadn't been touched. Weeks later, back in Cambridge, I transcribed the tapes from that day. I heard the sounds of axes, some singing, someone calling out, "Timber gettin' limber, timber gettin' limber, my timber gettin' crackin'," then several voices shouting, "Watch out, timber's limber, timber's crackin', watch out there, you with the camera, watch out, watch out there!" That was followed by a terrific crash and then a high-pitched voice saying, almost musically, "Heyyyy—it landed on his raydeeeooo."

Everything influences everything else. If you have a lot of equipment, you may need people to help you carry and set up and use the equipment. If you don't have help, you can't bring all those boxes. Linear increases in equipment introduce exponential increases in things that can go wrong--double the pieces of equipment you're using and you quadruple the problems you risk. If the machines are used interdependently, a malfunction in one can ruin the entire enterprise (if you're shooting sound film, for example, you're in trouble if there are malfunctions in the recorder, mikes, or camera).

If the elements of the recording system are used independently, then addition of new elements increases the failure risk only in regard to the information that would have come from that element and insofar as the attention of the recordist must be further divided. There are practical limits on how many machines anyone can properly operate at once. If, say, the fieldworker is audiotaping a discussion and elects to make some still photographs at the same time, the technical quality of the audiotape is not affected if the camera malfunctions, although the technical quality might be affected if necessary changes in the record settings aren't made because the operator is distracted while using the camera, and the content will surely be affected if the business of fiddling with the camera causes the operator to lose track of what's being said.

Finally, don't forget that the machines aren't neutral. They make statements of their own. If you're one person recording or photographing or filming an event being recorded or photographed or filmed by a hundred or a thousand others, then you have nothing to worry about. But the situations you'll be in will most likely be intimate; you'll be noticed; the number of people there will be small enough so what you do and what image you present will matter. "Consider," wrote the authors of one study, "a potentially nonreactive instrument such as the movie camera. If it is conspicuously placed, its lack of ability to talk to the subjects doesn't help us much. The visible presence of the camera undoubtedly changes behavior, and does so differentially depending on the labeling involved. The response is likely to vary if the camera has printed on its side 'Los Angeles Police Department' or 'NBC' or 'Foundation Project on Crowd Behavior.' Similarly, an Englishman's presence at a wedding in Africa exerts a much more reactive effect on the proceedings than it would on the Sussex Downs" (Webb et al., 1966:13).

Teams

Sometimes you can work better if you involve one or more other people in the fieldwork and divide the labor. One person might do all the videotaping or handle the audio recorder and still camera in a particular session, thereby freeing the other to concentrate on the conversation. If the equipment operator is unobtrusive, the interview proceeds almost as if the operator isn't even there. On the other hand, I have seen equipment operators whose every movement created such a flutter of motion and flurry of noise that real conversation was impossible. Don't work with people like that. People who know their equipment well and who understand what the field project is about are usually capable of blending into the woodwork. Informants quickly get bored watching someone load or unload the camera or deck and get their attention back to something far more pleasurable, like talking.

Projects defined as team projects from the beginning, with clear divisions of labor and lines of responsibility, can produce excellent results. These may be as simple as two people working together or they may involve separate teams coordinated in some grand design. They usually require a lot of time and a lot of coordination.

Adding more people to the collection team may create more problems than it solves. Having someone else to handle the camera and recorder frees one person to be "director," to maintain the continuity of conversation, but it also clutters up the set. Many field situations are destroyed by having too many outsiders present. Just one outsider—you working alone—changes the natural balance of things. In an intimate situation—a person's home or place of work, say—additional researchers puttering about intrude exponentially: two strangers can disrupt the natural sense of things far more than twice as much as one stranger. When the outsiders outnumber the insiders, the situation can be terrifically skewed. (Since 1972, I've done almost all my fieldwork in collaboration with Diane Christian. The collaboration has worked because we are both extremely sensitive to and aware of the other's nuances. Sometimes—as in the death row fieldwork—we did different kinds of work in different rooms at the same time; and other times—as in the work for *Out of Order*—we adopted different technical roles. When such collaboration works well it can be a delight, but as my words earlier about the self-aggrandizing filmmaker indicate, collaboration that doesn't work well can be a personal and professional nightmare.)

What Equipment Do You Really Need?

As little as you can possibly get away with. When I started doing serious fieldwork, I used to go off with the trunk of the car loaded with everything I might need and as many spares as I could get. Most of the time now I travel by air and, except when I'm shooting film, I can carry all the sound and photography equipment I need in a single shoulder bag. (It's not just that I've gotten more parsimonious about luggage; the equipment nowadays is smaller, lighter, and more reliable.) There's no limit to the amount or variety of equipment you might bring, but there are all kinds of reasons to limit the amount and variety of equipment you do bring.

The decision about equipment should be the last major decision of your planning phase. The reason it comes last is the equipment you have to a large extent controls the information you'll be able to capture (to say nothing of the information you'll think of capturing), so you want to be as sure as possible that you're picking equipment to deal with your research needs rather than defining your questions in terms of the equipment you've got. You could say, "I've got a video deck; what can I do with it?" But you should at least be aware of the strictures you're putting on your imagination when you become a servant of your machine.

Except for spectacularly rich folklorists (I know only three of these and one never does his own fieldwork anyway), most of us can't have the ideal equipment configuration for our fieldwork. And, except for the most depressingly poor and lonesome folklorists (who tend to do theoretical studies), most of us do own some equipment or have access to equipment we can borrow.

We might want to define our fieldwork project in terms of documenting the entire physical situation associated with tale-telling in Borneo, but if we don't have at least four fully equipped sound and camera crews, we're going to have to settle for something less. However the project is defined, we have to modify it to take advantage of the equipment we have or can get. If we happen to own a good video recording system, we're more likely to think of projects with a moving visual component than if we own no location equipment at all or no equipment other than a good sound recorder. We might decide we're interested only in narrative song, but if we've got a good camera we'll bring it along, and if we bring it along we'll take pictures, and if we're taking pictures at least part of the time we'll be thinking about what pictures we might take.

If we have barely functional recording equipment we're less likely to seek out and focus on technically splendid performers than we are if we have recording equipment good enough to use the field tapes for an LP or a radio broadcast. Or, to put that the other way around, if we're thinking about the information the informant has to offer rather than the broadcastability of the tapes we're making we're more likely to pay serious attention to informants who might not be as technically proficient or as charming as others.

There are no nice and easy answers as to what equipment you'll need. Certainly, you need the best equipment you can get, but you can get by with very little—a great deal of first-rate fieldwork has been done with no equipment other than pad and pen or pencil. Always be aware of the powerful influence on your field perceptions imposed by the tendency to think through the machines. We might decide, as Edward Ives did, that seeing is more worthwhile than capturing:

> We have seen thousands of photographs and have a pretty clear idea of what is or is not a good picture. First thing we know, we are looking at something not so much in terms of what it is in itself, but in the limited terms of whether or not it will make a good photograph. For example, I used to enjoy vistas (say, the view from the mountain one gets when he pulls his car over into the "scenic turnout"); but after a while I discovered that the pictures I took of such panoramas were usually dull and disappointing, nowhere near as good as that picture of the horse cropping grass

by the overgrown fence-post. It wasn't long before I began to lose interest in "scenic turnouts"—wouldn't even stop the car for them—and I'm sure that there were some I didn't even see because in a way they weren't there for me. Meanwhile, I developed a much keener eye for fence-posts and the like. The effects were two: I tended to look at the world around me as a means to an end, not an end in itself; and I frequently was more interested in the photograph than in the thing photographed *("I can't wait to get home and see how this one turned out")*. Since ultimately I found this limiting, if not a bit poisonous, I quit, and now leave the camera at home. I had become an artist, and I didn't like it. (1978:406)

Photographer Danny Lyon was working on a book of photographs in the Texas prisons about the same time I was finishing fieldwork for *In the Life.* We had the same publisher at the time and got to be friends. One night in a Houston diner Danny said, "The difference between us is I'm always looking for the beautiful convicts and you're looking for the intelligent ones." I told him that was absurd, neither of us was so narrowly focused. Later on, after I got serious about photography and had to decide sometimes whether I was going for words or pictures, I decided he was pretty much right. When I was taping interviews or just watching what was going on, I didn't care at all what anyone looked like or what the light was like or how the planes of light intersected each other; I just cared about what people said and did. And I know that Danny, for his prison book, spent very little time finding out what people were really thinking about things or considering what things people said to him were true and what things were said just to get his attention. The filtering wasn't deliberate on the part of either of us; that's just the way things were.

It was easier to do several kinds of documentation at once when I was less proficient in the use of the various machines. But now that I've worked as a professional photographer and professional cameraman, I'm no longer able to just point and shoot. I think about what the instrument is perceiving and, as I've said, the instruments perceive moments and spaces differently.

Now I know that I think of a room in radically different terms if I'm going to be recording sound in it, shooting film or video in it, taking photographs in it, or having a conversation in it. If I'm shooting film, I want all the areas in which action is going to occur to be lighted well enough for my film to record what's going on, and I want the movement limited so I can follow it without my sound equipment and without being obtrusive. If I'm doing still photography, I care only about the light in one place at one time. If I'm doing sound recording, I care about the sound character of the room and the comfort of the people. It's reasonable to focus attention on the factors that influence the information we're gathering at any particular time; but it's also important that we remind ourselves every now and then to take a look around at everything else.

Diane Christian and I made *Out of Order* with a very small crew—usually just the two of us with an occasional assistant. The nature of the conversations wouldn't permit a gaggle of strangers to be puttering about. Diane handled the sound equipment and carried on the conversations; I did the filming. I also planned on shooting stills, as I did for *Death Row,* but it didn't work. Someone else was doing the filming for *Death Row,* so taking stills was a simple matter. But when I was thinking in terms of a movie camera for *Out of Order* I couldn't shift, conceptually or physically, from the visions and movements of the film camera to the vision and planes of the still camera. I didn't take nearly as many stills as I'd planned when we set up the project, and the stills I did take weren't very good.

That doesn't mean you can't use different media to make a simple record of what's going on or where you've been. Even if you're working principally in sound, you can take photographs as aides-memoires, and some of them might very well turn out to be good. But unless you're exceptional in this regard, consistently serendipitous, or mildly schizophrenic, don't plan on dancing more than one step at a time.

Survival

Nothing lasts forever, though some things last longer than others. So fieldworkers should consider the life span of whatever recording media they decide to use.

No color film presently available has the life span of black-and-white film. That's because the three dyes in most color films deteriorate at different rates. (If you've ever seen an old movie on TV where everyone looks reddish or orangey it's because the blues have faded faster than the other colors.) Color prints don't last as long as black-and-white prints. In fact, the only kind of color process that lasts as long as black and white is one in which the three primary colors are separated and the information is contained on three black-and white negatives—which is the old Technicolor process. That's very expensive and not practical for fieldwork applications.

No one knows how long videotape images will last. Manufacturers are properly vague in their claims, for these tapes have been in use for so short a time there are no empirical tests of endurance, only projections, hypotheses, and desperate hopes. Video technology changes so quickly there isn't even any certainty that videotapes made now will find equipment that can play them twenty or thirty years from now. Videotapes made thirty years ago cannot be played on any modern equipment and they look dreadful when played on the older equipment still available. Since the basic process of projecting movie film has not changed in seventy-five years, old film that hasn't faded looks perfectly good on modern equipment, and the film can be projected and even edited on modern equipment.

Color film will deteriorate in the light or in the dark, but far more quickly in the light. If you have important slides you intend to project a lot, have them duplicated and use the copies for projection. If your slides are important to you, store them in chemically neutral sheets made expressly for archival preservation of slides. Store your negatives in acid-free sleeves. And be aware that most paper manufactured nowadays has so much acid in it that it will probably not last as long as you will. If you're preparing typed documents you want to be around for a very long time, use acid-free paper made for archival purposes.

I have some audiotape manufactured in the early 1960s that's no longer usable because the material bonding the oxide coating to the plastic backing disintegrated. ("On the other hand," notes Ives, "I have recordings made on 3M 111 acetate in 1957–8–9 or so that are still perfectly playable. And they weren't kept under ideal conditions, either.") Most quality tape manufacturers now claim their oxides will adhere "indefinitely." "Indefinitely" doesn't mean without limit; it means the limit isn't known. Use the best tape and film you can afford and store both as wisely as you can manage. Keep film and tape away from extremes of heat and cold and don't store them anywhere there are significant changes in humidity. If you collect materials you think are really important, contact one of the many archives in the country and see if they'll store your materials under archival conditions and make for you a duplicate set of everything that you can use without risk (see Kenworthy et al., 1985). If you'll be transcribing your tapes, you're better off doing the transcribing from a copy than you are cranking the original back and forth through machinery that sometimes gets hungry (see "Copying Tapes" in chap. 10).

Brains and Machines

The brain and its sensory apparatus form an amazingly sensitive and fast computer. With our eyes closed we can tell instantly when a nearby speaker moves a few inches to the right or left or nearer or further away. We can distinguish a million shades of color. We can instantly shift focus from an object in our hand to an object a mile away and from that to a mountaintop twenty-five miles beyond.

Our most sensitive recording instruments attempt to duplicate this capacity, and all of them fail. All of them present compromises of one kind or another, or they introduce distortions in the shape of reality. Many of the available instruments do single things better than we can—a telescope can see small objects further away, infrared film can see in situations we think totally dark, a well-designed microphone may hear sounds higher or lower than we can hear. But none of those instruments can do all the things our own instruments can do: the telescope can't focus on a hand at arm's length (you need another optical instrument for that); the infrared film can't record reliably within the optical spectrum (you need a different kind of film for that); the microphone can't tell the difference between a loud sound far away and a soft sound nearby.

A person with normal hearing can select one speaker among five or ten talking at once and, if all speakers are talking at the same level, actually hear what that one speaker is saying while ignoring what the others are saying. To accomplish the same with a microphone and recorder, we must either place the microphone very close to the speaker whose words interest us most or use a highly directional microphone that accepts audio impulses reaching it from only a very narrow frontal angle. That is, we must use a microphone that distorts significantly the natural sound of the event. The same microphone isn't capable of at once taking in the sound of the group and focusing in on the sound of one voice, though our ear/brain combination does that easily and without any conscious direction on our part or any delay in time.

Filters our subconscious mind provides are not provided automatically by any of the machines; they record anything, being omnivorous and stupid. The microphone connected to your recorder will feed to your recorder and your recorder will feed to your tape every single bit of sound that comes in above the minimal cutoff level. It's a function of air pressure entirely. The ear/brain complex is not only capable of sensing a far wider range of sound than any single recording system, but it's capable of making sense of and ordering those inputs far more efficiently than any recording system. The same thing applies to our visual apparatus and artificial visual devices such as film and video cameras.

What all this means is that every time we select an instrument to record a piece of the world we're making a compromise. We should be aware of the trade-offs taking place.

A filmmaker friend (I think it was John Cohen) said to me not long ago, "Ideally, I'd like to have a little camera in my eye. It would go on and off when I wanted it to. And that would make the movie." At the time I thought it a fine idea; now I'm not so sure. Cameras and editors can do some things the eye can't. The eye doesn't have to do all the things a camera and editor do because the eye has a brain hooked up to it. Cameras are mindless and editors come on the scene after the fact.

Here's an illustration of what I mean:

> You look out the window. You see the street, a few parked cars, a grove of trees beyond the street. A path weaves its way around the grove. Near the front of the grove you see a splash of yellow. The yellow moves, disappears, reappears someplace else. A figure on the right side of the grove moves and you realize it's a person. A young couple walks past the grove along the path. You follow their motion for a moment. You look for the yellow, but you can't see it now. Neither can your eye see the figure that you had first thought a tree and then decided was a person. You haven't moved. There hasn't been any sound.

Your brain processed all this with a single arc of view provided by your eye—approximately 100° to 120°, excluding the blurs at the periphery of your field of vision. The figures were all in consistent perspective. The only thing that changed, except for the moment you tracked the couple, was the point of focus, and you never consciously shifted that. When the brain is working normally, the eyes are *always* focused where you want them to be (drunks sometimes have to think about shifting focus; I'm assuming that you're sober and are using whatever corrective eyeglasses you might need). Eyes have very good depth of field and refocus instantly. The only way for your eyes to select among all those objects in their field of vision is by changing the plane of focus; everything else must be done by the brain without a return circuit.

If you put on your camera a lens with an angle of acceptance approximately equal to the eyes', and if you pointed it at the area you were looking at, and if you had enough depth of field so everything stayed in focus or if you changed the point of focus continually to approximate what the brain did for the eye earlier, almost nothing you had just noticed would be noticed by a watcher of a film of the same event. That's because the camera uses a specific language to bring things to our attention. The operator may throw most of the world out of focus so only one portion of the very deep area is clear. The operator may changes lenses or focal lengths so things that are small to the eye are rendered large to the viewer of the film. The operator may set the exposure to highlight or obscure portions of the image. Your brain does that stuff without you ever having to touch the dial.

The brain edits continuously. It selects from an enormous field of information things of interest and concentrates on them and on them alone. That's why you can look at a busy crowd of people and pick out and follow the motion of a familiar person. Vision is continuous, but consciousness isn't. Your eyes move across a field of things to see, looking for something, and your brain barely registers things it's *not* looking for. Did you ever look for your car in an airport parking lot? What were the colors and makes and years of the cars your eyes passed over immediately before you found your car?

Modern home video recording units are equipped with lenses that zoom from wide-angle to telephoto; they have directional microphones that hear better to the front than to the back; the lenses have automatic irises that set the system's optics and electronics for a balanced picture whatever the color and intensity of the light; they have automatic focusing devices that get things sharper than you can. They are marvels of electronic wizardry. Yet the human brain does *all* those things and does most of them better and faster and more efficiently than any single electronic device. The most highly automated visual and sound data-processing unit yet devised presently sits atop your shoulders and between your ears.

Television manufacturers not long ago introduced high-resolution receivers and monitors which are reported to deliver images twice as sharp as any television image previously available. Even so, nothing you ever see on video will be as smooth as the same object in the real world. Look at a television screen close up and you'll find tiny colored dots; look at a piece of cheese close up and you'll see cheese. Video equipment will never give you the nonvisual and nonaural information present in the real situation: when you videotaped the ice-fishing you were cold and you smelled the sharpness of the winter air; when you watch the videotape you made that day you've got your feet up, your shoes off, and a beer in your hand.

The human eye and brain handle a wider range of light than any mechanical or electronic reproduction device: you can see perfectly well in bright sunlight at the beach and you can read by candlelight; you can instantly shift focus from an object a few inches from your face to the Milky Way and you needn't ever tell your brain what object needs focus at any specific time. You select the specific sounds you want to notice in the mixed-sound situation and you no more have to tell your brain when you want to shift to another sound than you have to tell your foot to move from the accelerator to the brake pedal when the taillights of the car in front of you go red. If an object is far away, the image the object gives your eyes and the sound it delivers to your ears are coherent and consistent. If an object is in motion and you're in motion, your brain can cause your eyes to move so rapidly you can keep that object in the center of your field of vision.

For electronic devices to do these things you must tell them what you want and organize their controls so they can deliver what you need. There is, really, only one thing the machines do better than us: they can remember perfectly what they've seen or heard. The human mind exists always in the present; the recorded tape or exposed piece of film is forever locked in the past. That's the only reason we bother with them.

Scale, Pitch, and Speed

Our sense of size is comparative. An object standing alone is never large or small: it needs some other object to be larger or smaller than. The only way a photograph can give information about the size of an object is if it includes another object of known size.

Separate photographs of Kareem Abdul Jabbar (7'2") and Dudley Moore (5'2"), each standing alone against a plain background, with their feet reaching the bottom of the photographic sheet and the top of their heads reaching the top, appear to be of men of the same height—though Moore will seem in comparison the bulkier of the two. If both men are in one photograph with Jabbar standing twice the distance from the camera as Moore and no information in the picture lets us know that, Moore will seem slightly the taller. Put the two men next to each other in the same photograph and very different information is delivered, since Moore's head barely reaches the middle of Jabbar's chest. The photograph still wouldn't tell how tall either man is: one might be a giant and the other normal, or one might be normal and the other a dwarf. That is, it's possible to have the same discrepancy with one of the figures being that of a person of average height. A third object in the photograph—one of known size—lets us know how to interpret the discrepancy: a chair, a ruler, an automobile, a newspaper in the hands of one of the subjects.

In real life we interpret unconsciously those clues about relative dimension and distance and we use them to decide how big or small or near or far something is. The decisions are immediate and automatic. When part of our sensory apparatus isn't functioning—an eye or an ear—we're disoriented and must learn different techniques for determining distance and volume. People with one eye are dependent on memorized facts about the real size of objects to determine distance.

There are similar considerations with sound. How loud does a musician play or a storyteller tell or a priest utter? If we're physically present, we have an immediate sense not only of relative volume but of absolute volume: we know when we have to strain to hear or when the sound level becomes painful. But recorders don't have our ability to handle so great a range of sound levels at once, so recordists usually set the recording level so the meter barely moves into the overmodulation zone at transient high points. A whispering priest recorded at 0 db seems to be producing the same level of sound as a shouting politician recorded at 0 db; only the sibilants and plosives differ, and for all we know those differences result from speech impediments. Recorders aren't designed to capture *real* levels of sound, since no tape made has the dynamic range of the human ear, and the machines clutter up true silence with their own electronic noise. Rather, those machines are designed to capture an *acceptable* level of sound, which means far more signal (what you want) than background or system noise (what you don't want).

The potential source of sound ambiguity exists with pitch as well as volume. Modern tapes can record an extremely wide range of signals (far wider than we can hear), but if the tape player doesn't move the tape across the playback head at exactly the speed the tape recorder moved the tape during recording, there'll be a shift in pitch and in apparent elapsed time: a song actually sung in B may sound as if it were sung in B-flat or C; a story that required fifteen minutes for the telling may sound as if it took fourteen or sixteen minutes. Listeners will never know they're not hearing things as they were.

Since recording tape offers none of the referents we need to judge either absolute or relative volume or pitch, recordists often introduce them during the recording session. Some tape recorders and mixers have a signal generator that produces a tone of known frequency. When the tape is in the studio the electronic tone recorded at the head or somewhere else on the tape is played and switched back and forth with the same tone generated in the studio. If the two tones are identical, we know that the playback machine is running at exactly the speed of the recording machine, so the program material we hear will have the correct pitch. Fieldworkers recording a great deal of music often carry a small tuning fork or pitchpipe, and near the beginning and perhaps near the end of a tape they hold the tuning fork close to the microphone and strike it, or blow the pitchpipe; that provides a reference tone which permits any later user of the tape to know how to adjust the playback machinery. If we're careful to note in the field the volume level of the tone (always record at 0 db, say), then we can set our playback to reproduce that tone at the same level and know that we'll be playing the same volume area that was recorded. (That still doesn't mean we hear in the studio what we heard in the field, since the quality of sound is dependent on the microphones used and their locations, the characteristics of the recording and playback equipment, and the settings selected for the playback amplifier.)

Ethnomusicologists working with early field recordings made on cylinders are often unable to know what the performances on those early recordings really sounded like because the cylinder recorders had no fixed recording or playing speed. Both could be adjusted every time the machine was used. For recordings without a tuning fork or known pitch sounded, modern users can only guess at the proper playback speed—which means they can only guess at the pitch and tempo of the original performance.

Speed accuracy is a matter of critical concern for filmmakers because they usually record sound and picture separately. A difference of a half second (twelve frames) is enough to throw a film terribly out of synchronization. Experienced filmmakers can sense a film one frame out of sync (that is, the picture on the screen is one frame ahead or behind the sound coming from the speaker); nonfilmmakers who are paying attention can see two frames out of sync; drunks can perceive film three or four frames out of sync. For that reason, modern filmmaking equipment is crystal-controlled: the camera is driven at an exact speed of twenty-four frames per second and the tape recorder (which isn't sprocketed, hence isn't so easy to control exactly) has a recorded code that when played back through a device called a resolver ensures that the recorder plays back at the exact speed it recorded. Which means that if the record speed varied, the playback speed will vary in exactly the same way, therefore producing exact time rendition. More sophisticated equipment has "real time coding"—both the film and the sound tape are encoded with the same real time, which means they don't even have to be started or stopped at the same time. The editor later simply looks at the edge marking on the film and matches the number with the numbers printed on the sound tape; the scenes will be in perfect sync.

The best non-sync recorders lose or gain a few seconds over 1,200 feet of tape-running. The shift in pitch from degree of irregularity is imperceptible to the human ear; you don't know if the tone is one tiny bit above where it should be. But most machines gain and lose more than a few seconds, and they don't gain and lose consistently. The cheaper and smaller the machine, the greater the shift.

Parallel ambiguities exist with color. What is the "real" color of a red box? The technical answer—a wave of so many angstroms in length— is useful only if we walk around with an angstrom meter and if we can visualize what those wavelengths mean. The readings are transient anyway; the same red box produces different readings when illuminated by different kinds of light. The object is *not* always the same color, but our brains often make adjustments to convince us that it is. Under fluorescent light, for example, the skin of Caucasians takes on a greenish tint, but for most people "seeing" that green is extremely difficult. Snow, on a cloudless day, has a light-blue tint, but you don't see the blue (unless you look carefully into large shaded areas adjacent to "white" areas). The reason you don't see green Caucasians and blue snow is your brain has learned what those colors "should" be and makes the conversions for you. Except for the most grossly tinted light (say, a red spot on the dancer at a strip joint), the eye behaves as if all light were white and tints objects accordingly.

Film is incapable of making those conversions. It captures what the scene really consists of, and that's when photographers often learn for the first time that what they see and what's there aren't necessarily the same. If you want to know what the "real" color in a scene is, the photograph won't tell you unless you place somewhere in the shot a color scale or an object of known color which you can then place alongside the photograph for comparison. In that way you can adjust your photographic printing technique to make the rendition match your perception of the object. Without it, you're just guessing and hoping for the best.

While visiting an informant you find a hand-thrown pot you think worthy of documenting for your collection. How do you do it? An art photographer capturing an image of a bit of folk pottery for a gallery show might find the most beautiful pot and light it in the most beautiful way, then take the photograph and go on home. The photographer capturing an image of folk pottery in the course of a field investigation wants the photographs to show as much as possible about the pot itself and also about the pot's context. Several views of the pot are needed: front, sides, back, top. Some of those views should show the pot where it really is used: on a table, on a shelf, wherever it was when you came along. You also want to be able to know from the photograph the size of the pot. And you want a color referent to let you be sure that the photographs show the pot's real color.

You can (and should) measure the pot and put those measurements in your notebook. You can (and should) photograph the pot with something in the picture of known scale. Archaeologists include in their photographs rulers with clear markings. If you don't have a ruler, put anything of known and constant size in one or two pictures: a pack of cigarettes, a piece of currency, a coin (be sure to put in your notebook what coin you use—if the picture isn't clear a viewer who thinks the coin a silver dollar will read the photograph differently than one who thinks the coin a dime). The comparison object should be placed close enough so the lens doesn't introduce any distortion. If the ruler, for example, is only five inches from the camera and the object is a foot from the camera, the ruler will be blurry and it will suggest the object is far larger than it is. (The tip of your finger, held closely enough to your eye, seems larger than a distant mountain.)

Color scale is also important. If you're taking color photographs include in some of them an object of known color. You can purchase at photography stores a Kodak color and grey scale—a card with a series of colors on it and a range of greys between white and black. If you include that card in just one photograph on a roll (assuming the entire roll is shot under the same lighting conditions), you'll later know exactly how to compensate, if any compensation is necessary.

So far, we have a lot of information about what the pot looks like and how it relates to its physical environment—but we know nothing about how it figures in the life of the person who owns it. The art photographer is content to abstract the object from its world; the field-worker wants to locate it within its world. So after you've done all the fine documenting with your camera, you must have a conversation with someone.

In life, we almost always have referents to put things in perspective, to make them human and negotiable, to let us know how big or loud or far away or bright they "really" are. When those referents are absent, we suffer profound disorientation: there are impressive records of madness among sailors alone for a long time at sea or among Arctic explorers and among nineteenth-century travelers across the Great Plains. The brain is a context-seeking device. Our electronic and chemical recording devices care for context not at all, and they have none of the referents needed to let us know how to see and hear what they preserve. That's why, whenever possible, we introduce those referents artificially, to help the machines better approximate what the human brain does every waking moment without a conscious thought.

10/Recording Sound

Tape Machines

A tape machine is an information processor for a data storage device. The data are stored on a magnetic tape, either open-reel or cassette; the data are delivered to the tape recorder from an external source, a microphone or a preamplifier circuit carrying signals from a tuner or turntable or another tape recorder. The data are presented by the tape player to a speaker that's part of its own design or to a preamplifier circuit that will feed it to an external amplifier or to another recorder.

The job of the tape recorder is to encode on the tape with as much fidelity as possible the signal delivered to it; the job of the tape player is to decode with as much fidelity as possible the information stored on the tape. The recorder/player, then, is midway in a three-part system, bracketed on one side by whatever feeds its input and on the other by whatever makes use of its output. I'll say nothing in this book about the amplifiers and speakers you might use to listen to your tapes; those aren't critical for fieldwork since once a tape is made it can be played on the best or worst of playback apparatus with equal ease. Neither will I say anything about recording from phonograph records or television or radio broadcasts. The next chapter deals with the primary source of information for fieldworkers' tape recorders—microphones. This chapter deals with the recorders themselves.

Tape machines have up to four functional sections: transport, heads, preamplifier, and power amplifier. The transport mechanism moves the tape across the erase, record, and play heads. The heads get rid of a signal on the tape *(erase)*, place a signal on the tape *(record)*, or sense the signal already placed on the tape *(play)*. The preamplifier delivers

128

the input signal to the heads (in the *record* mode) or it reads the signal picked up by the head and sends it to an amplifier (in the *playback* mode). The amplifier makes the tiny preamp signal larger and channels that information and power to speakers. Portable professional recorders (when I say "portable" I mean a tape recorder that works on its own batteries), such as the Nagra, have small speakers and small amplifiers; these are used merely to check on the recordings made and aren't meant to provide the amount of power or quality of sound available when the same tape machine is connected to a good amplifier and studio-quality speakers. A *tape deck* is a tape machine without a power amplifier section. A *tape player* is usually taken to mean a tape machine that can play tapes but can't record them. The term *tape recorder* is used loosely by professionals and amateurs alike; it may mean a tape deck or a tape deck with a built-in amplifier. I use the term to mean a machine that records and plays tapes, whether or not it needs an external amplifier to feed the signals through a speaker system.

Track refers to the number of separate recorded paths on a tape. A *full-track* machine has one, a *two-track* (or half-track) machine has two, a *four-track* (or quarter-track) machine has four. *Channel* refers to the number of tracks a particular machine can play at once. *Stereo* is the same as *two-channel,* whether there are two or thirty-two separate tracks on that particular tape or readable by that particular machine. A two-channel tape recorder can feed two separate signals into two separate speakers; a four-channel tape recorder can feed four separate channels into four separate speakers. Your stereo cassette recorder is probably a four-track machine: it uses two tracks (and plays through two channels) when you play side A, and it uses two other tracks (and plays through the same two channels) when you play side B.

Tape Heads

Most portable tape recorders have two electromagnetic heads, one for erase and one for record and playback; more expensive machines separate the record and playback heads. Recorders designed to be used for film-synchronized sound recording may have a fourth head that places an inaudible synchronizing signal on the tape.

As the tape moves through the recorder it passes first across the erase head. The erase head is a broad magnet that scrambles the magnetic particles randomly, resulting in a set of signals that cancel one another out, leaving what on playback is a barely audible and unintelligible hiss. Erase heads are activated only when the recorder is placed in the record mode; they are inoperative in playback, for obvious reasons. You can get better erasure by using a bulk-erasing machine.

Most of the time when you're doing fieldwork you'll be using new tapes, which are supposed to be "clean"—that is, they're supposed to be silent. They aren't: "Tape, fresh out of the wrapper, is noisy. Heat and stray magnetic fields impress it with pops, clicks, and hiss, and not even the best erase head in the finest recorder can reduce the noise to the lowest possible level" (Honoré, 1980:72). Since bulk erasers bring the level of noise far lower than any erase head, tape used for recordings where high fidelity is important is often bulk erased before use. Many professional recording engineers are convinced audiotape stretches slightly during the first and second passes, so they like to run new tapes through the machine on fast-forward and fast-reverse before first use as well. When you're recording on location you don't have a bulk eraser (and you very well might not need that level of fidelity or your recorder won't be good enough for it to matter), and there isn't time to be running your reels or cassettes back and forth through the machine. If you have time before you leave the house, though, those run-throughs take almost none of your time (you can do something else while the tape machine is doing your work) and you'll know that the tape's pretensilizing will now be fixed at its operating length.

The erase head on a full-track recorder cleans (scrambles) the entire width of the tape. On half-track mono tape recorders, whether cassette or open-reel, the erase head cleans off almost the entire upper half of the tape (a small path between the upper and lower tracks isn't affected by any of the heads in order to prevent partial erasure of the wrong track on record and noise coming from the wrong track on playback). The operation is slightly more complex for stereo recorders. For open-reel stereo recorders that are also capable of operating in monaural, the erase head will usually parallel whatever record mode the machine is in: if the recorder is recording on one track only, the erase head erases that one track only; if the recorder is recording on both tracks, the erase head will erase both tracks. Since stereo tracks on quarter-track open-reel stereo recorders alternate, the erase heads are themselves quarter-track. They are set only on tracks 1 and 3 and their area of erasure is slightly wider than the record head's area of recording. When the reel is turned over to use the other side, those same heads now attack tracks 4 and 2, which are the left and right channels of the B side.

The stereo tracks of a cassette recorder are side by side and the tape is so narrow it's not practical to attack the individual tracks. You can't record single track on a four-channel stereo cassette recorder, and neither can you erase single track. The erase head is half-track wide and removes both the left and right channels at the same time.

The record head arranges the magnetic molecules so they record the signal delivered to it by the recorder's preamplifier section. The play head reverses the process: it senses the slight magnetization on the tape and feeds those signals to a preamp, where they are prepared to go into the amplifier that in turn feeds the speakers. Cheaper recorders combine record and playback heads and record and play preamplifiers; better machines use separate heads and separate electronics.

Noise reduction devices, such as the patented Dolby and dbx systems, treat the signal at the preamp phase before it's passed to the recording head and again at the preamp phase when it comes off the head and before it's forwarded to the power amplifier. They reduce significantly electronic noise created by the recorder itself but don't change the input signal in any way. The effect is a recording with far less audible noise during passages when the signal is recorded at a low level (see pp. 150–54).

Monaural cassette and open-reel machines work exactly the same way. If they are full-track, the record head puts on the tape a signal that covers the full width of the tape, and the playback heads read from the tape a signal imprinted on the full width of the tape. Several open-reel manufacturers offer full-track machines, but full-track cassette recorders are rare and must be specially ordered.

Half-track monaural recorders record and play only the upper half of the tape. When the tape has passed completely from the *feed* reel on the left to the *take-up* reel on the right, it can be turned over and the reels reversed (or the cassette turned over, which does the same thing to the feed and take-up spools inside the cassette) and another track can be recorded on what was previously the lower track. (Recordists often speak of recording on the "other side," but the term is inappropriate for tape, which records on one side only. What changes is *where* the signal is placed on the tape.)

Stereo (two-channel) open-reel recorders can be half-track or quarter-track. A half-track stereo recorder can apply a signal in one direction only: the recording head actually consists of two magnetic recording heads in one body, one placed above the other. One part of the head records the left channel on the upper part of the tape, the other part of the head records the right channel on the lower part of the tape. If you were to turn over a tape recorded in half-track stereo and put the recorder in playback, you would hear everything backwards; if you put the recorder in record, you would erase everything you just recorded. Most stereo open-reel recorders can be operated as monaural recorders, in which case the tape can be turned over and the other track used, just as with the monaural recorders described above. (Everything I say about recorders here applies equally well to players.)

On an open-reel quarter-track stereo machine, the erase head erases tracks 1 and 3, then the record head records on tracks 1 and 3. When the tape is turned over and the reels reversed so the tape is passing through the machine in the opposite direction, tracks 4 and 2 are now in the positions previously occupied by tracks 1 and 3. When you record on side A, track 1 is the left channel and 3 is the right channel; when you record on side B, track 4 is the left channel and 2 is the right channel. Between each track is a slight space not covered by the record or playback heads; that prevents leakage and keeps you from hearing faint signals of sounds going the wrong way.

It's possible, with a quarter-track open-reel machine, to record four separate mono channels, though I don't know why anyone would want to. The money savings doubles the mileage from your tape budget, but it clutters up the tapes. More important, if there's any tape damage, if a machine eats a few feet, you've damaged material from four recording sessions at once. (A friend suggests this as an economical way to "store old records where sound is poor—e.g., old 78s." I'd take exactly the opposite position: if you ever want to use your tape of those old 78s you very well may want to submit your tape to various kinds of filtering, enhancing, boosting, and equalizing. For that, you want to start out with as good a tape of your original information source as possible—warts and all.)

The usual tape for quarter-track recorders is 1/4 inch wide. Some studio machines have more tracks and use wider tape, but these are rarely used by fieldworkers. The width of the recorded areas are slightly less than 1/4 inch for full-track, slightly less than 1/8 inch for half-track, and slightly less than 1/16 inch for quarter-track. Cassettes utilize tape that's 1/8 inch wide, so the tracks are half the width of comparable open-reel configurations. A single track in cassette quarter-track stereo, for example, is slightly less than 1/32 inch. Fancy 32-track studio recorders that utilize 2-inch tape generate tracks no wider than the tracks on quarter-track stereo—slightly under 1/16 inch each. With modern technology, an awesome amount of information can be stored in a very narrow path.

Full-track	Half-track mono	Half-track stereo	Quarter-track mono	Quarter-track stereo
			1 ———▶	left A ———▶
	side A	left	2 ◀———	◀———right B
———▶			3 ———▶	right A———▶
	side B	right	4 ◀———	◀———left B

Figure 1. Track configuration for ¼-inch open-reel audiotape.

Except for specially made full-track models, all cassette machines record on the upper half of the tape only. If the recorder is mono, it uses the entire upper half (again, less a small space separating the tracks); if the recorder is stereo, it places the left channel on the uppermost track and the right channel on the track just beneath it. When you record stereo on side A, then, track 1 is the left channel and 2 is the right channel; when you record on side B, track 4 is left and 3 is right. I don't know of any cassette recorder that permits separate recording on the stereo tracks. The recording heads are quarter-track, but the erase head is half-track. That means if you're recording stereo the erase head will scramble the top track and the track adjacent to it. But if you have a signal coming into only one track—a mike fed into track 1 only, say—you'll get on playback sound coming from your left speaker and tape hiss coming from your right speaker, and perhaps a little sound from the left channel leaking over to the right channel.

Figures 1 and 2 indicate what a 1/4-inch tape and a cassette tape would look like if we could see the various configurations.

Head Care

The best preamplifier and amplifier and the most reliable transport system will be useless if the heads aren't functioning properly. If the record head is dirty, scratched, worn down, misaligned, or charged with residual magnetism, nothing you do will produce a decent recording. With the exception of a few recorders, head alignment isn't something users can do much about, but the rest is very much within your control. Heads are simple to clean: apply a little head-cleaning fluid or denatured alcohol with a swab to remove the accumulated gunk (the gunk starts to reduce the quality of your recordings long

Monaural	Stereo
side A ———————————▶	left channel side A ———————▶
	right channel side A ———————▶
side B ◀———————————	right channel side B ◀———————
	left channel side B ◀———————

Figure 2. Track configurations for cassette audiotape.

before you see it; be in the habit of cleaning recording heads on a regular basis). Sprays of solvent made especially for tape heads are available and are especially useful for cassette recorders, since the heads in cassette machines are often not as accessible as the heads in open-reel machines. *Never* scrape accumulated stuff off a recorder's heads. If you can't get deposits off with solvent, take the machine to a technician and get professional help.

Clean the capstan and tape guides whenever you clean the heads, using the same solvent. (Some solvents are bad for the rubber wheel that presses the tape against the capstan, so read the directions carefully.) Regular cleaning of the capstan and tape guides decreases the likelihood of tape wrapping around the capstan. (The other common cause of cassette tapes jamming is having the tape loose in the cassette at the beginning of play. If you're at the beginning of a tape, hit the rewind button for a second and you'll take up the slack; if you're replacing a tape and starting somewhere you stopped last time, use your finger or a pencil to turn one of the cores to take up the slack.)

Tape recorder heads accumulate small charges of residual magnetism. These charges interfere with recording and playback, so the heads should be demagnetized regularly. The process involves scrambling the accumulated magnetic charge with a small electromagnet applied directly to the heads. Some manufacturers recommend demagnetization after ten hours of use; some fanatics I know recommend demagnetization before every new tape is inserted in a recording session; I tend to demagnetize far more frequently when I'm recording in the field or doing serious editing than when I'm listening to things at home. I demagnetized the decks in my studio a few days ago; I don't remember the last time I demagnetized the deck in my living room.

The heads on open-reel tape recorders are demagnetized with a device that has a long thin tip coming out of the handgrip electromagnet;

the tip is moved slowly across each of the machine's heads. When using those, put a small piece of tape on the tip. The tape won't block the magnetic field, but it will keep you from scratching the tape head. Getting those devices in the right place is difficult in some cassette recorders, so many cassette owners use a battery-powered demagnetizer built within a regular cassette shell. Insert the demagnetizing cassette, push the play button to bring the heads in contact with the degmagnetizer, wait a few seconds, then remove the device. All tape recorders—cassette or open-reel—should be turned off when demagnetization is going on.

Head wear usually cannot be seen with the naked eye, but you can hear it. The highs go first. It takes a long time for modern heads to be worn down enough to cause you problems in the field, but if your field tape recorder is also the one you've been using to listen to music five hours a day for the past four years, you might have someone check it out before you do any serious work.

Tape Speed and Tape Length

Reel-to-reel or open-reel, tape play or record times are controlled by two factors: tape length and tape speed. Most open-reel recorders perform at two or more of the following four speeds: 7.5, 3.75, 1 7/8 and 15/16 ips (inches per second). Halving the tape speed doubles the tape's playing time; it also reduces significantly the quality of the recording. Professional machines record at 15 ips and some studio machines are used at 30 ips and even 60 ips. I don't know of anyone who records folklore or oral history material at 30 ips. Some years ago folklorists recording music might occasionally record at 15 ips, but that was rare. Nowadays, fieldworkers using open-reel machines generally record music at 7.5 ips and speech at 3.75 or 1 7/8 ips.

The speed you use depends partly on your budget but more on the use you have for the tapes. If you're planning on doing anything with them other than transcribing, you want the best recording you can get, so you want to record at as fast a tape speed as you can manage. If you're recording musical material and expect to transcribe it, record at a speed faster than the slowest speed of your recorder so you can slow the machine down on playback if you wish.

Don't change tape speeds in mid-reel. Tapes that are partly one speed and partly another are difficult to transcribe. More important, you can drive your informants crazy by constantly fiddling with speed controls. If you do shift speeds, you'll never be able to listen to the tape without hanging over the machine the entire time or making a copy and cor-

Table 1. Recording time per side for various tape lengths and recorder
          speeds.

Tape length (ft)	Recorder speed (ips)				
	1 7/8	3.75	7.5	15	30
600	60 min	30 min	15 min	7.5 min	3.75 min
900	90 min	45 min	22.5 min	11.25 min	5.62 min
1,200	2 hr	60 min	30 min	15 min	7.5 min
1,800	3 hr	90 min	45 min	22.5 min	11.25 min
2,400	4 hr	2 hr	60 min	30 min	15 min
3,600	6 hr	3 hr	90 min	45 min	22.5 min

recting for your mischief. The copy will have those whoops and grunts
common to tape sound when speed suddenly increases or decreases—
unless you cut them out, which is more work.

Set the speed to get the most important matter to be recorded. If
your recorder captures speech satisfactorily at 1 7/8 ips but you know
there's going to be important music that you'll want to transcribe, I'd
suggest recording the entire side at 7.5. Ives finds "that 1 7/8 is perfectly
adequate for almost any interview situation" and he recommends 3.75
ips if music will be part of the interview (1974:20). That's his preference. I would kick it up a notch: 3.75 for interview and 7.5 for music.
Tape doesn't cost *that* much and the difference in quality in most
machines is appreciable. To put this in some perspective: if the machine takes 7-inch diameter tapes and if a tape 1,800 feet long is used,
you get on each side 22.5 minutes at 15 ips, 45 minutes at 7.5 ips, 90
minutes at 3.75 ips, and 180 minutes at 1 7/8 ips (see Table 1). The
only open-reel machine that records well at 1 7/8 is the tiny Nagra
SNN, which costs about $5,000 with its various gadgets; I assume
you're not using a Nagra SNN. (It's a different story with cassette
machines. I'll get to them in a while.)

Tape decks are designed to accept different sized reels. Most home
machines will handle reels up to 7 inches in diameter. Nagras (except
for the miniature SNN) are designed to use a 7-inch reel with the top
open and a 5-inch reel with the top closed; special tops are available
that permit closed-top recording with 7-inch reels. Studio machines
take reels up to 10 inches in diameter. The advantage of the larger
reels is they permit more tape on a single reel without having to go

down to a thinner backing. The longest tape presently available for 7-inch reels is 2,400 feet on a 0.5 mil backing.

Tape that thin is more likely than thicker tapes to be tangled and to give *print-through*. Print-through results from a strong signal on one layer of magnetized tape transferring a weak signal to the covering layer; the practical effect is a faint pre-echo of the upcoming signal on playback. When tapes are recorded on one side only, the likelihood of print-through can be reduced by storing them tails out, which places print-through echo after the sound, where it makes sense and is therefore not disturbing. Tapes recorded on both sides should be rewound from time to time. I have rarely had print-through with tapes having 1-mil backing—1,800 feet on 7-inch reels or 900 feet on 5-inch reels—but some people have reported it. The open-reel tape least likely to suffer print-through or tangling is 1.5 mil—600 feet on 5-inch reels and 1,200 feet on 7-inch reels.

Cassette recorders are designed to record well at 1 7/8 ips. The better cassette recorders are capable of producing at that speed recordings that are better in all regards than any but the most sophisticated open-reel machines. A specialist in recording techniques for feature motion pictures wrote, "In the early 1950s it was unthinkable to master-record anything at a tape speed slower than 15 ips. Today, we accept the 1 7/8 ips cassette without flinching" (Honoré, 1980:54). Cassette machines have the added advantages of costing and weighing far less, taking up far less space, and needing far less power than open-reel machines.

A few cassette machines work at 15/16 ips or at 3.75 ips, but most operate at 1 7/8 ips only. Cassettes are available in four lengths: 15, 30, 45, and 60 minutes per side. Tape designations give the tape's *total* recording time: C-90 or SA-90, for example, are both tapes capable of recording 45 minutes on each side.

Unlike open-reel recorders, which use reels as small as 3 inches in diameter and, in some cases, reels as large as 10 inches in diameter, cassette recorders accept only one size tape holder—the standard cassette of 4 inches by 2.5 inches. The only way to increase recording time in a cassette is by making the tape longer, and the only way to fit longer tape into the same space is by making the tape thinner. As with open-reel tapes, cassette tapes with thinner backings are more likely to get tangled up and are more likely to suffer print-through.

When I'm shooting film and using a cassette recorder such as a crystal-modified TC-D5M, I find the 30-minute tapes just right for soundtracks because they are slightly longer than two 400-foot 16mm film magazines (12 minutes each). When I do interviews with a cassette recorder, I prefer the 45-minute tape because 90 minutes is about as long as I like to work in single interview segments. (Some people work differently. If you find you never go over an hour, then use C-60 tapes.) I don't know any fieldworker who uses C-120 tapes; they're so thin they print through strong signals and are very likely to get tangled in the capstan and be ruined.

Noise

If a recorder has more than one operating speed, it'll make higher quality recordings or provide better quality playback at the higher speed. A top-quality open-reel recorder gives better quality recordings than a top-quality cassette recorder. The reasons are purely mechanical. The same electronic devices are available whatever the transport speed and whatever container is used to hold the tape. The only real difference is how much tape the record head can influence in any moment in time. That's directly a function of the speed at which the tape moves and the width of the recording track.

A half-track stereo open-reel machine uses tracks slightly narrower than 1/8 inch each; a quarter-track stereo cassette machine uses tracks slightly narrower than 1/32 inch each; the open-reel tape moving at 7.5 ips is passing across the tape head four times faster than the cassette tape moving at 1 7/8 ips. The half-track stereo open-reel tape head is "seeing" sixteen times as much tape at any moment as the quarter-track stereo cassette tape head; a quarter-track stereo open-reel tape head (at 7.5 ips) is "seeing" eight times as much tape as the cassette head (at 1 7/8 ips).

For a variety of technical reasons the difference in signal quality isn't equal to the difference in the amount of tape seen. There are practical upper limits on how fast tape can be run and how wide it can be made: noise is reduced, but it's not cut in half if tape width or speed is doubled. Furthermore, certain design characteristics influence tape performance. Quality cassette recorders, which use narrower tracks than open-reel recorders, tend to be manufactured to extremely close tolerances and thereby obtain optimum performance from the heads and transport systems.

Some recordists say wider tracks and higher speeds provide more "headroom"—the tape is better able to handle transient periods of strong signal without *overmodulation* (when the input signal is so strong the information recorded on the tape is distorted). Headroom is an impressionistic quality; I don't know anyone who has measured it and I don't know anyone who sets the level controls intelligently at the beginning who has ever noticed any difference in the headroom of narrow or wide or fast or slow tapes. The real difference has to do with noise generated by the system itself, described by the *signal-to-noise ratio* (SNR), which is the relationship between the information sound output of a piece of electronic equipment and the noise generated by that equipment; or the ratio of the sound you want coming through to the sound you don't want coming through.

If you want to hear what electronic noise sounds like, turn on your amplifier and switch the selector to "tape" (with no tape on the deck but with the deck turned on). You'll hear both hiss and hum—the noise produced by the amplifier and the tape deck. Turn the deck off and both hiss and hum will drop significantly—but not totally. Now you're hearing the amplifier's noise. If you had a microphone cable plugged into the tape deck and had the deck on record or if you plugged the mike cable directly into the amplifier and then pulled the cable out, the same thing would happen. All electronic devices make noise; all pieces of loose wire in the system pick up extraneous signals. As long as the difference between the level of program material and system noise is great, you never consciously hear the noise; when the difference isn't great, you begin to hear the noise and the recording sounds dirty.

Performance specifications provided by manufacturers of open-reel recorders usually give SNR information in specific relation to one or more of the recorder's operating speeds. The electronics of the recorder are the same whatever speed the tape is going; the reason for different SNRs at different speeds is that the amount of noise added to the system by the tape itself differs at different speeds. Some recorders have electronic systems designed to compensate for the difference in performance at higher and slower speeds; these systems never compensate fully for the noise increase at slower speeds. Many tape recorders incorporate noise reduction systems. The two most common are those marketed under the names Dolby and dbx. The systems are being improved constantly: the original Dolby system, for example, was succeeded a few years ago by Dolby B, which was more efficient and which increased SNR slightly; in 1984 several portable cassette recorders (such as the Uher CR-160) were available with Dolby C, which improved SNR 8 dB further (dB—decibels—are a measurement of sound pressure, usually referred to as volume). These systems amplify weaker parts of the signal during recording and reduce the same parts of the signal during playback. The net effect is a significant reduction in the amount of electronic noise added during the process.

The amount of information delivered to the tape head—the signal strength—increases with the width and speed of the tape. All *system* noise remains constant whatever the speed and width of the tape. The amount of noise introduced by the tape increases the faster the tape goes and the wider the tape is, but if the tape has been bulk-erased that's probably the smallest portion of added noise. The best SNR, therefore, is achieved with the widest track possible. Full-track is better than half-track, half-track is better than quarter-track, and quarter-track on a 1/4-inch tape is better than quarter-track on an 1/8-inch tape. It works that way if everything else is kept equal. The thing is, everything else is *not* kept equal. There are considerations other than the maximum SNR possible, and those considerations influence the choice of machines all recordists at some point make.

Above a certain point, a high SNR is like owning a family car capable of going 150 mph: it's interesting that the car can go that fast, but if you're a rational driver you'll never have any use for the capacity, and acquiring it and maintaining it will squander a great deal of money you might use to better purpose. You won't hear the noise in a performance where the SNR is greater than 52 dB, even with superb speakers. Most quality home tape recorders—open-reel or cassette—perform far above 52 dB SNR. Better cassette tape recorders, with noise reduction on and with metal tape, routinely produce SNRs above 65 dB; Nagras produce SNRs well above 65 dB without noise reduction, which is a good thing because Nagra is one of the few recorder manufacturers that doesn't include one of the available noise reduction systems.

SNR is one of the things you pay for in a tape recorder. It costs more to make a system with little electronic noise than to make a system with a moderate amount of electronic noise; it costs a great deal more to make a system with extremely little electronic noise. If you can't notice the difference between the inexpensive machine that delivers 52 dB SNR and the expensive machine that delivers 65 dB SNR, why spend the extra money?

If you're going to make your tape and listen to it yourself directly, there's no reason at all to spend that extra money. It's like paying for the top 75 mph on that road car. The extra SNR matters if you're going to be making copies of that original tape or if you're going to be broadcasting it. That changes the game just as much as putting that road car onto a race track. ("What," asks Ellen Stekert, "of the people who come after who might use the tape?" Good question. I have just a fuzzy answer: Make the best tape you can manage to make, but don't feel guilty if you fail to provide all the nourishment a theoretical consumer might desire. This work is taking place in the practical world. Practically, every field tape might find extensive and unexpected utilization; practically, you can afford only so much precision. Know what you're doing, know what you might do, do as good a job as you can with the resources you have at your disposal. Then "the people who come after" can do their own work and solve their own problems.)

Every time a tape is copied (every time it goes to a new "generation," in the argot of the trade), there is approximately a 3 dB loss in SNR. If you start out with a tape having 55 dB SNR and make a copy you get a tape with 52 dB SNR; if you copy that copy you get a tape with 49 dB SNR. Three dB is the equivalent of a doubling or halving of volume; if you add 6 dB of noise (what happens in two generations), you have quadrupled the audible character of the noise on your tape.

Say you're planning on making a radio broadcast from your tapes. Generally you don't work with your originals. If the originals are 65 db, your working copies are 62 dB. (If your originals are on cassettes, make the copies on open-reel tapes if at all possible, since open-reel is far easier to edit accurately.) You cut and splice your copies and then remaster those into the broadcast tape, perhaps using an equalizer to correct some sound problems at certain points. That means your broadcast tape is 59 dB—still acceptable, but remember it has to go through the broadcast electronics and then through the receiver electronics before anyone gets to hear it. The sound quality for most radio news broadcasts is pretty lousy and people are conditioned to hearing a lot of noise; they're not conditioned to hearing a lot of noise on radio documentaries or radio music programs. The SNR of those broadcast tapes, therefore, should be as high as possible. (If you're taping off the air and then playing back your tape, a whole new batch of noise is added to the recording.)

The problem is more critical with film because film sound goes through more generations before it's used. The original soundtrack recording is copied onto sprocketed magnetic film (so it can be cut with the picture track). That's one copy generation. When the film is edited, two or more soundtracks are usually mixed together to make the final magnetic soundtrack. That's a second generation. (If more than three tracks are being mixed it's usually done in steps—two or three tracks are mixed and two or three other tracks are mixed, then the two mixed tracks are themselves mixed. That's another generation, but we'll forget about that option in this calculation.) The process doesn't stop with the final magnetic soundtrack, however. The sound must get onto the film itself. If the film has a magnetic soundtrack (which is rare), we have at least a 9 dB SNR drop from the original recording. If the film has an optical soundtrack (far more common), there are three more generations necessary—transfer of the magnetic track to an optical negative track, transfer of the optical negative track to the master from which prints are made (the color reversal intermediate or the internegative), and then transfer to the release print itself. That's five generations and 15 dB away from the original, and often more than that.

So the SNR of the original recording can matter a great deal, even though you can't hear it. But only if you're going to be making radio or television programs or phonograph records or films. For ordinary fieldwork, all that extra capacity is unnecessary, and even for most fieldwork in which extended use of the tapes is planned the extra advantage given by the Nagra isn't worth the cost or the trouble. Folklore fieldworkers' needs can be provided by recorders costing far less money and requiring far less attention. (Many independent filmmakers, whose recording needs are far more critical than folklore fieldworkers', have made the same decision: many documentaries are now made using crystal-controlled cassette recorders.)

In the next few years, all of this SNR and sound quality business is going to change radically. The change will happen when digital sound recording technology becomes generally available in field recording instruments.

Digital recording and playback technology is the most important development in electronic recording since semiconductors (transistors) freed recorders from the fragile, heat-generating, electronically noisy, power-hungry electronic tube. Digital made its first impact in the consumer market in the mid-1980s in the form of digital audio disks—generally referred to as *compact disks* or CDs (so called because they carry the amount of information on a 12-inch LP on a much smaller disk). Information on CDs is retrieved by a laser system rather than a needle moving through grooves. The section of the disks bearing information is never touched during playback, so there's no problem with mechanical surface noise, dust, scratches, and wear. Since the signal is transmitted numerically rather than mechanically, the amplifier gets exactly what's on the disk rather than an approximation of it. CDs are noted for spectacularly high fidelity and noise-free reproduction. Even though twice as expensive as ordinary LPs, digital disks were an immediate success, and many older albums have been re-released in the CD format. In 1984 and early 1985, several manufacturers announced production of digital video receivers. Audio digital recorders, curiously, were the last pieces of the sound-picture recorder configuration to be available for the consumer market, though they were available in laboratory-type equipment in the early 1980s.

Digital recording—more properly *pulse code modulation*—encodes and transmits information on tapes or disks (or any other storage and retrieval medium) in the form of pulses that represent numbers. Such recordings are free of the dynamic range limitations of ordinary video or audio recording tape and aren't subject to minor frequency variations that result in wow and flutter. In theory, audio frequency and dynamic range are limited only by the capacity of the microphones and speakers. No electronic distortion is introduced by the recording medium itself.

Many of us already use digital recording technology regularly—it's the basis of information storage, manipulation, and retrieval in computers. Because information is stored numerically, files on computer disks can be called up and rewritten and copied hundreds of times with no loss in signal quality. If there were signal loss, the information would soon turn to gibberish—which is what happens to even the best nondigital audio or video recording after twenty or thirty generations of dubbing.

The implications of this technology for fieldworkers is enormous. Lightweight and inexpensive field audio and video recording equipment capable of extremely high fidelity should be generally available within a few years. Recordings made on this equipment will be editable with virtually no generation loss. The first digital audio recorders reached the consumer market in 1985 when Sony introduced its 8mm video recorders, which were capable of recording up to twelve hours of high fidelity sound on a cassette only slightly larger than an ordinary audio cassette.

Cassettes or Open-Reel?

The best-quality tape recordings are made on the best-quality open-reel recorders, so there's no question about what kind of tape machine should be used in a studio. In a studio all the equipment is in place and the performers come to it; size and weight are irrelevant. Fieldwork is just the other way around: the performers are in place and the fieldworker brings the equipment to them; size and weight can be very important. The quality of recordings made by cassette machines now is so high and the difference in cost, weight, and bulk between cassette and open-reel machines is so great that only rarely is the open-reel machine a sensible or practical choice for fieldworkers.

Because of the way recording technology has developed in the past decade, cassette recorders provide higher quality recordings than open-reel recorders in the same price range. The fieldworker's concern, however, isn't just getting the most value for the dollar; the concern is getting the best recordings possible given the resources available and the reasons for which the fieldwork is being done. The answer to the question, "Which is better—cassette or open-reel?" is, therefore, "It depends on what you can get, what you want to do, and why you're doing it."

A decade ago, no professional folklorist found cassette recorders acceptable for serious use, and some archives refused to accept cassette tapes at all. Now, few folklorists who record in the field use anything else. The American Folklife Center (in the Library of Congress) uses Nagras (the best portable open-reel recorder available) on many of its field projects because its staff believes the Nagra produces recordings more likely to be suitable for record release and radio broadcast than cassette recorders. There *are* differences in the quality of the tapes made by the Nagra and the best of the portable cassette recorders, but they matter only in special circumstances. Most fieldworkers are after data, not materials that will be converted into other products, and the slight technical advantage afforded by the Nagra may not be worth the great difference in cost, weight, volume, and ease of use. Furthermore, fine record masters and radio tapes and film soundtracks have been made with cassette recorders in recent years. I don't know anyone who can by listening distinguish among original tapes made by a competent recordist on a Nagra 4.2 and on a portable cassette recorder with Dolby C noise reduction.

I noted above that many independent filmmakers now use cassette recorders for their location soundtracks. Some Nagra fans say film-makers can get away with that only because the 16mm optical track produces a fairly narrow range of sound frequency. They're right about the limitation of the optical track but not about the reason for liking cassettes. Filmmakers need very good original recordings because their recordings go through at least three tape and three optical generations before reaching a speaker. Recorders like the Sony TC-D5M, the Sony WM-D6C, and the Uher CR-160 produce recordings good enough to handle that, and they have the additional advantage of being extremely portable. Hollywood film crews use Nagras—but Hollywood film crews consist of a lot of people, many of whose jobs consist of nothing but carrying things for other people. Few independent filmmakers, and even fewer folklorists, have someone to fetch and carry.

A nonfolklorist who does technical work for the American Folk-life Center points out to anyone who'll listen that the Nagra is very portable when compared to studio machines. It surely is portable compared to those beasts that must be mounted on large frames. But if you're on the move all day, the Nagra can become a real burden, especially if you're carrying tapes to feed it. I can go out in the field with my cassette recorder, enough tape to record all day, enough batteries to power the machine several hours longer than I expect to be recording, two mikes with cables, a Leica with an extra lens, film, notebook, pipe, tobacco, and a few cigars for long breaks—and carry it all easily in a shoulder bag of average size. That, for me, isn't an insignificant consideration.

The Nagra 4.2L weighs 15 pounds with batteries and tape, occupies 468 cubic inches of space, and costs well over $6,000 (the stereo version, the 4.2S, costs over $1,000 more); the Sony TC-D5M, a stereo cassette recorder, weighs 3.75 pounds with batteries and tape, occupies 115 cubic inches of space and costs less than $600. The Sony WM-D6C cassette recorder (the "Walkman Pro"), which has crystal-controlled speed and Dolby C noise reduction, weighs 1.5 pounds, occupies 44 cubic inches of space, and sells for about than $200. That makes the stereo Nagra 4.2 ten times heavier, ten times bulkier, and thirty-five times more expensive than the WM-D6C. The Nagra's power supply alone—twelve D-cell batteries—weighs more than a WM-D6C, two quality microphones, and a half-dozen cassette tapes. The Nagra claims an SNR "in excess of 68 db"; the WM-D6C with Dolby C and metal tape has an SNR of 71 db. The SNR of the Nagra could be boosted by the addition of a noise reduction system, but for field recordists that provides further complication, bulk, weight, and cost. Some of the Nagra's specifications are superior to those of the WM-D6C—slightly wider and slightly flatter frequency response, for example. If one has the money and can manage the weight and cost and the loss in flexibility, the Nagra makes sense. But for most fieldworkers a machine like the Sony WM-D6C or TC-D5M or the stereo Uher CR-160AV (which has a 74 db SNR with its Dolby C on metal tape) is far more practical.

Nagra makes a miniature open-reel recorder, the SNN, but I don't know any fieldworkers who use it. Filmmakers used to use it for hiding in people's pockets before good radio mikes became available. The SNN uses 3-inch reels and is slightly smaller and slightly lighter than the Walkman Pro. The two machines have about the same frequency response and the same SNR. The Nagra SNN, with all its gadgets, lists for over $5,000 and is just about never discounted. That means it costs about twenty-five times as much as the Walkman Pro.

(I've given a lot of detail here about specific machines. My intention is to use them as examples only. By the time you read this, other models of the Nagra and the Sony and other cassette machines will be available. Perhaps inexpensive digital field recorders will be available. The specs will be better and the prices of the best cassette machines will probably be even lower than they are now.)

The cassette machines are not only lighter, they're also faster to use. To change the reels on the Nagra, the operator must take the full reel recorded off the right-hand spindle (after fast-forwarding it to get past the last segment of still-unrecorded tape), move the empty reel from the left-hand spindle to the right-hand spindle, place a roll of fresh tape on the left-hand spindle, lace the tape through its path, and start the machine; the process takes an efficient and experienced operator a minimum of thirty seconds. To change reels on any cassette recorder the operator pushes a button to pop out the cassette, slips in the new cassette or turns over the one that was being used, pushes the rapid advance control momentarily to get beyond the leader, and starts the machine; the process takes an operator who has practiced for only a few minutes about five seconds—and it can be done with one hand.

Some things can't be done well on cassette machines. You can't edit on them; if you want to edit material on cassettes you have to copy the originals onto open-reels and cut those up. (I'm talking about cut-and-splice sound editing, not dubbing segments from one tape to another, work which can be done quite well with two decent cassette machines.) For serious editing, for cutting out bits of tape to make things move more neatly, for shifting things around, open-reel is by far preferable. But even when working with open-reel originals from the field, you don't come home and cut up the *field* tapes. You come home and copy the open-reels onto other open-reels or you come home and copy the cassettes onto open-reels. Same difference.

I know people who've had problems with tapes jamming in cassette machines. It's never happened with my WM-D6C or TC-D5M and it never happened with my TC-158SD. But it can happen. A big Nakamichi in my office started getting hungry for tapes a year ago. The same thing can happen with an open-reel machine: the big Crown I used to use for editing developed a penchant for wrapping tape around its capstan not long ago. I've spent far more hours unwinding tape from the capstans of open-reel recorder spindles than I have unwinding tape from cassette machine spindles.

You're better off with open-reels if your tape breaks when you're on location. You don't even have to splice it: just wrap it around a few turns on the take-up reel and its own friction will keep it going properly again so you can finish recording on that side and make the splice when you get home. Cassettes are very difficult to splice: the tape is very narrow (1/8 inch) and you often have to take them apart to get the ends of the tape out. Cheaper cassettes don't come apart: the halves of the cassette are held together by glue rather than screws; if you want to pry them open you usually have to wreck the cassette in the process. But I think this is something that's far more a problem in the abstract than in reality. How often does a cassette tape break in normal use?

If your recorder is working properly, if you keep the machine clean and don't use cheap or very thin tape (not more than forty-five minutes' capacity per side), the machine won't get hungry; if you're using cheap tape, it doesn't matter what kind of tape recorder you're using. When I advise you to avoid "cheap tapes" I mean *really* cheap tapes—those that come without a brand name you've ever heard of. Lately, I've been using TDK SA-90 and Maxell XLII-90 for interviews (the tapes cost less than two dollars each); for critical stuff I use TDK MA-90, which provides a slightly better SNR and now costs only a little bit more than the SA. The tapes are high quality and the cassette shells are well made and held together with screws. I've never had one break in use or jam in the machine. Friends who use the other major tape brands have similar success with their tape of choice. (Cassette tape prices are widely discounted. If you live in a small town where everything goes for list price, look at a recent copy of *Rolling Stone* or the arts section of the Sunday *New York Times*. Both regularly carry ads from mail-order places that sell brand-name audiotape and videotape at large discounts.)

Ives argues that "the biggest problem with cassette tape is that it's a poor medium for preservation. For long-time archival storage—an important consideration—the best advice I can give is that open-reel tape is still by far the best. Therefore, even if your field recordings are made on cassettes, you or your archives should make provision for transfer to open-reel tape as soon as possible. This is a bit of a nuisance and it costs you a generation, but provided that you have good transfer equipment, it's hardly a compelling reason for not using cassettes in the field" (1980:4–5). I've never seen any evidence that cassettes are any more likely to have storage problems than open-reels; I've never had a print-through problem on any forty-five-minute cassette tapes and some of them are now ten years old. I have had print-through problems on some open-reel tapes of the same vintage.

Print-through is generally a function of two factors: thickness of the tape backing and strength of the signal put on the tape. It's similar to light that does or doesn't get through a piece of material: the brighter the light and the thinner the material, the more likely the light is to get through. Whether you use open-reel or cassette tapes, use the thickest tape you can (if you're going to record an event that's twenty minutes long, there's no need to use an open-reel tape that's 1,800 feet long or a cassette tape designated C-90 or C-120) and avoid putting too strong a signal on the tape. Modern tapes and recorders can tolerate far stronger signals than tapes and machines of a few years ago, but if you'll be storing the tapes for long periods of time, try to have nothing but occasional peaks record beyond the 0 db point on your recorder's meter.

There's convenience in identification with cassettes: you write on the cassette itself and don't have to worry about someone later slipping a reel into the wrong box. Cassettes also have a device to prevent accidental recording over material you want to preserve. If you look at the back of the cassette you'll see two small tabs. When these tabs are in place they depress a pin at the rear of the cassette chamber in the tape recorder that allows the record button to engage. If the tabs are taken out, the pin isn't depressed and the record button can't be engaged. If the tabs are facing you (and the tape opening, therefore, is away from you), the tab on the right will protect the upper side and the tab on the left will protect the lower side. If side A is up, break out the tab on the right and you won't be able to record on side A unless you cover the hole with a small piece of tape.

Everything I've said so far about the differences in the two kinds of machines is minor or arguable or a matter of taste: some people want the extra cushion in SNR and others don't care about it; some people like the lightness of the cassette machines and others don't mind lugging the Nagra. There is, however, one important difference between the Nagra and the top portable cassette machines presently available: the Nagra is a three-head machine and it permits the operator to perform A/B tests; neither of the Sonys I've mentioned here nor any other high-quality portable cassette deck has separate record and playback heads, which means you can't perform A/B tests on any of them.

The term *A/B test* as applied to sound recording means simply that the recordist monitoring the recording switches back and forth from the signal produced by the record preamplifier (the signal going to the record head) and the play preamplifier (the signal taken off the playback head). The test may be done using meters (which tell the recordist how closely the recorded signal level compares to the input signal level) and with headsets or monitor speakers (which tell the recordist how the sound of the original and the taped version compare). If a recorder doesn't have a separate playback head, A/B tests are impossible during recording.

You can't know for sure that the level of sound the meters say is going in is in fact what the tape has recorded on it; and you can't know until you play the tape back if the tape was defective. With a machine with separate heads, switching the meter from record to play mode lets you compare instantly what's going on the tape with what the tape is preserving. When you're doing interviews, it's unlikely that you'll spend much time with the earphones on or doing A/B checks anyway. But if you're recording a complex performance you might very well have headsets on the entire time. The Nagra and any other three-head machine permits you to check the recording at any time in the recording session.

I said the capacity to perform A/B tests is an important difference in field recorders, but like those extra 3 db of SNR, it may not matter to you. With a good headset you can monitor the quality of the input signal as it's processed by the preamp feeding the record head, as well as the adequacy of mike placement, the level of noise, and, with stereo recorders, the character of the separation. That's what you hear when you plug into the headphone jack when the machine is in record.

If not having the A/B capacity leaves you feeling insecure, then portable cassette machines aren't for you. I should note that I've done more than 300 hours of field recording on my TC-D5M and the recorder that preceded it, the TC-158SD, and the only trouble either machine ever gave me was when I forgot to check the batteries and once when I forgot to depress the record button. Those are not equipment problems.

The comparisons above all deal with Nagras and machines like the TC-D5M. Most people don't have access to Nagras. Students doing fieldwork projects for class are not likely to be running around taping their family with a machine costing more than $6,000. Few professors off on field trips, for that matter, are likely to have Nagras at their disposal. If you're buying a machine for your own use in fieldwork, on a dollar-for-dollar basis you're almost always better off, given the current technology, with a cassette recorder. There aren't many good, inexpensive, battery-operated open-reel recorders available, and, except for the Nagra, none of them perform as well as cassette machines in the same price range. If you're borrowing a recorder from someone else you'll probably have to take what's available. Don't despair if you get open-reel when you've decided that cassette gives you a better chance of getting what you want, or if you get cassette and would have preferred open-reel. Within any quality bracket the differences are far less important than the similarities.

The reason, by the way, most recordings done on inexpensive recorders sound so awful has little to do with the recorders at all. Those tapes sound bad because lousy microphones are usually used with them and the mikes are incorrectly placed. If you use the best recording machine available and you use lousy mikes or don't use the mikes correctly, you might as well be out there with the cheapest machine you can get. The next chapter will deal with microphone type and placement.

For some things I would use an open-reel recorder. I think cassette machines are terrific, but I'm not maniacal about them. The only open-reel machine I would use for location work is the Nagra; it is, as I've said, the only battery-operated open-reel machine that makes recordings better than I can get from the best portable cassette machines. I would use a Nagra if I were recording something for which the sound was critical, complex, and enormously wide in dynamic range, and if the stuff was going to go through several generations before final use. I might use a Nagra to record Wagner or a gun-battle where I was in a safe enough position so I wouldn't have to move quickly or when continuing A/B checks were essential. But I wouldn't use a Nagra or any other open-reel machine for an interview, even if I had someone to work it and carry it.

Setting Levels

The recordist's goal is to record as high an input signal as possible on the tape without overmodulating—without imposing so strong a signal the tape's image of the sound is distorted. Most tape recorders have meters to let the recordist know the strength of the signal being applied to the tape. Older tape recorders had VU (volume unit) meters with pivoted needles registering on scales that usually ran from -20 on the left to $+5$ on the right. If the recording level was set so the primary signal didn't go over 0 (except for extremely brief moments) and didn't drop below -10 (except for moments of relative silence), the tape would be getting the level of input it needed to store information without distortion and without an inordinate amount of tape noise. Newer recorders have peak meters, which have much faster transient responses than VU meters, hence are more likely to indicate momentary overloads glossed over by the slow-moving VU meter. Some newer machines indicate recording levels with bars of light emitting diodes (LEDs). Some LED bars are peak meters and some operate as VU meters; read the recorder's manual to find out what any specific machine has. Some machines, such as the Sony TC-158SD, have VU meters and in addition a single LED that indicates peak overmodulation. The background of most tape deck VU meters changes to red above 0 VU, and the LEDs on most LED recorders are green below 0 and red above 0. As in personal economics, you want to stay out of the red.

Recording levels are always a compromise. You want to be able to get the faintest bits of sound that matter to you, but you don't want to set your volume level so high that in the process you overmodulate (and turn to annoying fuzz) everything else. You want the loudest bits of sound that matter to you, but you don't want to set your volume level so low that you lose everything soft and gentle and simultaneously increase the relative portions of noise. I can tell you to set your meter so you're recording at 0 VU or no more than 100 percent modulation, but to know what really works you'll just have to experiment with the recorder, microphone, and tape you intend to use. Plug in a mike and carry on a conversation. Set the volume control so you get a reading below -10, then set it up to 0, then move it up to $+5$. As you make each change say what you're doing. Go out in the street and do the same thing with passing traffic. Put your mike next to someone hacking away at an electric typewriter and do the same changes. Then go to the best playback amplifier and speaker system you can find and listen to what you've done. You'll learn quickly enough how far into the red you can afford to go and how low on the scale you can afford to work. (See Ives, 1980:29–30, for his version of this kind of test.)

Cheap tape recorders have no VU meters, no LED bars, and no record level controls. They set their levels automatically. Many have built-in microphones. They're easy to use but they make lousy tapes. The reason is their automatic gain controls get as uncomfortable about a silence as they do about a scream. They bring the scream down to conversational level and they bring a whisper up to conversational level. Since many of these machines have a slight delay in their adjustment to level changes, you may not even be able to know later what was a constant sound and what was a sound on the move. Tapes made on such machines will never tell you what the original situation sounded like, and the upward and downward rush of room noise as conversation runs on and takes pauses can drive you crazy when you're listening to them later. The built-in mikes don't just record the room sounds, they also record the machine noises of the tape recorder itself, since they pick up even faint amounts of mechanical vibration from the motor. If such machines are all you can get, good luck with them; they'll get the words you want but not much else. If you can lay your hands on a machine with a manual record level control, grab it.

The way you set the level is simple: you have the microphones and people in the positions they're going to be in during whatever event you're going to record—conversation, performance, religious shrieks of ecstasy—and you adjust the level until your VU meter or LEDs are just not going into the red. If nothing else changes during the recording situation, keep your hands off that control for the rest of the session. If you do fiddle with the control you'll never know later when things got louder or quieter, when background noise increased or when it just seemed to increase because you had kicked up the total recorded level. If there's a choice between undermodulating (recording to the left of 0) or overmodulating (recording in the red), always opt for undermodulating. With good filters and equalizers you can minimize some of the effects of excessive tape and electronic noise created by recording at too low a level, but you can never clean up the fuzziness of a tape recorded at too high a level.

Some recorders have manually controlled devices to control the input signal. The *automatic level control* (ALC) lets you elect to do what cheap tape recorders force upon you; it's for lazy recordists who don't care at all about the quality of their recordings or for people recording in total darkness. I've never recorded in total darkness, so I've never found an occasion that called for using the ALC.

Noise control switches, found on a few recorders, let you cut out high, low, or both high and low signals; they're useful in outdoor situations where there's danger of a lot of wind noise. They should be used only when necessary because the signals they keep from reaching the tape can never be put back. It may be that part of your program material is in the same range as the noise you want to avoid. Some noise can best be filtered out later. The kind of noise most important to avoid is from gusts of wind, which tend to overmodulate the tape and which can't be filtered out later. (On most tape recorders, the tone controls are inoperative when the machine is in the record mode.)

The *limiter* doesn't affect recorded levels so long as the sound stays out of the red. It comes into play when there are peaks that threaten to overmodulate. A microsecond after the signal begins to overmodulate, the limiter reduces it to a safe level; when the input signal goes back to normal, the limiter cuts out. The limiter comes into play only when the recording level threatens to overmodulate, while the automatic level control operates constantly. If the presented sound is lower than the ALC thinks adequate for a good recording, it boosts the sound level; if the sound is higher, it reduces it. The disadvantage of the automatic level control is it changes the relative sound levels as individual sound levels change. The limiter does that too, but only at the high end, which means it doesn't introduce annoying electronic noise to your recording when your subject is silent for a long moment.

Here's an example of how the limiter and the ALC work. Say you're recording a voice interview: you and someone are talking on a street-corner. A truck goes by, making a lot of noise.

— If you're recording with the record level set *manually* and the limiter *off,* the truck will be very loud, as it is in life, and it may or may not drown out the voices, and the recording may or may not overmodulate.

— If you're recording with the record level set *manually* and the limiter *on,* the truck will be very loud, it will reach a certain level and then not get any louder, the tape won't overmodulate. But the sound of your voices will seem to drop significantly until the truck sound attenuates, whereupon your voices will seem to get louder.

— If you're recording with *automatic level control* you don't have to worry about overmodulation. But if you whisper, the ALC will amplify your whisper so it sounds conversational and at the same time amplify the sound of any background noise and any electronic tape noise; if you shout, it will reduce the shout so it sounds conversational and at the same time reduce any background noise and any electronic tape noise. The total signal strength will stay about the same whatever happens, but the level of ambient noise will shoot up and down un-naturally.

I use a limiter only when there's a chance for sudden unnatural surges, and I know those surges will be rare. If there are going to be a lot of surges, I just set the overall recording level lower.

The monitor speakers on most recorders are cut off in the record mode; if you want to listen to what you're getting you must use head-sets. If your recorder's speaker can be left on during record, be sure to turn it off or to turn down the play volume control, otherwise you'll get the annoying squeal known as audio feedback.

All portable VHS and Beta video recorders presently available are made with ALC: the recorder "knows" what the optimum sound level for the videotape is and adjusts the recorded sound to hover around that point. The problem is, those electronic devices hear only the *total* sound; they can't focus on what sound is important. Controlling sound and picture at the same time is a complicated business and the man-ufacturers of those machines didn't want the amateur market to be put off by a lot of failure. In order to make the machines more generally useful, they made them less specifically accurate. Some, but not all, of the limitations can be managed by using an external microphone rather than the one those machines have built in. (More on this in the next chapter.)

Two other controls influence the quality of the signal delivered to your tape: *bias* and *equalization*. Most quality recorders now have a switch that tells the recorder what kind of tape is being used. On cassette recorders this switch is usually marked Type I, or Normal; Type II, or CrO_2; Type III, or FeCr; and Type IV, or Metal. Each of these types requires a different bias, a high frequency and inaudible signal involved in the recording process, and a different equalization, the adjustment of the preamplifier to compensate for different tape types. (Equalization is also necessary to compensate for differing electronic performance at different speeds; many open-reel recorders automatically change equalization when tape speed is changed.) A few recorders are capable of sensing the kind of tape passing across the heads and automatically set their bias.

Bias controls on professional open-reel machines must be set manually, a simple process. You need a tone generator or something that will provide a constant tone signal to the input. Many microphone mixers have such a generator to be used as a reference on tapes recorded with them. If you don't have anything that fancy you can put the mike close to a telephone and use the dial tone. (Don't take too long because in most places the dial tone goes to screech if the telephone company's machines decide your phone is off the hook.) Set the record level on the machine to a reasonable level, say -4 dB. Then switch to the playback head (you're still in the record mode—you're looking at the B side of an A/B check) and adjust the playback signal (using the playback volume control) to about the same level as the record signal. Now turn the bias knob all the way to the left, then slowly rotate it to the right (clockwise). Go .5 dB *beyond* the maximum level on the meter and stop. You've set the bias for that tape and won't have to adjust it again unless you're changing to a different brand or type of tape or you suspect someone has fiddled with the knob. If your recorder has a bias switch that sets the VU meter to reading bias and if you know the tape's required bias, the process can be done directly.

Copying Tapes

Original tapes, if at all possible, should be used only for making copies. Blank tape is cheap; lose the original and you've wasted all that field time. Open-reel tapes are not cut up to make master tapes for LPs or radio programs: they're dubbed (copied) and the dubs are cut. Sophisticated editing equipment makes it possible to edit tapes electronically with no physical cuts at all; few folklorists have access to such equipment, so they do their cuts with single-edged razor blades and splicing tape. If things go wrong, it's easy enough to make another dub and start the cutting all over again.

Since cassettes can jam or wrap around the capstan when they're being jockeyed back and forth, it's a good idea to copy them before transcribing an original. If money is a problem, one cassette can be used for the transcribing copy of each tape in succession.

As any other kind of recording, the quality of dub you need depends on the use to which it will be put. If you're making the dub to have a tape for transcription purposes, you can often get rid of annoying noise by using the tone controls on the source machine: cut down on the highs and the lows and you'll make the voice far more distinct. If you're making the dub to have an archive copy, then you want a copy that matches the original as closely as possible. If the dub is to be used for broadcast or other distribution, then you may want to clean up the signal using an equalizer or a filter.

Any two machines can be used to make copies: a cassette can be played back on any cassette player, and the copy can be recorded using any other recorder (cassette, open-reel, even the audio track of a videotape). I've heard some people say that the dub should be done using the original machine for the source and as good a machine as you can get for the copy recording. (I'll refer here to the machine on which the original tape is played as the *source,* the machine on which the dub is made as the *target.*) The justification for using the original machine is most cassette recorders and many low-end open-reel recorders combine record and playback heads, which means any error of head alignment or azimuth that affected recording quality should reverse itself in playback.

That's the theory. My experience has been that you're just as likely to have the problems doubled, especially if the original recording was made on a cheap recorder. If the originating machine has a problem with wow and flutter, those will be much worse the second time around because wow and flutter don't occur in the same places every time the tape is run through the machine. The potential advantage to using the original machine comes only in regard to head alignment. When I've had the original recorder and time to spare, I've tried it for the dub, and I've also tried a dub on the best machines I had available. Whichever sounded better, that's what I went with. When there wasn't time, I just used the good machines.

For my own work, I dub using the original machine as source and my best other machine as target. I do that because I generally use very good recorders for my original recordings, so they're good dub sources anyway. If there's any advantage from coming and going through the same head configuration, I get it; if there isn't, nothing is lost.

I would *never* use a target machine with automatic level control, especially if the original was recorded with ALC. The electronic noise on the dub can be just awful. But if you're making a quick dub to use for transcribing words, you can get by with just about anything.

All my recorders have VU or LED level meters. When dubbing, I set the playback level on the source machine so the signal peaks rarely but high enough so the signal rarely drops below -10 dB. That minimizes the amount of electronic noise added in playback. I usually set the level of the target machine so it's exactly the same, which is easy to do: just place the machines near one another and adjust the level control on the target machine so the swing parallels the source machine.

I'm usually careful about setting sound levels in my original recordings, but sometimes I have to deal with a tape that's significantly over- or undermodulated. If I'm making a straight dub, I set the source by ear (I listen through monitor speakers, so I can crank up the source signal through the amplifier), then I set the target as if it were making an original recording—that is, so the signal rarely goes into the red. That way, I don't compound any of the original tape's problems by introducing new mush from added overmodulation or new electronic hiss from added undermodulation. Nothing will get rid of the mush in an original recording, but electronic hiss can be reduced using a filter or an equalizer.

Connect the output terminals of the source tape recorder to the input terminals of the target tape recorder. If the original was recorded in stereo be careful to connect the left channel output of source to the left channel input of target, and the same with the right channels. If those lines are reversed, the position of the sounds is reversed and there's an audio hole in the middle and a sense of illogical placement at the far left and far right.

I generally make dubs flat—that is, I don't boost or reduce any segment of the signal spectrum. If there's noise I don't want, I use a graphic equalizer, the same kind many hi-fi addicts have as part of their home equipment. The source output is plugged into the equalizer's input, the equalizers output into the target recorder's input. The problem with using equalizers or filters to get rid of noise is they get rid of information you want that occupies the same frequency zone. If the noise is at a higher frequency than the voice or music or other sounds I want, I'll reduce the higher end only slightly. I don't like to reduce it too much because those reductions sometimes cut out harmonics that provide an important component of tonal quality. If the offending noise is below the signal I want, I cut it all.

The equalizer I use lists for $250 but I bought it at a discount store for $150. It has an LED visual display so I can see where the important part of the signal is located, and it's capable of boosting or decreasing segments of the signal 15 dB, which is more than enough for most of my purposes. If all the problem sounds are at just the high or low end, I can begin work with the controls all the way up or all the way down and thereby get a full 30 dB of boost or reduction. The equalizer works in octave ranges and covers all of the audible spectrum. When I tinker this way with a copy tape, I use my best sound-isolating headset (not the lightweight headsets used with Walkman-type tape players); if I'm using speakers, I set my playback amplifier very loud so I'm not adjusting the tape in terms of room and machine noise. I also do a lot of A and B switching to be sure I'm not losing more than I'm gaining.

Very specific filtering equipment is available. If the offending noise occupies a very narrow band, you can use what's called a *notch filter,* one that can be set to cut out sound occupying a bandwidth as narrow as 1 cycle. Set the brackets for 512 and 514 cycles and the copy tape won't have anything at 513 cycles. If a tape suffers from 60-cycle hum (one of the more common interference conditions), the octave-wide operation of my equalizer would cut into the male vocal range; the notch filter would cut out the hum and leave everything else alone. These machines are expensive—I don't own one and I don't know any other individuals who do. Many professional recording studios have them. I've had a few occasions when I would've found the notch filter useful, but not enough to buy one. You can, as I've said several times, go goofy if you try to get every piece of equipment you might need. Almost always, the simple equalizer has been more than adequate.

Batteries

Fieldworkers use a lot of batteries. We use them for our tape recorder, condenser microphone, camera meter, motor drive (if our camera has one of those noisy devices), flashlight, calculator, wristwatch—and probably some other gadgets I've missed or haven't gotten around to using.

The most expensive item in your field trip is usually not your equipment or supplies or even getting there and staying there. Rather, it's the uniqueness of the situation itself. Few field situations can ever be repeated exactly. Having the same informant tell the same story or sing the same song or explain the same process again another time isn't a repetition of the first time. If you're re-recording materials it should be because you want more versions of whatever it is you're re-recording, not because you screwed up mechanically.

Unless you're really broke, I recommend always going into the field with fresh batteries. There's no economy in using a half-dead battery if it gives up the ghost in the middle of a one-time event you'll never get to record again. The difference in cost between a half-used battery and a new one is only the price of half a battery. Big deal. If your recorder operates on four batteries, you can go into the field with confidence for the price of two batteries. (Use the half-dead batteries for the kids' toys or for playing music tapes when you're at the beach.) Fresh batteries are the Ultra Ban of the fieldworker's world. I don't mean to be fetishistic about this: if you record for a while on Tuesday with fresh batteries and you're going to be recording on Wednesday, of course you can keep the same batteries in the machine. That's safe enough because you know how much more work you can expect from those batteries and you won't be taken by surprise when they give out.

(The best single article I've seen on the subject is "Batteries," *Consumer Reports* 48, no. 11 [November 1983]: 588–92. Much of what follows is based on that article.)

Six kinds of dry-cell batteries are currently available: regular (zinc carbon), heavy-duty (zinc chloride), alkaline (alkaline manganese), rechargeable (nickel cadmium), mercuric or silver oxide, and lithium. Lithium batteries have the greatest shelf life and contain the most energy; presently they're generally available only for very small devices such as watches and hearing aides, as are mercuric and silver oxide batteries.

Batteries behave differently according to the way they're used. A battery used for a while then put aside before it's discharged will usually regain part of its charge. For that reason a battery used intermittently will deliver far more service than one used continuously. In intermittent use, *Consumer Reports* concluded that the same total service would be delivered by 1 alkaline cell, 1.5 heavy-duty cells, and 2.5 regular cells. In continuous use the alkaline gave the longest service; the same operating time was provided by 1 alkaline, 2.5 heavy-duty, and 5 regular cells. The performance of various brands of alkalines was very similar but there was great variation in the performances of different brands of regular and heavy-duty batteries.

Not only are alkalines cheaper to use for long sessions, but they're more reliable. They retain their shelf life far longer than regular or heavy-duty batteries, and they work better in very hot and very cold temperatures.

What about rechargeables? *Consumer Reports* says they last about as long as heavy-duty batteries, which means in continuous use they deliver only 40 percent of the service of an alkaline. They're cheaper if you reuse them a lot, but economy isn't the fieldworker's only consideration.

A few years ago I used rechargeables a great deal; now I never use them for anything important. The change came when we blew a filmed interview because some rechargeables went dead far sooner than I'd expected. It happened when Diane Christian and I were making *Out of Order*. We used radio microphones for several interviews in that film. The radio mikes saved us a lot of trouble: a few minutes of set-up business early on—when we were doing business anyway setting up the recorder and getting comfortable—meant we wouldn't have to bother with cables or connectors for the rest of the conversation. We could move about as much as we wished and the sound would always come from a mike eight inches from the speakers' mouths.

The instructions that came with the radio mikes said we were to use alkaline batteries. A lot of batteries were involved: each microphone transmitter had one nine-volt battery and each receiver had five more. After our first location work with the equipment I decided to save money by using rechargeables. Nine-volt batteries are expensive and I knew that the rechargeables would pay for themselves quickly.

The first time I used the rechargeables everything worked perfectly. It was a short filming session, perhaps two twelve-minute reels, and both of them were done quickly—perhaps an hour or a little more of work time. The second time was a disaster. We were working a two-person crew—just Diane and me—and after we got started Diane did the interviewing while I did the camerawork. The sound, we assumed, needed no attention once the initial levels were set. But some time shortly after the start of the second reel the rechargeable battery in our interviewee's transmitter gave out. It just went. If we'd had a third person in our crew we would've known there was a problem because that person would've seen that channel's VU meter drop and would've monitored the earphones and realized we were just getting noise. But we didn't have one, nor did we want one—this was intimate stuff and a third person would've been an intrusion, and an intruder's presence would've kept us from getting anything important. As it turned out, we got nothing anyway, because the conversation couldn't be repeated. We wasted time, money, and an unrepeatable opportunity.

Rechargeables, like alkalines, go dead very quickly, but they die far sooner. They don't do that slow fade characteristic of zinc-carbon batteries: one minute you've got enough power to operate, the next minute nothing works at all. Even at their peak, rechargeable batteries don't put out the same voltage as their nonrechargeable counterparts. G.E.'s rechargeable C batteries put out 1.2 volts; zinc-carbon and alkaline C batteries put out 1.3 volts. You'll *see* the difference if you're using a flashlight. That difference might not matter to some field recording instruments; it might matter to others. None of the technical manuals I've seen discuss the effect of slight consistent variations in line voltage. The difference might not matter in machines with a hysteresis-synchronous motor, which is designed to operate at constant speed regardless of line fluctuations, but it might matter a great deal in devices that are power dependent, such as microphones and transmitters. Rechargeables are great for kids' toys, for pocket calculators, for devices you always have plugged in when you're not using them away from an AC power source, or for devices that can go out of service now and then without causing real problems. For fieldwork, rechargeable batteries don't save you anything at all.

Batteries provide direct current (DC) power; wall outlets in most parts of the world provide alternating current (AC) power. Almost all portable tape recorders work equally well on AC or DC, and they don't care which power source is feeding them. If you're running on batteries and the batteries are getting low, you can plug the machine into a wall outlet and it'll switch over with barely a glitch. If you're abroad, check the line voltage before you plug your recorder into the wall outlet. Many countries run on 220 line voltage. If you attempt to power a tape recorder designed to run on 110 volts (the North American standard) with that line power, you'll blow out the power supply—as I did in Paris one summer. Inexpensive transformers will convert the power for you, if you remember to use them.

I know one folklorist who uses batteries for field recordings so he won't impose on his informants by upping their electricity bills. That's not much of a reason, since most transistorized portable recorders use less power than a 60-watt lightbulb. Some fieldworkers use batteries rather than AC because they worry about fluctuations in tape speed caused by changes in line current. I don't think that's a useful worry either, since most modern recorders have hysteresis-synchronous motors. One fieldworker uses batteries in the field because she worries that transient power surges will blow out her transistors; she's considering buying a surge suppressor, like the one she bought for her computer. She needn't worry or buy the suppressor: tape recorder circuits aren't nearly as fragile as computer circuits. Do you know anyone whose home tape recorder ever blew out because of transient line surges?

I like running my recorder on batteries because they let me be totally portable. I don't have to fret about locating myself near a wall outlet or carrying (and cluttering the room with) extension cords. I don't have to say, "Do you mind if I unplug that lamp for a minute?" I can just take the recorder and mike out of my shoulder bag and go to work. Sometimes I'll use AC if the recorder is going to be in one place for a long time and if AC is convenient. It means I don't have to worry about the time several hours down the line when the batteries begin to give out and I won't have to stop the action, turn the machine upside down, take out the old, put in the new, and ask my host, "Anyplace I can dump these?"

The manual that comes with most tape recorders specifies how long they'll perform with different kinds of batteries. If you have a chance, it's a good idea to check that specification out yourself: time one set of fresh batteries in continuous use. Since batteries tend to recharge themselves partially when they're resting, that continuous use test will tell you the minimum safe time you've got.

If you do use nickel-cadmium rechargeable batteries (nicads) be sure to read the manufacturers' instructions carefully. Some recorders will recharge those batteries while they're inserted: you plug in the recorder or camera overnight and a slow charge is put on. Other recorders won't recharge batteries and you must purchase a separate charger. Leaving some batteries plugged into the charger past full charge may cause damage, so most manufacturers recommend that you unhook the charger after a certain period of time. If your nicads are the kind that can be stored charged (most are), you'll find that topping them off when you're ready to use them again won't take nearly so long as bringing them up from being fully exhausted. Most manufacturers of nicads recommend never letting them go completely to zero and that they be brought to full charge whenever they're partly discharged. If your rechargeable is the kind that should be stored at zero charge, discharge what's left in it by letting the machine run it down, not by shorting out the terminals (that is, don't run a wire from the positive to the negative terminal). Shorting out will discharge the battery quickly; it may also generate sufficient heat to do permanent damage. Most manufacturers recommend a full charge before storage.

Nicads have the curious property of learning how to behave. Their first several cycles teach them what to expect and forever after they perform most efficiently in that kind of service. It's often useful, therefore, to fully charge the nicad, run it down until it's fairly low, fully charge it again, run it down again, then fully charge it again.

Never leave any battery in any piece of equipment if you're not going to be using it for a long period of time. Zinc-carbon batteries will leak and can destroy your machinery; alkaline batteries don't leak, but they can cause electrical corrosion anyway. If you're putting a tape recorder away for more than a month, take the batteries out. If you're worried about forgetting to put them back in, tape a note to yourself on the recorder. The only equipment I own in which I leave batteries between uses are flashlights and my camera meters, and on occasion I've had to scrape corrosion out of those. The little mercury batteries in watches are about as safe as batteries get; I've never heard of any of them causing damage. (The reason watch batteries don't cause corrosion is because they're operating constantly, so the electrical energy is going into the circuits.)

All batteries are polarized, which means they have a positive and a negative side, a side from which electrons go and a side into which electrons come when they're part of a completed circuit. If you put batteries into some mechanical equipment the wrong way, the equipment may work backwards; if you put batteries into transistorized devices the wrong way, you may do permanent damage to the fragile electronic system. All batteries are marked for the positive and negative sides or ends, and all battery-using equipment I've seen has a map somewhere indicating the direction of battery placement. On some camera meters the map is on the underside of the cap you unscrew to get to the battery compartment. On most recorders the map is inside the battery compartment itself. Sometimes you can tell when you've screwed up: the light meter moves in the wrong direction when you turn it on. Some instruments are keyed so you can put the batteries in only the right way—the nicads made for Vivitar flashes and Nikon motor drives, for example, fit the camera equipment and the rechargers in one position only.

ALWAYS beware of false economies. Cheap tape and tired batteries may save you a dollar or two for every several hours you record, but they may also make your recordings useless for anything but a partial trip down memory lane. Since you don't know what ultimate use you'll have for your materials, and since there are so many things that can and will go wrong anyway, opt for everything that gives you the best possible chance of getting the most reliable information: good tape, fresh batteries, and fresh film. Always buy film, tape, and batteries from stores that sell a lot of them. That way you'll be fairly certain what you're getting is fresh. If you're going to be doing a lot of field recording and want added security, you might invest in a battery tester. These inexpensive devices can be purchased at places like Radio Shack and K-Mart; the doubts they abolish are more than worth the small purchase price.

And don't try to save money by recharging batteries not meant for recharging. They blow up.

11/Microphones

What Microphones Do

Some things the brain knows so well it doesn't even bother asking us for instructions when they come up. Sound is one of those things: most decisions about the nature of sound are made before we turn our heads to look there or there or there.

The brain associates certain characteristics with distance or volume and locates sounds nearer or closer depending on the presence or absence of those characteristics. Sometimes that knowledge is based on concurrent information: the eye sees the shouting man across the street. Or it may have to do with direction. Most of us hear binaurally: sound arrives from two sides and is captured by curved and channeled devices mounted on the sides of our heads. The shape of the ear introduces microsecond delays in the time some sounds require to reach the ear canal. By cocking our heads slightly we can change the balance of sound information with which our brain gets to deal. By paying more attention to one part of the sound than another, the brain can zoom in on certain sound sources and ignore others. The brain is great at filtering out clutter. That's why you can have a conversation in a subway or at a football game.

Microphones and recorders do none of that; they process everything they get and they don't discriminate. All sounds hitting a microphone at the same time appear in the circuitry at the same time and are placed on the tape at the same time. They won't filter out irrelevant information unless they're ordered specifically to do so. The mike and its coil respond to air pressure and nothing else; the recorder responds to electrical impulses sent to its preamplifier circuit by the microphone

164

and nothing else. The tape is totally passive: it accepts and repeats what the preamp circuits have given it. If audio tape recorders are to capture what we want from the world, their sensing devices—microphones—must be manipulated by us so the tape recorder hears what we want it to hear.

A microphone is part of the class of devices called *transducers,* which change one form of energy into another form of energy. A solar panel on the roof of a building changes the sun's radiant energy into thermal energy; an electric motor changes electrical energy into mechanical energy; a generator changes mechanical energy into electrical energy. A microphone is a kind of generator. It responds to variations in air pressure and changes those variations into electrical energy. That's why the output of microphones is expressed in *millivolts.* (Voltage is a unit of electrical pressure, just as pounds per square inch is a unit of mechanical pressure.)

Sound consists of pressure waves in the air. A microphone in that section of air responds mechanically to the varying pressure created by those waves; the response is translated by the microphone into electrical impulses. Those impulses are fed to an electronic system that amplifies them immediately (a P.A. system), transmits them elsewhere (from a distant telephone's mouthpiece to your telephone's earpiece; from a radio announcer's microphone to your radio), or stores them (on a magnetic tape).

There are several systems by which microphones change air pressure to electrical energy and the various systems have different properties. These systems, or types of microphones, are carbon, crystal, ceramic, dynamic, condenser, and electeret. Carbon, crystal, ceramic, and dynamic microphones are the cheapest to manufacture and provide the strongest signal, which is why they're provided with many inexpensive tape recorders. They don't produce very high quality sound, which is why serious recordists use condenser and electeret microphones. Condenser and electeret microphones require small electronic amplifiers (usually built into the microphone system and powered by a battery or the recorder or amplifier system) to increase the signal strength before the signal is delivered to the tape recorder or power amplifier. The dynamic microphone produces a signal by the motion of a coil through a magnetic field. Carbon, crystal, and ceramic microphones produce a signal through the piezoelectric effect—the ability of certain substances to produce minute electrical impulses when they're subject to small changes in pressure.

Some microphones hear a very wide range of frequencies; others have mechanical limitations or built-in filters that make them more responsive to some parts of the audio frequency spectrum than others. Some microphones hear equally well in all directions *(omnidirectional)*; others hear in variations of a heart-shaped pattern with better receptivity in some directions than in others *(cardioid)*. Microphones may be held in the hand, clipped to clothing, suspended by a string around the speaker's neck, supported by a boom, or mounted on the recording device itself.

Folklore fieldworkers typically record speech and music; they may also record mechanical and natural sounds. The microphones they need, therefore, must cover a wide range of frequencies. Male voices run from about 80 to 400 Hz (cycles per second); female voices run about 190 to 1,050 Hz. "Both men and women produce sounds past 6,000 Hz, when pronouncing 'C,' 'S,' 'X,' and 'Z.' But, in addition, there are multiples of the basic frequencies that are present, known as 'harmonics' or 'overtones.' These go far above the normal speaking range, adding a fullness and 'presence' to the voice" (Gifford, 1977:135). Most musical instruments generate their primary tones at the lower and middle parts of the audible spectrum, but the instruments, like human voices, get their character from harmonics, tones that are multiples of the basic tones. For that reason, it's always more important for recording instruments—microphones, recorders, players, and speakers—to have accurate frequency rendition than it is for them to have exceptionally wide frequency capacity.

We don't hear all the sounds things make. It's not just a matter of volume—it's more a matter of frequency. Human frequency response typically declines with age, with women being able to hear higher frequencies than men at any age. The total documented range of human hearing extends from 20 to 20,000 Hz, but hardly anyone hears either of those extremes, let alone both of them, and they don't carry much useful information for us anyway. There are no speech sounds and almost no musical sounds below 50 Hz, and few electric speakers handle tones that low with any accuracy. Rarely are any of the critical harmonics of anything fieldworkers record found above 15,000 Hz, and even if they were it wouldn't matter because hardly any sound speakers produce good tones above that and very few adults hear tones above that. "Actually, most natural sounds have hardly any low frequencies and quite often what you'll find down at the lower end of the frequency scale is noise. This is important, for it establishes a practical set of margins for microphones" (Clifford, 1977:90).

Folklore fieldworkers do quite well with microphones having a response between 50 and 15,000 Hz. There are microphones available with wider frequency responses, but it's like buying that 150 mph car for city driving. You can't use it, it costs more money to get, it's likely to introduce special problems—so why bother? What matters most with a microphone, if it has a reasonable range of frequency response and is reasonably accurate within that range, is how you use it.

Before we discuss the placement of microphones, we must first consider two technical matters—*ambient sound* and the *inverse square law*. Ambient sound is important because it supplies much of the context in which the sound you want to record exists; the inverse square law is important because it explains how the sound you want to record relates to sounds produced by other objects or persons.

Ambient Sound

Ambient sound is the sound that's there all the time. It's the sound you don't hear because you get used to it. It's the sound you notice only when it goes away. If you don't force yourself to check for ambient sound when you're recording, it can overwhelm the sound you're really after; if you don't have ambient sound in situations where it belongs, your recordings will sound unnatural.

The difficulty in dealing with ambient sound arises from the brain's ability to ignore sound it doesn't perceive as supplying essential information. If you're in a place long enough, you'll stop hearing the place's constant noise so long as that noise remains below the level of pain and below the level where it interferes with whatever communications you want to carry on.

When I returned to Cambridge from my first field trip to Texas prisons, I played my tapes through my sound system and received a terrible shock: on all the tapes recorded of the work crews in the Brazos and Trinity bottoms there were constant rushing and buzzing sounds, sounds I hadn't heard at all when I'd been there. At first I thought my playback equipment was defective—but a quick check with a pre-recorded tape showed the equipment worked fine. Then I thought something was wrong with my recording equipment that I hadn't noticed when I'd checked playback on location through headsets. But I'd checked the sound on the headsets a lot while I worked: the sound quality had been good, the mix was good, the level was right, it was fine stuff. It was only home in Cambridge coming through my AR speakers that it sounded so weird. Then I realized that the rushing and buzzing noises had been present in the forest the entire time I was there, but I hadn't heard them with the headsets on or off because my brain knew it was ambient sound and it did what brains always do with ambient sound: it filtered it out and paid attention only to the sound information I was really after. The microphone and the recorder don't have that capacity; they capture and preserve everything they can. On those July Gulf Coast days they picked up the worksongs of the convicts well enough, and they also picked up the steady noise of wind in the live oaks, insects in the grass, the distant and constant chatter of birds, the constant curtain of sound in those trees and that brush, sound that became quickly transparent to consciousness.

We're more likely to notice ambient sound when it stops than when it continues. If you've ever spent a lot of time in a room with a "quiet" air conditioner you know what I'm talking about. A "quiet" air conditioner is simply one that doesn't make so much noise you must consciously raise your voice to communicate. You don't consciously hear it until it goes off, in which case you're aware of a sudden silence. Have you ever gone to sleep with the television set on and waked up with a start, knowing something was wrong but not knowing what? Then you realize the room is quieter than it had been, that the only sound is the hiss of the empty channel coming through your TV set's small speaker. I've heard that sometimes before a tornado birds and insects fall silent and that people know something is up even though they don't yet have any idea why they know something is up.

Ambient sound doesn't have to be constant—it can be irregular at a constant rate and can produce the same transparent effect. When I was very young we lived near the Myrtle Avenue elevated train in Brooklyn. Our apartment was on the fifth floor, in the rear of the building; my bedroom window was two stories above and perhaps a hundred feet away from the trains. The buildings on the street facing the trains were only three stories high, so my window had a clear line of sight—and sound—over them to the train tracks. Friends who came home with me after school would sometimes say, "How can you stand that noise?" "What noise?" I'd ask. Then one summer my parents got me out of the city for two months. When I came home in late August I nearly went crazy because of the trains. I heard every one. Conversation and sleep were impossible. I heard them whenever I was in the apartment; I heard them all night long. That lasted perhaps a week, then the sound disappeared again.

If you've ever taken a plane trip you've dealt with ambient sound. When the plane takes off, you're probably conscious of the noises the plane makes, even if you're an experienced traveler. Three or four minutes after takeoff the pilot changes the contour of the wing; if you're sitting over the wings, you hear a grinding sound from the retractor motors, followed by so great a reduction in noise that inexperienced flyers sometimes worry if one or more of the engines has failed. (After a moment they realize that it's only the wing noise that has changed; the engines still whine loudly. They relax.) Then the plane achieves its cruising altitude, the sound steadies, and after a while you don't hear the engines or the noise of air rushing over the wings at all. If you force yourself to pay attention, you hear them and you realize they're quite loud, but in a few seconds you forget the sound again. But if the noise of the engines changes, you may be suddenly yanked back to an awareness of the sound, you may see people sound asleep suddenly sit bolt upright with their eyes wide open. When the change stabilizes, the sound again becomes functionally invisible.

If you're recording outdoors in a city, there'll always be a great deal of background noise. You may want it for verisimilitude; if so, no problem. But if what you want is the conversation going on or the rhyme recited or the song sung, you must get your microphone close enough to the source or get a signal powerful enough to your microphone or use a microphone narrow enough in angle of acceptance so the signal going into your recorder consists of what you really want. If you're recording an athletic event and you're in the stands, the microphone in your hand will do a far better job picking up the quiet question of the person next to you than it will the shouts and grunts from the field. Your brain selects what it wants from the mass of data available to it; the microphone and recorder do none of that, so in a situation with a great deal of ambient sound they may very well put gibberish on your tape. Folklorist Neil Rosenberg uses omnidirectional microphones to record everything in a public place where a performance is going on, rather than tapping into the performers' sound system or using a shotgun microphone to cut out as much room noise as possible (Ives, 1980:57n).

Rooms sound different at different times of the day; they sound different with windows open and windows closed. If you're recording to make a commercial record or a radio broadcast, you probably want as little room sound as possible. If you're recording to capture a sense of the time and place and persons and situation, you want the ambient sound to reflect the reality. You might record a person talking in a room and hope later to intercut pieces from your various recording sessions. If there are no transitions, nothing between the various cuts, your audience will hear differences even though your actual tape splices or electronic splices are silent. Filmmakers always record the sounds of the spaces in which action has taken place while they're on location in case they need some fill or transition sound when they're editing later. Even when no one is talking movie soundtracks are never truly silent.

Unless you are or have been deaf, you've never experienced silence. True silence can seem louder than a trumpet. "There is always something to see, something to hear," wrote John Cage. "In fact, try as we may to make a silence, we cannot. For certain engineering purposes, it's desirable to have as silent a situation as possible. Such a room is called an anechoic chamber, its six walls made of special material, a room without echoes. I entered one at Harvard University several years ago and heard two sounds, one high and one low. When I described them to the engineer in charge, he informed me that the high one was my nervous system in operation, the low one my blood in circulation. Until I die there will be sounds" (1966:8).

Microphone movement can introduce to your tape apparent increases or decreases in ambient sound. Say the person you're recording with a directional microphone moves from left to right. To the left is a highway with a fair amount of traffic; to the right is a grove of trees presently inhabited by a great many blackbirds; directly ahead, between the grove and the highway, is the desert. As you track your informant the noise of the highway—at first quite loud—will disappear nearly entirely and be replaced by the faint hiss of wind, and that faint hiss will then be replaced by the far louder sound of the wind in the branches and the birds chattering to one another. Nothing on your tape will give any reason for the change. (If you're filming, the changing background might indicate why the sound is changing, but it still won't sound natural because the change isn't so radical to the human ears.)

The most important thing for you to remember about ambient sound is that it's there. Always. After you have several times forced yourself to listen to it deliberately, you'll become used to checking for it when you're recording and you'll be able to deal with it without difficulty. You wouldn't want to be aware of ambient sound all the time; the noise would drive you crazy, and that's why the brain filters it out. But you do want to be aware of it when you're working with electronic recording equipment that doesn't have the brain's good sense.

The Inverse Square Law

This isn't something you need worry about a lot, but awareness of it might help you avoid some difficulties or solve some problems with sound and also with light.

Light and sound intensity fall off at a rate equivalent to the square of the change in distance from the source. (Intensity, not frequency: a middle C stays middle C the length of its passage; it just gets softer and softer. And a coral blue stays a coral blue the length of its passage, so long as no filters get in the way; it just gets dimmer and dimmer.) If you double the distance from the light source or from the sound source, the light level reaching you and the sound level reaching you are reduced by a factor of four; if you triple the distance, the levels are reduced by a factor of nine; and so on. It works the other way too: cut the distance in half and the sound volume or light intensity increases by a factor of four.

In the previous chapter I said that a 3 dB difference in sound pressure level represents a doubling or halving of the amount of sound reaching a point. Every time you double the distance between a sound source and a sound receptor, there's a 6 dB decrease in sound pressure level—that is, double the distance and the sound level goes down by a factor of four. The converse is the same: cut the distance in half and the sound pressure level goes up 6 dB, a quadrupling of the sound level. (This is what happens outdoors or in an acoustically dead room. In ordinary interior spaces the changes aren't so exact because the surfaces in the room are reflecting sound back into the signal path. The decrease in sound level isn't quite so great as it should be in theory when distance is doubled, and the increase in sound level is a little more than it should be in theory when distance is halved [see Clifford, 1977:129–30].)

The reason for this relationship between distance and signal strength can be visualized. The amount of light emitted by a flashlight is constant as it moves away from the flashlight. If the flashlight puts out 200 units of light, 200 units of light from that flashlight will hit an object 6 feet away or an object 12 feet away or an object 100 feet away. (We're ignoring the reduction caused by interference of dust in the air.) But the light, if it's not a laser, doesn't go forth in a narrow cylinder. It traverses a cone that spreads out uniformly, which means the same amount of light covers wider and wider circles the further it gets from its source. If the light forms a circle 6 feet in diameter at 10 feet, it forms a circle 12 feet in diameter at 20 feet and 24 feet in diameter at 40 feet. The changes in diameters are linear, just as the changes in distances; but the changes in the *areas* of the circles created vary by the *squares* of the diameters—that is, double the diameter and you quadruple the area. The area of the 6-foot circle is 28.27 square feet, the area of the 12-foot circle is 113.09 square feet, and the area of the 24-foot circle is 452.36 feet. A square foot of surface area in the 6-foot circle receives 7.07 units of light (200/28.27), a square foot in the 12-foot circle receives 1.77 units of light, and a square foot in the 24-foot circle receives only 0.0796 units of light. Some devices control the distribution of sound and light so they're effective further. They still fall off according to the inverse square law, but the intensity at the point of issue is so great and the circle of issue so small that they seem more powerful. They're not, it's just that the narrowness of angle to start out with gives the advantage of a few doublings along the way. Some sirens are highly directional, and so are trumpets and trombones. Some flashlights have reflectors designed to keep the light in a very narrow angle as it leaves the flashlight itself. None of these devices keeps the emitted signal from dispersing at the usual rate; all they do is make sure that the emitted signal starts life as brightly or loudly as possible.

The inverse square law has several implications for a fieldworker. If the distance between microphone and subject is small, then small changes in distance can make large differences in sound levels. If you have an interviewee positioned two feet from your microphone with the sound level of his or her voice well over double the sound level of ambient noise, the recording you get won't be clean; you'll hear the background noise, but you'll also hear the voice clearly. If the interviewee moves directly back two feet, doubling the distance to the microphone, the sound level will be reduced by a factor of four, which may be enough to let the ambient sound overpower the voice, leading to a "dirty" recording. A shift in position several times will make the voice level rise and fall noticeably. If you're using a directional microphone and the person moves to the side two feet, the reduction in recorded sound might be greater because of the microphone's reduced sensitivity to sound off center.

The reverse of this is also true. If you're recording a person in a noisy situation, moving the mike closer may be enough to let his or her voice overpower even very loud ambient sound. You see this on television when the reporter in a busy crowd or battle scene talks at a normal level into a mike held close to his or her mouth and the words comes through with clarity, or the reporter at a legislative hearing stands at the back of the room and whispers to the mike and records clearly enough to broadcast well without bothering anyone in the room. Rock performers facing a screaming audience and backed by a mountain of overdriven loudspeakers hold mikes within an inch or so of their mouths and their mikes don't pick up other performers or yelling fans. (Rock vocal mikes are specially built to be less sensitive than usual to plosives—to *p* and *b* sounds; those mikes aren't good for recording conversations or anything ordinary.)

The goal of the fieldworker is to place the mike near enough to the sound source so the recorded sound is primarily what's wanted rather than ambient sound, and far enough away so normal movements (a person leaning back in the chair or leaning forward toward you) won't distort the level enormously. It may be necessary to use a highly directional microphone positioned some distance away to accomplish this; or it may be necessary to use an omnidirectional lavaliere or lapel mike attached to the informant's body or clothing.

Microphone Patterns

All microphones are designed for a specific kind of hearing and each represents a specific compromise. There are two basic microphone types: *omnidirectional* and *directional.* Omnidirectional mikes hear equally well in any direction. Put one in the middle of four people speaking at the same volume and it will record them all at the same volume. On playback, you can't tell if the omni was facing, sideways to, or pointing away from the source of sound. "With an omni, it's *working distance* that counts, not the way the microphone is positioned" (Clifford, 1977:133). The omni sees the world as a sphere of indeterminate size. It has no sense of direction; it senses only sound level.

Directional microphones have the strongest response to sounds directly in front, somewhat reduced response to sounds coming from the sides, and significantly reduced response to sounds coming from the rear. Microphones in this group are often referred to as *cardioid, supercardioid,* and *shotgun* mikes. Each is a variant on the basic cardioid (heart-shaped) pattern. The supercardioid elongates the cardioid pattern, with more discrimination against sound from the sides; the shotgun elongates the pattern even further so it's more like a long balloon. Sennheiser and a few other firms also produce what they call a *spot microphone,* which is simply a shotgun with greater discrimination against signals from the side than the regular shotgun mike. (A few companies manufacture *bidirectional* microphones; these have figure-eight patterns and the electronic equivalent of two cardioid mikes attached back to back.)

Several times when I've been working with a shotgun mike people have asked, "How far does that mike hear?" That question is no more meaningful than "How far does the eye see?" The eye doesn't see any distance at all and the mike doesn't hear any distance at all; both instruments respond to whatever signals reach them and distance has nothing to do with it. On a clear moonless night I can see objects a million light-years away; on a foggy night I can see only a few feet away. I can see a tall building a mile away—unless a hill or a tree or my hand blocks the view. In similar fashion, I hear a person talking in a normal voice across the room—unless the stereo is on or someone next to me is also talking in a normal voice or a police car is going by with its siren on. We hear something if nothing gets in the way of the signal reaching us or if noise doesn't prevent our hearing it. (A good definition of noise is "sound we don't want.")

All microphones types respond to whatever sound reaches them. The only difference between them is how wide an angle they "see" well. If we point each of the mikes—omni, cardioid, supercardioid, and shotgun—at a sound source ten feet away, each will capture the sound of that source at exactly the same level. The mikes with the heart-shaped and elongated heart-shaped patterns won't get a stronger signal than each other or than the omni. But they'll get progressively weaker signals from *other* sound sources outside their cones of greatest sensitivity, such as the room's ambient sound or people chattering behind us. Sometimes we want all the sound going on in a place; in such circumstances we use the omnidirectional microphone. Other times we don't want the clutter, so we use one of the cardioids.

If we can record a performer well with an omnidirectional mike at one foot without troublesome reverberation or background noise, we can record that performer equally well and with just as little noise if we use a cardioid at a distance of two feet (Clifford, 1977:69). The sound level of the performer picked up by the mike two feet away isn't as high as the sound level picked up by the mike one foot away; the cardioid doesn't hear important stuff better. What it does better is ignore noise from the sides. The cardioid "is programmed for maximum sensitivity in the forward direction and gradually reduces its sensitivity a little to sounds arriving at 90° and becomes relatively weak to any sounds arriving from the rear of the microphone." The rear shutoff isn't perfect, sound from the other directions isn't entirely cut out, but it can reduce room noise or external noise. "Because it does collect far less sound from the rear, however, the cardioid can suppress more room sound and noise than an omni in the same position subjected to an identical sound field (Clifford, 1977:134).

Supercardioids are like cardioids except their pattern of side cutoff is more severe. You can move even further away from the performer and be untroubled by room noise. They're not perfect: the supercardioids and shotguns have lobes of sound sensitivity to the rear, so sometimes they're less effective at cutting out rearward noises than a simple cardioid.

The shotgun has the narrowest pattern of all, but its pattern isn't constant. "It has reception patterns that vary between modified cardioid shapes at low frequencies to elongated pears at high frequencies, with first a *doughnut* and then a *tear drop* attached to the stem. Rejection of side sounds is much greater than with a standard cardioid. The directional efficiency is even greater than the supercardioid and is narrower. The rear end of the pattern sometimes shows a number of small lobes. .... The higher directional efficiency of a shotgun microphone means, in the end result, that for the same microphone to source distance, the direct signal will be equally loud as a standard directional microphone, but ambient or background noise will be less with the shotgun" (Clifford, 1977:81).

The shotgun mike is good for recording sounds at sporting events (it cuts out much of the crowd noise) or at public interviews in large rooms or outdoors (it cuts out the chatter of other reporters) or in special situations where ambient noise can be otherwise controlled by the recordist but placing a microphone near the speaker is impractical (as in filming a movie). But the shotgun has problems. It's most directional for high frequencies and nearly omnidirectional for low frequencies, so it exaggerates voice sibilance and accentuates room boominess (Honoré, 1980:38, 97).

I learned about the shotgun mike the hard way—by nearly wrecking a filmed interview that couldn't be repeated. I was recording in the small recreation room on death row in Texas. The room had a concrete floor, brick walls, a low ceiling, and metal tables; the only place with worse acoustics on death row was the shower. When several conversations were going on at once, the room was an impossible mess of noise. I was just talking with one man, but I knew there would be a problem with the room's reverberation. I decided to use my shotgun mike, which had worked perfectly well on many outdoor recording sessions when I was trying to keep down ambient noise. The man sat at one of the tables and I put the mike directly in front of him, with its tip elevated about two inches; we covered the mike with a white prison jacket so it would be out of sight. I was certain that the shotgun would cut out the echoes from three sides of the room and from the floor and ceiling.

I had it wrong: the shotgun *exaggerated* those echoes and produced the worst possible recording under those circumstances; I'd made almost every mistake possible. First of all, placing the shotgun on the hard table increased the amount of phase cancellation (I'll get to that term in a few pages); even without the boominess of the room that would've made the speech unclear. Second, the shotgun is especially sensitive to boom, so even though it wasn't getting boom from the sides, it was multiplying the boom coming from the front. Third, the shotgun has responsive nodes at the back, so it was picking up more unwanted boominess from the far side of the room.

I would've been far better off hanging a small omnidirectional lavaliere mike around the man's neck or clipping a mike to his shirt. That would've picked up some of the room's noise but not nearly as much as my fine shotgun did. And the lavaliere or lapel mike would've been far closer to his mouth, so the echo and boom would've been far less significant a part of the overall signal.

Omnis are the littlest mikes; the shotguns, which are longer the more directional they are, are the sexiest. You feel like you're really doing some serious recording when you're pointing that long tube with its sinister dark foam filter at someone or something. But it often turns out that the simple omni does a far better job.

For interviews, the omni is often the best mike to use. If you're recording monaural, you can put one between you and your informant and it'll pick both of you up equally well. If there's minor troubling noise from the sides, use a cardioid. Use cardioids if you're recording stereo interviews. Use the supercardioid or shotgun only when they're absolutely necessary and only when you know what you're doing. (I say that, but I *thought* I knew what I was doing in that death row rec room. Sometimes you don't know what you didn't know until later. As I've said before, the important thing to do then is try to learn from the blunders and avoid them the next time out.) The mikes with the elongated patterns are far easier to use outdoors than indoors, and they're far easier to use with a stationary subject than a moving subject. When you use them, try to keep the headphones on all the time, and use headphones with good sound insulation around the ears so you know you're hearing the preamp or the tape and not the live sound.

The best way to learn about a mike's patterns of response is by using it. If you can, borrow several kinds, and even if you have just one kind, take the time to play with them or it seriously. Set up as many weird conditions as you can. Have people talk to your mike from different places and different directions, talk to the mike in a car with the windows open and the windows closed, record your TV set and stereo and washing machine, have someone talk near one of those devices and move closer and further away with the mike and point it in different directions. Clifford (1977:98) suggests "repeating the number 7, selected since it contains both low and high frequencies." When you go through all this apparent foolishness be sure to tell the mike what you're doing, otherwise it will all be meaningless to you later. (Ives calls his version of this "The Game"; 1980:29–30.) If other people are around, tell them what you're doing too, otherwise they'll think you've gotten very weird.

Remember that all of the microphone types hear best what fits their pattern of acceptance best. They don't choose the things that matter most to you—you have to know what sort of thing you want to record, then select the kind of microphone that will best help you get it. If you're buying a microphone and can't spend much money, get a good omni or a good cardioid. If you can afford a little more, consider something like the Sennheiser K3N/K3U electeret condenser system, which has a basic powering module and accepts interchangeable heads for omni, cardioid, supercardioid, shotgun, and spot patterns. You can start out with the powering module and one head, then acquire others when you need or can afford them.

With the quality of tape recorders now available, even a relatively mediocre recorder will produce good tapes if you use a decent microphone and use it correctly. If I were buying a recorder and mike and didn't have too much money, I would probably buy a recorder a little less fancy than I preferred and get as good a microphone as I could afford.

Microphone Placement

What kind of sound do you want? If you want "studio sound" take your informant to a studio. You won't get it anywhere else. Studio sound is atmospherically dead; all the sound quality is produced by the machines of sound production and the electronic devices processing the signals. If you want to record the sounds as they seem to the performers in life, studio sound is the last thing you want.

You should place the mike close enough to the source of sound so it will deliver to your tape a clear rendition of the sound. You don't want it so close that it unnaturally cuts out ambient sound; neither do you want it so far away that ambient sound seems louder than it really is. If the mike is too far away you may also increase the apparent room echo.

Recording close may seem the more attractive option, because it's more likely to provide a "clean" recording, but the results may not be satisfactory. "Recording very close" writes Clifford, "is equivalent to putting your ears very close to a sound source. This is an unnatural listening position, for you will hear the pure, direct, dry sound of the instrument or voice sounds just as though you had decided you wanted to do such close-in listening. We're much more accustomed to sound at spectator distance" (1977:131).

The model for "good sound," unfortunately, tends to be what we hear on records, tapes, and FM radio. If you intend to make a commercial record of your field tapes, then that's the sound that should be attempted. But if you're attempting to capture folkloric data as it really sounds, then it's necessary to relax, to be willing to let the world intrude now and then just as it does in real life. As I've noted several times before, folklorists collect in two kinds of situations: set-up situations, where someone is performing or talking specifically for the folklorist, and natural situations, where the folklorist is documenting what's going on. You can be as finicky as you wish in the set-up situation, because that's unnatural anyway, but in the natural situation you should preserve some of the event's real quality, otherwise your tape will be documenting a fiction.

Recordists spend a great deal of time figuring out ways to get rid of all of the natural sound in an environment, and they spend a great deal of money on special microphones and filters and equalizers that will help them accomplish that end. But folklorists often want those natural sounds so their recordings will be a fair record of the real conditions under which performance occurs. Ives cites folklorist Neil Rosenberg, who suggests that collectors who are after musical performances in their natural contexts should "place the microphone where it can pick up the full ambience of sound—audience coming and going, people talking and ordering drinks, pinball and cigarette machine operating, etc." " 'Whenever possible,' writes Rosenberg, 'I recorded events: Dances, fiddle contests, jam sessions, house parties, radio sessions, and rehearsals. In most of these situations I used an omnidirectional microphone and set the recorder at slow speed, so as to record the total audio event' " (Ives, 1980:57n, quoting and paraphrasing Rosenberg, 1976).

The optimum distance between a microphone and the person or object being recorded depends on the sound being recorded, the microphone, the recording situation, and your own requirements and taste. For normal speech, one to three feet produces the best results with an omni. Mikes used by rock vocalists, as I noted earlier, are designed to be used within one or two inches of the mouth so the singer's voice will produce a strong signal relative to the sounds of the instruments coming from the nearby stage monitors and audience noise; if the vocalist works too far from the mike the likelihood of feedback squeal is greatly increased. Those microphones are especially designed to be insensitive to the pops created by plosives and to wind noise from the breath.

Sudden bursts of air, whether from a speaker's mouth or from wind, can be a problem anywhere. Air movements you don't hear (but which you can feel on your skin if you pay attention) play havoc with sound recording because the mike translates them as very loud low-frequency sounds. If your mike has a windscreen, use it indoors or out. The screen is transparent to sound but it reduces the sound distortion introduced by air currents. These are far more a problem outdoors, but they can affect recording quality indoors too. If you have a wind problem and don't have a good windscreen designed for your microphone, you can reduce the effect of wind somewhat by covering the mike in two layers of pantyhose. If you don't have a windscreen or pantyhose, find a drugstore and buy a pack of nonlubricated condoms. ("The gel on the others," Honoré points out, "will gum up your microphone" [1980:45].) If you don't have any of those devices and if you can't record somewhere else, check to see if the microphone has a low-frequency roll-off switch, which allows the recordist to reduce significantly the strength of signal below a certain frequency, usually 100 or 50 Hz.

Different musical instruments require different mike positions for optimum recording quality. Record a brass solo instrument from the side with a cardioid mike and a reed instrument closer to the holes than the bell since that's where more of the sound comes from. "To record the sax, put the microphone about halfway between the topmost finger holes and the bell of the instrument, with the mike position above the instrument and the head of the microphone facing down toward it" (Clifford, 1977:151). For a clarinet "you will get the true character of the instrument by aiming the microphone at the main sound source ... the halfway point of the finger holes" (1977:152). Banjoes should be recorded close to the head, the acoustical guitar about the twelfth fret. To avoid pops from plosives, singers should record across the top of the mike, not directly into it. (See Clifford, 1977:144–71, for a detailed discussion of mike placement for various instruments and groups.)

Every room has its own sound characteristics (see Figure 3). A room with hardwood floors, no curtains, and little furniture will be very "live"—it will perhaps even seem echoey. A room with thick rugs, padded furniture, curtains, and people will soak up sound; it will be "dead" or flat. When people talk about a "good concert hall" they aren't saying the seating is comfortable or even that the lines of sight are easy, but rather that the hall's sound characteristics are such that music performed on the stage reaches most segments of the hall about the same time, that there isn't a lot of bouncing around, and neither

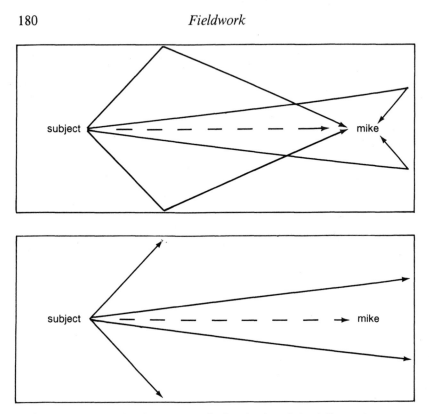

Figure 3. Sound reflection patterns in live (*top*) and dead (*bottom*) rooms.

is the room so absorbent that the music is flat and lifeless. A good room needs some resonance but not so much that sounds duplicate and linger and thereby muddy sounds coming along next.

When you're doing fieldwork you usually won't be able to control the acoustics of the rooms in which you record, but you can adjust your recording to fit the acoustics. The boomier the room, the closer you should work to the sources of sound; if you don't, you'll pick up a lot of echo and the tapes will sound dreadful. Your brain works very hard to filter out those superfluous signals, but the tape recorder doesn't have the brain's capability—it takes in everything fed through its microphone cable.

Proximity to hard surfaces may cause phase cancellation problems (see below), so avoid placing a microphone on a table if at all possible. Usually, the best recordings are obtained when the mikes are on booms because they can be positioned where they'll get the best signal from the source and be least subject to phase cancellation from hard-surface reflections. In formal interviews that's easy enough to manage because people expect the hardware and the clutter; in more casual interviews the mike stand and boom may intrude more than they're worth. In such circumstances go ahead and put the mike on the table, if you're sitting at a table, but don't have the mike parallel to the table's surface the way I did in the death row recreation room. Get a small mike stand that will permit you to put the mike on the table and have it tilt up toward the speaker's mouth. Glue to the bottom of the mike stand rubber pads or a foam rubber base of your own to reduce mechanical noise transmitted by the table. If you don't have a mike stand or a boom or a lavaliere mike you can always use a coffee cup or table glass for a support. If you use a glass, make sure all the holes and slots of the mike are outside of it, otherwise you may get some nasty cancellation from sound bouncing around in that little space. Place a napkin in the glass or cup first so the body of the mike isn't resting on anything hard; if you don't, you'll record a terrific clatter every time the table shakes the least bit.

I like to use lavaliere mikes for interviews because they let the subject (and me, if I'm using two and recording stereo) move around a fair amount without creating unnatural signal falloff. Radio announcers always use mounted mikes, but announcers in a studio position themselves close to the mike and maintain that distance carefully. Ordinary people move around, so their voice level with a mounted mike can vary considerably. If that variation reflected accurately the change in sound level we hear in real life, there would be some justification for capturing it on tape, but microphones, especially directional microphones, don't work that way. Their falloff is far greater than the falloff sensed by our ears. Lavalieres, since they hang around the speaker's neck or are clipped to the clothing, are always the same distance from the mouth. With a lavaliere, the voice signal will remain constant, the only changes in recorded level will result from changes in the volume of the voice itself, not from slight shifts in body position. Furthermore, I don't have to worry about a mike hanging in the air between us or getting knocked around on the table. The convenience isn't free, though: because lavaliere mikes rest on or near the chest, they're generally designed with low-frequency cutoffs or attenuators to reduce boominess or resonance from the chest cavity. Full-size mikes on a table stand or a boom will generally produce a recording of fuller range. I've found that the trade-off in loss of very low tones is generally negligible because those tones are below the vocal range of women and most men.

If you must be outside the action and you want the sound to come from within the action, put a cardioid or omnidirectional microphone in the middle of the scene and run a cable to your audio or video recorder. If you're using a video recorder, its internal microphone will be cut out of the circuit once you plug in the cable from the external microphone. Any shop that sells microphones also sells shielded coaxial or triaxial cable to use for those extensions. (Because a microphone generates a very weak signal, the signal is susceptible to interference, so never use speaker cables or lamp cord or telephone wire for microphone hookups.)

If you're just recording sound, it doesn't matter what your microphone looks like in the scene, but if you're videotaping or filming and don't want the mike to show you can cover it with anything porous. If the people you're recording are at a table you can cover the mike with a napkin or put it in a bowl of fruit. If you don't want to see the wire and can't hide it, suspend the mike from overhead using a boom. Or you can use a shotgun mike mounted on the camera (better doing this with video cameras, which are silent, than with film cameras, which make mechanical noise). Or you can have an assistant point the microphone wherever your camera is pointing.

If you're videotaping one person with a home VHS or Beta video deck, mike placement is usually easy. Unless there's a great deal of background noise and you can't get close enough with your camera to have the voice be the louder signal, you can use the mike on the camera. If you're videotaping or filming and want to use a detached microphone, you might use a cardioid mike on a table or a boom near the speaker, or a lavaliere or lapel mike. If you don't want such mikes to appear in the shot, you can hide them under the speaker's shirt or blouse, but watch out for two potential problems. If you bury the mike under too many layers of clothing, the sound will be muffled; and some fabrics, silk especially, make a great deal of surface noise when they pass across the microphone shells. That's why newscasters wear lapel mikes on their outer clothing.

If you're using a directional microphone and recording several people at once—a conversation, say—you might be tempted to point the mike at whomever is speaking. Suppress the urge whenever possible. First, ambient sound is rarely the same in all directions, even inside a room; when you swing the mike back and forth the ambient sound will change in volume and character. This can be terrifically annoying on playback. Second, whipping the mike back and forth can drive the people you're recording crazy. I said earlier that most people forget early on about the recording machines; if you use the mike like an accusatory pointer, they'll never forget it. And third, in normal conversation people regularly interrupt one another. What do you do when

A is speaking and B interrupts and A goes on talking? If you've been swinging back and forth and you don't do it now, B's voice will sound different than it does when the mike is pointed at B, but if you do point at B then A's voice will fall and rise again when you repoint at A. In such a situation you'd be far better off using an omni or wide cardioid, or using two microphones and feeding them into separate channels on your recorder. And if you can't do that, move a little further back and resign yourself to having some of the voices a little off-mike; that's better and easier than jerking the mike around constantly.

Sometimes, however, moving the mike is appropriate. If you're recording a group of people spread out along a table and you're far enough away to be using a supercardioid, your moving the mike won't interfere with their talking and the movement of the mike across that flat plane probably won't move into areas of significantly different ambient sound. Or if your subject is moving and what your subject is doing is worth the shifting ambient sound or loud enough to be significantly louder than the ambient sound, then follow away.

For recording certain kinds of groups, such as choirs and folk-type groups, Clifford recommends what he calls the "X-Y configuration." Place two mikes on a bar with the mike on the left angled so the head points to the right, and the mike on the right angled so the head points to the left. Connect the mikes to the recorder reverse of normal: the right mike goes to the left input and the left mike goes to the right input (1977:185). It sounds goofy until you realize that the left mike is really looking toward the right side of the noise-producing action, and the right mike is looking toward the left side, so connecting the left mike to the right channel and the right mike to the left channel makes sense.

Whenever possible, practice with the mike you'll be using in the place you'll be recording. If you can't manage that, practice in a place like the place you'll be recording in. And if you can't manage *that,* practice anyway and anywhere you can. *Never* use in the field recording equipment you haven't played with long enough so you're comfortable with it.

And remember that all recording situations are a compromise. No microphone or combination of microphones can accomplish what your ears and brain can accomplish. Your task is to know what you want so you can know what kind of compromise will cost you the least.

Video Sound, Film Sound, and Sound Perspective

Home video recorders and cameras won't produce videotapes of broadcast quality, but they will produce tapes that can be of great value.

Such machines, as I point out elsewhere, are relatively inexpensive (compared to professional equipment, to 16mm equipment, and to what was available only a few years ago) and can do a surprisingly good job of capturing live situations under a great variety of physical conditions.

Sound functions on the VHS and Beta machines are automated: the sound recorders set their own recording levels just like inexpensive cassette sound tape recorders with their automatic level controls. All these cameras have microphones mounted in fixed positions alongside or above the lens. The person operating the camera doesn't have to think about what those devices are up to. The operator sees the scene through the camera's viewfinder (usually, though not always, in black and white); rarely does the operator of such equipment use earphones. Hearing the sound and seeing the picture together usually happens only later, at home, and the results are frequently disappointing. Some of the problems result from the performance characteristics of the microphone and the automatic record level mechanism; others result from the way the equipment was used.

Two of the most common problems are too much garbled noise and too little sound connected with what the lens is seeing. Disconnected sound happens when the lens zooms in on a faraway subject. The image is big and clear on the screen, but the sound is being captured at the camera position far from that action, so it has little or nothing to do with the image. The garble happens because of the difference in the way the ear and the microphone work. As I noted earlier, you can stand in the midst of several people speaking at once and, with no particular difficulty, hear whichever of those speakers you wish. The brain is very good at filtering and selecting and compensating for directionality. You can stand in a room that's very live or boomy and still understand conversations; you can carry on a conversation in a subway without having to shout or be shouted at. Put a normal microphone in those situations and you get a mess: the roar of the subway overwhelms the words of conversation; the echoes in the room turn the voices to mush.

The problem created by having the picture and sound not coming from the same location at the same time is usually referred to as a problem of *sound perspective*. As the source of a sound moves farther and farther from us, its level (assuming it continues emitting sound at the same level) falls off and its relationship to ambient sound changes. At a dinner table, someone sitting next to you can whisper and you can hear the words perfectly well but you may not be able to hear at all words spoken at normal conversational level by people five or six seats down the table. The difference creates no discomfort in real life because we expect sound emitters farther away to deliver less sound volume and less sound clarity, and we expect distant sounds to be overwhelmed by nearer sounds. (The visual equivalent is being able to blot out a mountain with your finger held close to your eye.) But when we film with a zoom lens set on telephoto (which produces the effect of being nearer the object than we are) and we're using a microphone positioned at the lens or near it, then there's a sense of something wrong. That's because the sound isn't appropriate to the image.

The sound perspective problem has to do with the relationship between a sound and the distance from the observer of the object making the sound. In real life, when a person or object moves away from us, the sound generated may be the same but the level of sound reaching us decreases according to the inverse square law. If we listen to a man singing as he moves away, we hear more and more background noise as the distance increases because the *relative* strength of the background noise (which is constant) increases as the actual level of the sound reaching us decreases. If there's little background noise—a city street with no traffic late at night—we might hear the singing for a considerable distance. If there's a great deal of background noise—the same street during the day or the shore near the surf—the singing quickly drops below the level of audibility. Sound is part of the information we use for determining an object's distance from us. If in the deep dark of night we hear the screech of tires and the crunch of metal, the levels of that screech and crunch and their relationship to the normal sounds of night give us a fair idea how far away someone's car just got itself wrinkled. We don't think about this; the brain just does the calculation on its own.

All that is obvious enough. Here's how it matters in fieldwork. If we film or videotape a person moving away and keep the focal length of the lens constant (that is, if we don't use the zoom), then the sound recorded will seem normal. But if we do use the zoom lens to keep the subject about the same size in the frame, then the sound and picture will seem unhooked. The man who's seen in close-up because you've been zooming with him may be 100 feet away, but the picture will make him seem much closer; his lips move and he's obviously speaking, but a microphone at camera position will pick up nothing of his voice.

Imagine videotaping or filming a group singing in a church. You and your camera are tactfully positioned at the back. If you use a cardioid microphone, the sound and picture when you're shooting wide-angle will be commensurate with each other; but if you zoom in for a close-up of the preacher or choir, then the sound won't feel at all right. If you use a supercardioid, the sound might be acceptable on close-ups but inappropriate on wide shots.

One solution is to place a microphone at the point of most sound interest and do your pictures from wherever is most convenient. That complicates your work because long cables might be tripped over by someone else or by you. You might also use a radio microphone, which frees you and the performer of cables but which introduces several other devices that have to be monitored.

Folklore fieldworkers are not usually trying to make professional films or videotapes, which means they and their audiences need not seek the visual and sound perfection sought by makers of commercial films and videotapes. Once again, the fieldworker decides what's most important and tries to locate the machinery to capture as much of that as clearly as possible. I said earlier that recorded sound always represents some kind of compromise; recorded sound joined to recorded picture represents a double compromise. Don't expect the impossible or improbable from the equipment and you'll find it can be enormously valuable. Try to mime what you're used to seeing on television or at the movies and you can expect a great deal of frustration and wasted time and annoyed informants.

Radio Microphones

Many times the most important source of sound will be one person speaking. If that person is in motion, or if the recordist for some reason can't be close enough to that person to make a microphone connection with an ordinary cable, radio microphones may provide a convenient solution.

A radio microphone introduces two additional pieces of equipment to the recording event. The microphone (usually, but not necessarily, a small lavaliere or lapel mike) is plugged into a transmitter, a device about the size of a package of cigarettes. A receiver is plugged into the tape recorder. The microphone feeds its information to the transmitter, the transmitter broadcasts to the receiver, the receiver provides input to the tape recorder. If filming is going on and the fieldworker doesn't want the transmitter to show, it can be hooked to a belt, carried in a pocket, or even taped to the body. (Taping transmitters to bodies is more likely to be done by cops and spies than folklorists.)

Radio mikes operate in the FM range, which means they're line-of-sight; if your informant turns a corner or if a truck moves between you and the informant you're apt to lose the signal. The operating distance is fairly short—100 feet or so, farther under certain conditions. Sometimes radio mikes pick up harmonics of local radio stations, which means you can be recording someone telling someone else how to operate a piece of machinery and suddenly have an announcer selling soap join in the conversation. Many people using radio mikes have two complete rigs with them, each operating on a different frequency. That way, if a radio station intrudes you can switch to the other frequency.

Radio mikes are expensive and they're two more things that might go wrong; they involve a lot more business—more arranging things, more setting up, more batteries to check and monitor. I wouldn't use them unless I absolutely had to, but when they're necessary and when they're used properly they can extend the fieldworker's options enormously because they can go places you can't and be in the middle of events you might not be able to join.

Acoustic Phase Interference

Sound exists as a wave in the air, as varying moments of pressures in different directions. If the sound produced by a source arrives at a microphone and is followed very closely by a second set of the same sounds from the same source (which happens when sound reflects off hard surfaces), a condition known as *acoustic phase interference,* or *phase cancellation,* may occur. The multiple waves hitting the mike at different times add to and subtract from the basic and desired information wave, and that causes the recorded signal to be louder or softer than it should be in an irregular fashion. The audible effect, what you get on the tape, is distortion. (Clifford, 1977:136–42, discusses the problem at some length.)

The problem can occur when you're using one microphone and when you're using multiple microphones fed into the same channel through a mixer. Earlier I described a situation involving a single microphone—the muddy recording in the death row rec room. What happened there was the head of the microphone picked up the speaker's voice and some room echo, and the tail of the microphone picked up reflections of the speaker's voice and room echo as well, but the distance between the head and tail of the mike was great enough for there to be a practical difference in arrival time when those signals were fed into the electronic circuit. Furthermore, both head and tail of the microphone picked up voice and echo as they were bounced off the table.

If you watch Johnny Carson or any other talk show where the host stays in one place and the guests come and go, you'll notice that the host uses a table or lavaliere mike and the guests are picked up by a mike on an overhead boom. Carson and those other talk show hosts have in their control booths sound technicians expert in the mixing of those two microphone sources; another technician handles the boom. The equipment those people use costs a fortune. They don't have problems for several reasons: the mikes are far apart, the rooms are acoustically dead, and those technicians are on the job. Folklorists in the field have none of those options: we work in normal rooms, we don't have technicians in soundproof booths monitoring things, and we usually can't keep all the action in the positions determined in advance by the engineers. So if we're using multiple microphones, or if we're recording in normal situations where there might be phase interference problems, we have to protect ourselves.

"It is easy to run a quick check, taking just a few minutes, to determine if you have this problem," Clifford writes. (I wish I had read his book before the death row trip.) "Mount the microphone in the position in which you expect to use it. Talk into the microphone and take a VU reading. If the mike was positioned on a tabletop, lift it about a foot above its surface and repeat your test. If you get a reading of a few decibels more, reflections from the tabletop are causing phase cancellation. The solution in this case, as in other recording situations, is a matter of common sense. If the phase cancellation is due to reflection from a wall, just move the microphone away from it" (1977: 141).

The reason for acoustic phase interference when multiple microphones are used is the same sound wave reaches the microphones at different moments and the resulting signal on the tape is distorted when the signals from those microphones are melded together. I also fell into this problem. I was recording two women talking in a breakfast nook. The space was boomy enough anyway, but I compounded the problem by putting a lavaliere mike on each, combining the two signals, and feeding the mix to my tape recorder. Both mikes picked up the speech of *both* speakers, but not at the same time. The mike on each speaker was about eight inches from her mouth, but the speakers were perhaps five feet from each other. So when speaker A said something, her mike picked it up clearly and the microphone on speaker B picked it up a little off-mike and a little bit later; compounding the problem, the two mikes picked up the reverberated sound at even larger time gaps. Clifford says phase cancellation can be avoided if "the distance between microphones is at least three times the distance between each performer and his individual microphone. If the separation between performer and mike is one foot, then set up the mikes for a separation of not less than three feet" (1977:137). He is generally right—but this situation was made more complex by the echoes off the two walls and the table in the breakfast nook. Sounds were coming from everywhere. I would have done far better with a single omnidirectional microphone in the middle of the table.

But what if, in that situation, one of the speakers had a loud voice and one had a soft voice? Two solutions. The simplest and probably best would be to move the omni closer to the soft voice until a reasonable balance was achieved. The final recording *should* show some of the difference in those two voices, but not so much that one was overmodulating or the other was disappearing in ambient noise. Or use two cardioid microphones aimed away from one another, each of them close to a speaker. Working this way, Clifford says, you need have the mikes separated by only 50 percent of the distance required by omnis—that is, 1 1/2 times the distance from speaker's mouth to microphone head.

Phase cancellation is often very difficult to detect in the earphones. I'm not sure why. I know that in the death row rec room and the breakfast nook situations things sounded better in the headsets than they did from where I was standing when I took the headsets off. It might be that my brain, knowing how far I was from what I was looking at, accepted a higher degree of muddy sound in the headsets than it would have accepted if I were as close to the speakers as they were to each other.

If you think there's a chance you may be running into the problem, you can check for it with your recorder's VU meter. Clifford outlines a procedure that's complicated to read but simple to do if you do it with the equipment in front of you. Using a normal speaking voice for the signal, set the level for the right mike to zero and adjust the level of the left mike for a reading on your VU meter—any level will do. Then drop that to zero and set the right mike to the same level. Then bring the first mike's level control back up to where it was set for the initial reading "and speak into the area between them. If they're in phase, the resulting signal should be 3 dB higher than that produced by one microphone. To see if this is so, switch one microphone off and talk into the area between the two microphones. Make a note of the VU meter reading. Now switch on the unused microphone so you have both mikes working. Talk and note the VU meter reading. If the microphones are in phase there should be a 3 dB increase" (1977:139–40).

If the microphones aren't in phase, they'll fuzz the sounds of voices and they'll kill many of the harmonics generated by musical instruments. If you're going to the trouble of using multiple mikes and mixing them down to a monaural channel for recording, it's worth a few minutes of your time to make sure that you're not doing more harm to yourself than good. If you can't take the time to do the checking or if the recording situation is such that the test would be awkward, think seriously about recording with one microphone.

Stereo

I love recording in stereo. It has nothing to do with playing back through separate speakers and getting that lifelike stereo effect. Rather, it has to do with the greatly expanded options for accurate data collection provided by the ability to record two simultaneous channels of sound information.

Most of the phase cancellation problems in interviews I mentioned in the previous section disappear if the two microphones are going into two channels on the tape. There's no electronic phase cancellation because the signals aren't adding to or subtracting from each other. (The only phase cancellation problems that remain are those common to the use of one microphone, which you have anyway.)

Stereo provides a wide range of options to the recordist. One microphone might be placed in a "normal" listening position, thereby getting the sound a real listener at that position might get; the other microphone might be placed near a performer of special interest, thereby making it possible for the transcriber later to single that performer out from the others. Or the other microphone might be located some distance away to pick up room sounds and other ambient noises not picked up by the first microphone. Or one microphone might be directed toward the performer, the other at the collector (see Polunin, 1965).

If you want to approximate what the brain picks up, the kind of data with which the brain normally deals, the microphones should be fairly close together. Our sense of binaurality depends on two factors: directionality (based on what our senses tell us about tiny differences in volume and the relation of the sound to other present sounds, which is one function of the shape and direction of the ear) and time delays (based on microseconds in sound arrival time). Most of that information is blended together and dissolved in a monaural recording; much of it is preserved in a stereo recording.

Stereo is far preferable to two mikes mixed down to one channel for several other reasons. Feeding several mikes into a mixer, controlling the level of each, then feeding the mixer output into a recorder and controlling the recording level is a complicated business and is usually, for fieldwork purposes, impractical. Recording stereo is a relatively simple affair. Stereo recordings are far easier to transcribe than mono recordings.

And, finally, stereo can give you a measure of protection: if one mike goes out or if one mike is stupidly placed, the other mike is still there working for you, and it might be intelligently placed. Since the tracks are totally separate, you can select the better track for dubbing later. Stereo adds one mike and one cable to your bundle of things to handle and place, and using it means you have one more dial to watch on your tape recorder. It also means you're far more flexible in how you can operate and your tapes can be far richer in what they contain. If all you have is a monaural tape recorder, by all means use it; but if you can manage to work with two mikes on a recorder with two channels, do it.

Microphone Supports

The element in a microphone that picks up sound and converts it to electrical impulses is built to respond to changes in air pressure. The same element will respond to any other kind of vibration. If you hold a mike in your hand and move your fingers, the friction of your fingers is translated into a slight vibration in the microphone's barrel, and that appears on your tape as a rushing noise. If you have to hold the mike in your hand, keep your fingers absolutely still. If your mike has a low-frequency roll-off switch, use it. Better yet, find some other way to hold the microphone.

Generally, in field situations, the microphone is supported by something other than the hand. Some manufacturers make pistol grips with rubber shock mounts that isolate the microphone from vibration introduced to the grip by finger movements. Those are fine for situations in which the source of sound is on the move (you're walking along with your informant) or where you're moving to different sound sources. More commonly, the mike will be in place for a long time and if you're holding it you can't very well work the recorder or make notes or pour coffee. Many folklorists use small table stands—a heavy base with a clip of some sort that grips the microphone; these should have a rubber or foam base or set of feet to isolate the stand from table vibrations. Fancier versions have center sections that permit raising or lowering of the mike. In a fix, the mike can be put on a table in front of the informant with its business end raised by resting it on a few books or newspapers or magazines, or it can stand in a glass. In such cases do what you can to insulate the mike from table vibration noise made by moving cups around or simply by moving elbows or anything else: wrap the parts that touch anything else in a napkin or something else soft. (Some folklorists hang their microphone from the back of a chair. Since the backs of most chairs have a slight slant, this method of support can avoid the problem of mechanical noise sources, but if the mike is at all directional its business end is pointing at the floor—the one place in the room least likely to be occupied by anything you might want to record.)

Lavaliere and lapel mikes present a problem only if the speaker is in the habit of touching his or her chest for emphasis. I had that happen once: it was a politician, and every time he wanted to demonstrate sincerity he pounded his breastbone with his clenched fist. The tape is so sincere it's hardly bearable: "I want you to know that I mean this! *Kathump!* No one has fought harder for this than *kathump!* me!" I wrote that interview off to experience. Lavalieres, as I noted before, can produce noise if silk or certain other materials rub across them, but that doesn't happen if the mike is worn on the outside of the clothing.

I use a shock mount whenever possible. Shock mounts may consist of a simple rubber cylinder that comes between the microphone and whatever is supporting it; they may also be a complex web of rubber cords that hold the microphone suspended away from any direct contact with anything hard. The simpler kind is integral in the Sennheiser K3N/K3U series, which is the microphone system I use most when I'm not using a lavaliere.

Manufacturers of most home video cameras mount microphones on the cameras with a short boom, a device that holds the head of the mike a foot or so from the camera's body. You're supposed to get the impression that this boom will help you get more professional sound. It does nothing of the kind; it's cosmetic only. Booms are useful when mounted on film cameras because film cameras make a lot of noise, but most video cameras have no moving parts and they don't make a sound. Having the mike on a video camera on a boom means nothing except that it juts out and looks sophisticated to someone who doesn't know any better. It's also something else that can bend or break.

Booms in serious recordings are more complex affairs. The boom operator in a Hollywood movie gets a credit with the other technicians, and often that credit is really deserved. The boom operator has to move the mike near where the sound is but keep the mike and boom out of the camera operator's frame. That requires a high sensitivity to the action of the film and the angle of view of the lenses being used in each shot; it also requires an ability to maintain consistency, since you don't want the sound to change radically when you move from a close-up to an extreme close-up or when you change the point of view slightly. Sometimes those booms are large heavy poles and are balanced with counterweights; more often they're long poles held by hand.

(You can see one of the Hollywood overhead booms in the video version of Arthur Penn's *Night Moves*. It appears in the scene in which the detective, played by Gene Hackman, has his first interview with the woman who wants him to find her missing daughter. The reason you can see that dangling mike and boom shock mount isn't because cinematographer Bruce Surtees made a mistake. It's because *Night Moves* was shot for wide-screen projection, which means the normal 35mm frame is partly masked when the film is projected in a theater. The boom man brought his mike down just a few feet above Hackman's head—not out of the negative's frame but out of what would be the projection frame. But the video transfer of that part of the movie seems to have been made nearly full frame, so you see the device in the shot.)

Often news and documentary filmmakers use a simple hand-held boom to get their microphones closer to a speaker. In an emergency a broomstick will do: just tape the mike to one end. The most common news and documentary film boom is a collapsible tube with a microphone cable inside, a mike mount at one end, and a connector for the mike cable to the recorder at the other end. The most common boom used by folklorists, oral historians, and anthropologists is connected to a floor stand by some kind of T-mount. It lets you have the microphone close to the performer or sound source without having the stand itself in the way. Some recordists say the best place to put the microphone for an acoustic guitar is about six inches directly above the twelfth fret; a mike on a boom attached to a floorstand lets you do that easily. The floorstand/boom/shockmount rig is the best all-around way to manage your microphone in a field situation—unless you're trying to be unobtrusive, in which case you might use a pistol grip of some sort.

Whatever kind of support you select or have to use, try to use the shockmount. Few things are more destructive to a recording than wind-blast and mechanical vibration transmitted through the mike's body; both are nearly impossible to get out afterward, even with the best filters and equalizers. Both can be avoided, or in the worst of situations at least minimized.

12/Photography

Documentary Views

Two very different approaches have developed toward documentary photography and filming. One has it that the photograph or film should be a transparent document, that it should reveal something significant about the scene being recorded but not about the recordist, who is as irrelevant as the camera. The other takes the position that since the recordist is very much a part of the event, he or she should be included in the recording wherever appropriate. Filmmaker Les Blank, for example, will film himself in a mirror if a mirror happens to be in the room; filmmaker Fred Wiseman will never have a trace of his own presence noticeable in his films. Wiseman's aesthetic in documentary still photography was probably best expressed by Walker Evans, who wrote: "I think I incorporated Flaubert's method almost unconsciously, but anyway I used it in two ways; both his realism, or naturalism, and his objectivity of treatment. The non-appearance of author. The non-subjectivity. That is literally applicable to the way I want to use a camera and do" (1982:70).

The styles represent two very different goals—one of art, the other of diary. Most fieldworkers are probably best served by going for diary: it's more likely that someone viewing your images will want to know where you were in all of this than that your images will take on the kind of abstract value that permits them to exist completely independently of you and what you want them to say. And it's more likely that you'll use your photographs as sources of factual information than as the stuff of an independent display.

Recording the facts isn't the same work as making fine images. The image-maker (which is what Evans was) is concerned with the relationship between lines, planes, colors, shadings, and shapes within the frame of the photograph; factual content, if not irrelevant, is secondary to order. The fact-recorder is concerned with the information an event or object has to offer. You may make beautiful photographs while you're doing fieldwork, but if making beautiful photographs is your primary concern, you're not doing folklore or ethnology or anthropology. Both can occur at once (viz. the Peruvian photographs and films by John Cohen), but serving the double master isn't at all easy.

The mechanical parts of the two kinds of photography, however, are exactly the same. The same devices are used—cameras, lenses, meters, filters, film, lights—and the same natural conditions are negotiated or incorporated or manipulated. The sections that follow are about basic aspects of photography. This chapter deals with devices, problems, and techniques common to any kind of photography; the next chapter is about still photography, and the one after that deals with special problems of shooting film and video. If you're thinking about doing professional quality work in any of these photographic fields, you'll need far more information than these pages can provide; but the information on these pages is nonetheless basic to whatever level or kind of photographic work you do.

You can make pictures, sometimes good ones, without most of this information. Modern cameras are largely designed for people who know very little about what they're doing. You can buy cameras you don't even have to focus; cameras that sense for themselves the film's speed; cameras that rewind themselves when the roll is finished. That's very much like using one of those tape recorders with a built-in microphone and no record level control: those recorders will make tapes, just as those automated cameras will take pictures, but the tapes and pictures will be made on the machines' terms, not yours. If your terms happen to agree with theirs, fine; go out and have a simple and successful time. If you want more choice, if you want to control the images that document what your eyes are seeing out there, then spending some time with the technical matters on the following pages will help you achieve what you want.

How Pictures Are Made

Cinematographers often speak of their work as "painting with light," and it's not a bad metaphor. All photographers manipulate light to create a chemical change in the emulsion on a photographic film, which is then developed. If the film is itself a positive print it's usually referred to as "reversal film"—not because it's a reverse of what you saw, but because it's a reverse of what's usual in photography, where each stage normally reverses all the tones of the previous stage. If the film requires another printing step before a normal image is achieved, it's referred to as "negative film." (In video the change is magnetic, not chemical, and is effected not by light hitting the tape itself but rather by transducers that respond to light energy by emitting electrical energy; the signals produced by those transducers are amplified and fed to the magnetic tape.)

All film cameras perform exactly the same operation: they focus light in the space where the film is being held. The most primitive cameras—pinhole cameras—don't even use a lens. Most cameras do three things:

—control the light information admitted to the film chamber (their lenses adjust to admit greater or lesser amounts of light and can be focused so objects at selected distances appear in sharp focus on the strip of film; their shutters control the amount of time that light is passed along to the film);

—keep the film in darkness until it's developed and will no longer be acted upon by light (35mm cameras take film out of and then put it back into a small can, which is later opened in a darkroom for development; instant print cameras, such as the Polaroid, perform the development operation themselves);

—transport the film (large view cameras handle one sheet of film at a time, but 35mm cameras have a film transport controlled by a lever or motor, and most instant print cameras have motors). Movie cameras differ from still cameras only in that they're built to take a rapid succession of images; each individual image in a movie is made the same way each image is made in a roll film still camera.

Film must be exposed properly if the photographer is to have any control over the images that result. Modern cameras are capable of exact exposures. The proper exposure is determined by use of a light meter, either built into the camera or used separately. Four factors control exposure:

—the speed of the film (which indicates how much light the film needs to see to make a proper exposure, expressed in ASA, EI, or DIN);

—the speed of the shutter (how long the camera lets the film be exposed to light, usually expressed in seconds and fractions of seconds: 1/30, 1/60, etc.);

—the speed of the lens (how much light the lens will pass through to the film, expressed in f/stops);

—the amount of light reflected by the object to be photographed (expressed in footcandles or their metric equivalent, lux).

In order to get the *same* exposure, any change in any of these factors must be compensated for by an equal and opposite change in the other factors. If the lens is "stopped down" (the hole is made narrower) so half as much light passes through, then the outside light must be doubled or the shutter speed must be halved or film with twice the speed of the original film must be used. If the sky darkens and the photographer wants to preserve the same negative contrast and density, then a slower shutter speed, wider lens opening, or faster film must be used.

Eyes

No optical device has everything in focus at once. Your eye can focus on an object a million light-years away (a star), fifty miles away (a distant mountain peak on a clear day), or in the palm of your hand, but it doesn't focus on all those things at the same moment. We're not aware that most of the objects in our field of view are out of focus most of the time because when our brain/eye mechanism is working properly our eye is focused at exactly the point in space that concerns us. It takes no conscious message from us to tell the eye muscles that they must change the shape of the eyeball and thereby change the shape and point of focus of the lens. It's instantaneous and, in a normal eye, perfect. No machine comes close.

Neither can any optical device accept at once all degrees of light available. The human eye functions in near darkness and in brilliant sunlight, but not at the same time. Its diaphragm—the pupil—automatically contracts or expands in terms of the eye/brain's sense of how much light the optical nerves need to develop an accurate picture. (If you've ever had a glaucoma test on a bright day you know what happens when that mechanism is temporarily disabled: normal daylight is painful and details are impossible to see.) No single photographic device made can accept the range of light with which the normal eye deals every day. Films capable of working in near darkness can't be used in bright sunlight without requiring such dense filtration on the lens that focusing is impossible; films capable of working in bright sunlight can't be used in near darkness. "The eye was the first lens, and it's still the best," wrote photographer Aaron Sussman.

> The most perfect lens ever made is just a clumsy affair compared to the sensitive, self-adjusting, *apochromatic* zoom mechanism that functions as the eye.

The curious thing about man's long search for the perfect lens is that he pursued this search with the only perfect lens there is, and never realized it. Each new basic discovery in lens design was just a rediscovery of optical and mechanical principles already at work in the eye. Some of these are the *diaphragm,* which is the *iris* of the eye; the *compound lens,* which duplicates the *liquid* and *crystalline* lens formations of the eye; the *shutter,* which is a mechanical eyelid. The eye even has an *anti-halo* backing, a layer of some black substance behind the retina which absorbs all rays not needed or not wanted to create vision. Also, it has a built-in *UV absorption filter,* is *self-cleaning,* and doesn't suffer from *shutter fatigue,* provided you get your quota of sleep each day. (1973:44)

F/stops

Lenses differ in two important regards (assuming they're of the same optical and mechanical quality): their *speed* (which has to do with the maximum amount of light they can pass through to the film) and their *focal length* (which, functionally, has to do with the angle of view they see).

F "is an abbreviation for the term *factor* and symbolizes an arithmetic proportion; the relation between the diameter of the widest lens opening, or *effective aperture,* and the *focal length* of the lens. . . ." A 1-inch lens with an aperture of 1/2 inch, a 3-inch lens with an aperture of 1 1/2 inches, and a 6-inch lens with an aperture of 3 inches all are f/2 lenses (Sussman, 1973:82).

The maximum f/stop of a lens is an indication of the maximum amount of light it will let in. When photographers speak of a lens's speed, they express it in terms of the widest f/stop. A 35mm lens with a maximum aperture of f/2 is "faster" than a 35mm lens with a maximum aperture of f/3.5. In practical terms, an f/2 lens will make acceptable images in less light than an f/3.5 lens, an f/3.5 lens will make acceptable images in less light than an f/8 lens, and so on. This difference in speed matters only when the lenses are opened to their maximum apertures. An f/2 35mm lens set at f/8 will admit exactly the same amount of light as an f/3.5 35mm lens set at f/8 or an f/8 35mm lens set at f/8.

Almost all modern lenses have adjustable diaphragms that control the amount of light they'll pass through. These diaphragms are adjusted by a ring on the lens barrel. (Such adjustments are done automatically by automatic cameras and by most Polaroid cameras.) The ring is calibrated in f/stops or, in some movie lenses, *T/stops,* which are determined by actual measurement of light transmission; an f/stop is based on a mathematical relationship. T/stop transmission is therefore always slightly smaller and slightly more accurate than f/stop theoretical transmission, so for lenses calibrated in T/stops and f/stops, the T/stop should be used for setting exposure. Meters give information in f/stops—simply use the indicated f/stop setting on the T/stop scale on the lens barrel. Light transmission has nothing to do with depth of field, so in depth-of-field calculations always use the f/stop. (This description is more confusing than the reality: with any particular lens, you'll be using either an f/stop or a T/stop ring.)

Generally, each f/stop position on a lens represents a halving or doubling of the light let through the lens. The usual stops, in sequence, are f/1.4, f/2, f/2.8, f/4, f/5.6, f/8, f/11, f/22, f/32, f/45, and f/64. Few 35mm lenses go beyond f/22. If film speed and light are kept equal, each step in that sequence requires a doubling or halving of the exposure time to provide the same exposure to the film. If f/1.4 requires 1 second, then f/2 requires 2 seconds, f/2.8 requires 4 seconds, and so on. (Novice photographers are sometimes confused because the smaller numbers—f/1.4, f/2—represent larger lens openings, while the larger numbers—f/16, f/22—represent smaller lens openings. If you keep in mind that these are fractions it makes better sense: 1/2 is a bigger hole than 1/22.) Lenses are available in other f/stops: very fast lenses with ratios lower than 1 (f/0.8, etc.) were developed by Zeiss for Stanley Kubrik's *Barry Lyndon*. And some lenses have half-stops—clicks between the major f/stops.

The usual term for making the aperture smaller—going from f/2 to f/5.6, say—is *stopping down*. The usual term for making the aperture larger—going from f/5.6 to f/2—is *opening up*.

Depth of Field

Changing the f/stop not only changes the amount of light reaching the film (and therefore the amount of light you need or don't need from other sources to make a proper exposure), it also changes what photographers call the *depth of field*. Depth of field is the area between near and far points from the camera in which objects are acceptably sharp. In theory, a lens is perfectly focused for only one distance, but because of the limitations of resolving power of film, printing paper, and projection screens, there's a far deeper zone in which images *seem* to be in focus. This has to do with a quantity referred to as *circles of confusion*, which I won't discuss here. (But see Pincus and Ascher, 1984:65–68, or almost any technical manual on lenses.)

With any particular lens the field in which objects appear to be in focus increases as the lens is stopped down and decreases as the lens is opened up. If the maximum aperture of the lens is f/1.2 and the minimum aperture is f/22, a picture made at f/1.2 will have the least depth of field and a picture made at f/22 will have the most depth of field. More of the world is in focus at f/22 than at f/1.2.

The importance of depth of field may be clearer in the context of specific examples. Let's examine how depth of field is affected by (1) changing the lens (while keeping the same point of focus and the same aperture); (2) changing the aperture (while keeping the same lens and the same point of focus); and (3) changing the point of focus (while keeping the same lens and the same aperture). (The numbers that follow were taken from lens tables in Clarke, 1980:249–55).

1. If you were shooting at f/8 and had the lens focused at 15 feet, these are the depths of field you would get from different prime (non-zoom) lenses:

25mm	3'10"–infinity	75mm	11'4" –22'2"
35mm	6'0" –infinity	100mm	12'8" –18'4"
50mm	8'8" –55'5"	150mm	13'11"–16'4"

That is, the 150mm lens would give you a depth of field only 2'5" deep, the 100mm lens would give you a depth of field 5'8" deep, and so on. Furthermore, the closest point of focus, with the lens itself focused at 15 feet, moves from 13'11" to 3'10".

2. If you had a 50mm lens focused at 15 feet, these are the depths of field you would get at different apertures:

f/2	12'8" –18'4"	f11	7'6"–infinity
f/4	11'11"–20'2"	f/16	6'2"–infinity
f/5.6	9'11"–30'9"	f/22	5'0"–infinity
f/8	8'8" –55'5"		

The same lens focused at the same point 15 feet away gives you a depth of field ranging from 5'8" to infinity, and the point of closest focus ranges from 5'0" to 12'8".

3. If you had a 50mm lens with the aperture at f/8, these are the depths of field you would get for different points of focus:

50'	10'4"–infinity	6'	4'2"–10'11"
25'	8'7"–infinity	5'	3'8"–8'0"
15'	7'0"–infinity	4'	3'1"–5'8"
10'	5'8"–41'1"	3'	2'6"–3'10"
8'	5'0"–20'2"	2'	1'9"–2'4"

The closer the point of focus, then, the narrower the depth of field; the farther away the point of focus, the deeper the depth of field. Notice that there is more distance in acceptable focus *behind* the point of focus than in front of it. If the lens is focused on an object 4 feet away, for example, the depth of field ranges from 3'1" to 5'8"—11 inches in front of the object and 20 inches beyond it. Depth of field is always approximately twice as deep behind the point of focus as in front of the point of focus.

Clarke summarizes the relationships between f/stop, focal length, distance, and depth of field this way: "The smaller the f/stop and the shorter the focal length of the lens, the greater the depth of field. The further away the subject, the greater the depth of field. Conversely, the opposite is also true. The larger the f/stop, the longer the focal length of the lens, the closer the subject to the lens, the smaller the depth of field" (1980:243).

Depth of field isn't just a technical consideration. If you're photographing objects on a table, say, the depth of field of that lens at that aperture controls how many of those objects will be in sharp focus; it may even control whether all or part of an object is in sharp focus. If you want as much as possible to be in focus, you'll shoot with as small an aperture as possible. If the background is full of irrelevant things that will just clutter up the shot, you might want to shoot with the lens wide open so you can throw the background out of focus.

Say you want to photograph a fiddler playing his fiddle. Three feet behind where the fiddler stands is a wall covered with family photographs. Because of the light conditions you have to shoot at f/8. If you take your photograph from a distance of 4 feet, you can't get the fiddler and the photographs in focus at the same time, since the depth of field for that lens at 4 feet is 2'7" (3'1" to 5'8"). To get the space from the wall to the fiddler's hands in focus you must have a depth of field of about 6 feet. If you step back just 2 feet, so you're focusing at 6 feet, your field of focus will range from 4'2" to 10'11".

It might be just the other way around. Your fiddler might be standing in front of a wall cluttered with stuff you don't want in your picture. In that case, you'd find a depth of field that gets the object into focus but leaves the background out of focus. If you photographed your fiddler from a distance of 3 feet, the wall would be a blur.

You don't have to figure this out every time you go to take a picture and neither do you have to lug around depth-of-field charts for each of your lenses. There's an easier way. With single lens reflex cameras (SLRs) you can *see* depth of field. All 35mm SLRs focus with their apertures wide open. That is, if you have a lens with a maximum aperture of f/2 and you have the camera set at f/11, the camera doesn't stop down to f/11 until you press the shutter button. That means you're looking through the lens with its aperture wide open, which provides its *minimum* depth of field. If everything you want seems to be in focus at that point, fine; go ahead and shoot. You can check the depth of field at the aperture you'll be using to photograph by pushing the button on most 35mm cameras that closes the lens down to the preset aperture. Your field of view will darken (each f/stop you shut down from the maximum cuts the light in half, so if you're going to f/11 from f/2 you've reduced the light by a factor of sixteen), but you'll see distant and near objects suddenly come into focus. That's what will be in focus on your negative. Your negative and print will never be sharper than what you see in the viewer at that moment.

You don't even have to look through the viewfinder to get an idea of depth of field. Most interchangeable lenses for 35mm cameras have depth of field indicated on the lens barrel. Nikkor lenses, for example, have pairs of colored lines keyed to the colors of the lenses' f/stops. Those lines are opposite the distance scale on the focusing ring. Once the lens is focused and the aperture is set, everything between those lines will be in focus. You can't stop down a rangefinder camera to look at depth of field because in a rangefinder camera you focus through a different optical system. That's why many photographers put up with the extra weight and noise and bulk of SLRs. But better rangefinder lenses have those parallel lines on the lens rings. Many less expensive cameras without interchangeable lenses have charts in the instruction booklets giving the camera's depth of field at various aperture settings. If you have that kind of camera, read the instructions.

Focal Length

The shorter the number for focal length, the wider the angle of the lens: 50mm is usually considered a "normal" lens for 35mm cameras; 28mm is wide-angle; 300mm is telephoto. For 16mm cameras the effect of the lenses is doubled, since the image is contained on a much smaller frame of film; therefore, a "normal" lens for these cameras is 25mm. From the same position the normal lens might see a building, the wide-angle lens might see the building and the buildings surrounding it, and the telephoto lens might see one window of the building. A "longer" lens sees a narrower angle; a "shorter" lens sees a wider angle.

The focal length is determined by this equation: focal length = distance $\times$ aperture size/object size. You don't have to worry about the equation because focal length is engraved on all lenses. Focal lengths are expressed in millimeters or inches, depending on the manufacturer. A 50mm lens is approximately a 2-inch lens and a 75mm lens is approximately a 3-inch lens. The best lenses are made in Europe and Japan, as are most still and film cameras, so the focal lengths of most modern lenses are given in millimeters. For a 35mm camera, the relationships between focal length and horizontal angle of view are as follows: a 21mm lens sees 91°, 28/76°, 35/64°, 50/45°, 90/27°, 105/23°, 135/18°, 150/16°, 250/10°, and 500/5° (Sussman, 1973:52).

Wider angle lenses have greater depth of field than normal lenses and far greater depth of field than telephoto lenses. They're also more likely to introduce distortion in near objects. If you photograph a face with a wide-angle lens, the face will look odd because the nose seems larger in relation to the face than it really is. This is because the nose is proportionally so much closer to the lens. Many portrait photographers use a focal length of 90 or 105mm, which permits them to fill the frame with the face but be far enough from the subject so that distortion isn't introduced. Wide-angle lenses also magnify the sense of depth because of the way they sharpen perspective; objects appear more distant than they really are and, in motion picture filming, persons or objects moving toward or away from the camera seem to be moving far more rapidly than they really are.

Extreme wide-angle lenses introduce *spherical aberration:* straight lines seem to curve and perspective is accentuated even more radically. Photographers trying to make pictures of real objects showing the actual physical relationships of objects to one another rarely use lenses wider than 35mm with 35mm film.

Lenses of enormous focal length—300mm and more, say—introduce another kind of distortion: *depth compression.* Objects that are really separate from one another seem very close because they don't fall off in size the way they do with normal perspective. Perspective is reduced, so distance seems compressed. Moving persons or objects in motion picture films seem to be covering less distance than they really are.

Zoom lenses are available for all 35mm and 16mm reflex cameras that accept interchangeable lenses. Zoom lenses are not used with rangefinder cameras because the photographer has no way of knowing what the lens is seeing. (Rangefinder, reflex, and other type cameras are discussed in the next chapter.) Many manufacturers provide zoom lenses in several ranges. Nikon, for example, makes a 43–86 zoom (not quite wide-angle to not quite portrait) and an 80–200mm zoom (just below portrait to moderate telephoto). Zooms tend to be slower and heavier than prime lenses (lenses of fixed focal length), but they offer versatility that can sometimes be useful because the photographer confronting a wide range of photographing situations doesn't have to carry many different lenses or constantly be changing them.

Films and Film Speeds

There's as much difference in film made by different manufacturers as there is in cannelloni made by different cooks. The difference is most obvious in color films. According to David Leitner, optical technician at DuArt labs in New York, Kodak film (American) produces images rich in color saturation, Fuji film (Japanese) makes images with subtle tonal gradation and great sensitivity to pastels, and Agfa film (German) produces images that are literal—closest to reality.

"The *speed* of a stock," write Pincus and Ascher,

> is a measure of its sensitivity to light. The *exposure index* expresses the speed as a number that can be used with exposure meters to help determine proper exposure. The film manufacturer recommends an exposure index for each stock that is usually given in the form of an *ASA number* (American Standards Association, now American Standards Institute or ANSI). It's printed on the data sheet and often on the film's packaging. The metric equivalent is a DIN number marked with a degree sign. An *ISO number* (International Standards Organization) gives the ASA number first, then the DIN number (for example, ISO 64/19° means ASA 64, DIN 19). (1984:104)

Doubling the EI (or ASA or DIN) cuts in half the light required to shoot the scene; halving the EI doubles the amount of light needed to shoot the scene. If, say, you have film rated at EI 100 and your light meter says you need 100 footcandles of light to expose the film properly, using a film with an EI of 200 would require only 50 footcandles, using a film of EI 400 would require only 25 footcandles, and so on. It works the same way in the other direction: if you went to a film with an EI of 50, you would need 200 footcandles to illuminate the scene adequately. (There are four ways to manage the amount of light needed to photograph a scene: changing the amount of light illuminating the scene, changing the film to one with a higher or lower EI, changing the camera's shutter speed, or changing the aperture of the camera's lens. It's also possible to change the film's EI by requesting the lab to "push" it in development—a film with an EI of 400, for example, can, with special chemical developers or longer developing time, be made to behave like a film with an EI of 800 or 1200. Most modern films can be pushed one stop, that is, their EI can be doubled, with little or no increase in grain size. Beyond that, grain size increases and image quality decreases.)

European films are rated in DIN (Deutsche Industrie Norm) rather than EI or ASA. The difference is that the DIN scale is logarithmic rather than linear, so an increase or decrease of three digits of DIN rating is the same as the doubling or halving of an EI or ASA rating. A film with DIN 20 is twice as fast as a film with DIN 17 and half as fast as a film with DIN 23.

Black-and-white film, such as Kodak Plus-X and Tri-X or Ilford HP-5, is panchromatic. That is, the film is balanced to "see" the entire range of the visible spectrum equally well. (Specialized films—such as those used for photocopying documents, aerial surveillance, infrared work, and such—are especially balanced to see only certain colors or to be especially sensitive to colors in certain parts of the visible spectrum.) Since black-and-white film sees the entire visible spectrum evenly, it can be used without filtration indoors or outdoors, in tungsten or fluorescent light. The photographer must consider the *amount* of light illuminating the object and reflected to the film, not the *color* of light.

Not so with color film, which comes balanced for tungsten illumination or for daylight illumination. (Some amateur films are available that are a compromise—somewhere between the two.) Photographs made outdoors with a tungsten-balanced film produce images with an unnatural bluish color; photographs made indoors with tungsten illumination on daylight balanced film will take on an unnatural reddish color.

Most photographers can't afford the luxury of having separate cameras for different film, nor can they afford to change film every time they move into a different lighting situation. What they do instead is filter the light to bring it into balance with the film. They do this in one of two ways: by filtering the light at the source (putting a tinted gel over the lamps or over the windows) or by filtering the light as it reaches the camera (mounting a filter on the lens).

If the camera contains tungsten-balanced film, an 85 filter (pale orange) will make the film usable in daylight; if the camera contains daylight-balanced film, an 80 filter (dark blue) will make it usable in artificial light. The 80 filter is so dark it soaks up the equivalent of two stops of light (it cuts the film speed to 25 percent of its rated value). Since there's generally far more light outdoors than indoors, most photographers who'll be working in both situations use tungsten-balanced film and use the 85 filter outside. The 85 only reduces light hitting the lens by two-thirds of a stop, so it's far less troublesome than the 80 filter.

If you do use the 85 filter so you can use the same roll of film in both situations, remind yourself to check the lens to be sure the filter is off when you're photographing in tungsten light. The effect of the 85 through the viewer is a mild pink/orange tinting of the scene, so mild it's sometimes easy to miss. Every so often I forget, and I get color pictures of people who are far rosier than they ever were in real life.

Black-and-white film (B&W) is by far the easiest to shoot but it's not necessarily the easiest to see. The decision about whether to shoot in color or B&W is made on the basis of what use will be made of the images. For research, accurately balanced color slides or negatives provide the most information. For publication in a book or journal, B&W is more practical. B&W is also usually far less expensive to buy, process, and print.

Color slides or negatives can be printed in black and white, but few photographers use those films that way. That's because a photographer thinks differently when shooting color than when shooting B&W. B&W film sees differences in planes and shapes; color sees differences in fields of color. An image that might be boring and uninformative in B&W might be interesting and informative in color. This sounds obvious, but in practice it isn't. That's because we see the world in color and have to make a conscious shift to think about what things will look like in black and white. Since we think differently when using the different films, we tend to seek out different kinds of things to photograph with them.

Until not very long ago there prevailed the curious notion that B&W was a more serious or artistic medium than color: color was for tourists documenting the family trip or for hacks doing advertising copy, while the great photographers—Evans, Lartigue, Steiglitz, Strand—did their visions of the world in black and white. Those artists produced wonderful images in black and white, surely, but the choice of film stock wasn't theirs. Color stocks were not commonly available in the early part of this century, though the process had been invented, so the photographic explorers had to develop aesthetic criteria in terms of the film stocks that were available—black-and-white stocks. Those photographers sought out subjects that would render well within the limitations of black and white, and their images were organized in terms of the sensitivity of B&W film to planes and textures. Had Paul Strand, for example, been using color film when he was photographing in the Hebrides, his images would not just have been more colorful, they would have been of different things differently composed. (Cinematographer Nestor Almendros says that black-and-white film distorts reality: "Black and white can make a film seem strange and stylized. Since reality exists in colors, just by doing without them, one immediately achieves an extremely elegant aesthetic transposition of things" [1984:83].)

Say you want to photograph a large quilt. It's made of beautiful patches of deep purple, deep red, dark blue, and bright yellow. If you photograph the quilt in color, you'll see all of that. If you photograph it in black and white, you'll see a large rectangle of dark grey with a few bright areas (the yellow). That's because B&W film doesn't care about color, it just cares about how much light is reflected by the surface—how dark or bright it seems.

Some fieldworkers carry extra cameras so they can be ready to shoot B&W or color at any moment. I've tried that, but I haven't been happy with the results. Constantly shifting from thinking in terms of planes of light to fields of color can be confusing; the pictures I made when I deliberately worked with two cameras loaded with different films were not, generally, as good as the pictures I made when I worked with just one kind of film stock. Many photographers can't afford the extra camera or don't want to manage the extra weight. My preference is to work with one stock at any one time; if something comes along that demands the other kind of stock, I take out what I've got in the camera and shoot a roll of the other kind of film. If I *have* to be ready to shoot both, I'll have a Nikon loaded with color and a Leica loaded with B&W. This helps me make the shift from one style of visualizing to the other and it keeps me from getting confused about what I'm doing. It works pretty well, but I still prefer working with one camera and one kind of film. That's me; you might be perfectly comfortable shifting back and forth—or you may decide to work in one kind of stock exclusively.

A decade ago, the decision about whether to use color or B&W was made on the basis of film speed as much as end use. Older color films needed far more light than B&W films. But that difference no longer exists. Kodak makes a color print film with an EI of 1000 and Fuji introduced, in 1984, 35mm color print and reversal films rated at EI 1600. If you can see something, you can probably photograph it.

Polaroid produces a line of 35mm film which makes it possible to shoot 35mm and have it developed immediately. Polachrome CS is transparency film (ISO 40/DIN 17), Polapan CT is continuous tone black-and-white transparency film (ISO 135/DIN 22), and Polagraph HC, used for copying black-and-white print documents, is high-contrast black-and-white transparency film (ISO 400/DIN 27).

The Color of White

No, it isn't the same all the time. The color of true white is the same, but what strikes your mind and eye as white rarely is true white. What *seems* white to you—a shirt, say—doesn't reflect the same colors outside on a cloudless day, outside on a cloudy day, in a room illuminated by incandescent lights, a room illuminated by fluorescent lights, when you move from a room with yellow walls to a room with green walls. We don't "see" color; we see light reflected by objects. The color we see depends on the color of the light hitting the object and the light-absorbing and light-reflecting qualities of the object.

The brain does a balancing act. It "knows" what certain objects should look like and it corrects everything else in terms of them; it acts as if all incident light was white. That works fine when we're considering a person's perception of color, but it doesn't work at all well when we're considering a film's rendition of color. Film has no brain; it just produces what it sees. Snapshots taken in the snow often have a curious bluish tinge because snow, on a cloudless days, has a bluish tinge. The brain suppresses that data, but film doesn't. Film shot under fluorescent light produces people with a slightly green hue because people under most fluorescent lights have a slightly green hue. The brain won't have that either.

Sunlight at sunrise or sunset has a color temperature of 2,000° Kelvin (color temperatures tell us the length of light waves emitted or reflected by an object; the length of those waves is interpreted by our eyes in terms of color). An hour after sunrise or an hour before sunset the color of sunlight is 3,500°; a little later in the morning or a little earlier in the afternoon it's 4,300°; at noon in Washington, D.C., in the summer, sunlight is about 5,400°. Skylight (which isn't the same as daylight, since daylight consists of sunlight plus skylight and incorporates the blue light created by dust and other particles in the air) is even cooler. Overcast sky is 6,000°, light summer shade is 7,100°, and average summer shade is 8,000°. Average summer skylight ranges from 9,500° to 30,000°. Different artificial light sources produce extremely different colors of light: a match flame is 1,700°, a candle is 1,850°, a 100-watt incandescent tungsten lamp is 2,865°, and a daylight blue photoflood lamp is 4,800°. Fluorescent lamps range from 2,700° to 6,500° (Clarke, 1980:305–11).

If we take pictures of objects, using outdoor film outdoors and indoor film indoors, our pictures will produce color renditions far closer to what those objects "really" look like than what they seem to look like to us when we're there looking at them. Sometimes we want to capture the different color; we may want the greenish tint of skin under fluorescents, or the reddish hue cast on everything at sunrise or sunset. If we don't want those tints, if we want the objects or people to look more like we think they should look, then we must somehow control the light reaching the film.

There is, as I said earlier, no problem in black and white since you just have to worry about the amount of light reflected and not the color of light reflected. Photographers working in B&W may use filters to enhance parts of the image. They may, for example, use a light yellow filter when working outdoors to compensate for the film's ultraviolet sensitivity that results in rendering the sky slightly lighter than it really seems. A yellow (K1) filter makes clouds stand out better; a red filter (25) does that to an extreme: it makes the sky dark but keeps everything else pretty much the same.

The problem is easily solved in video because video cameras are capable of adjusting themselves or being adjusted to maintain consistency in the way they see white, whatever color the source light. At the beginning of a shot, the camera operator adjusts the camera's *white balance,* which means only that the camera will produce the same white this time as it does every other time; since white is a combination of all colors, the other colors will be reproduced consistently as well. Many cameras that come with home video units do this automatically.

Color correction is a minor problem for fieldworkers shooting color slides; if the image is off-tint slightly it's usually no great problem. I suggested earlier putting a color scale in some of your color pictures; that will let you know exactly what kind of color shift you've encountered and will let your lab know exactly how much color correction to do if you ever want to reproduce the colors exactly.

The problem is greatest for filmmakers, not so much because they want to get colors exactly right (sometimes they do, sometimes they don't), but because they often have to put next to one another shots of persons or objects taken under slightly differing light conditions. Audiences don't think, "The person is now being illuminated by tungsten rather than skylight so he looks a little redder." They think, "Something is screwed up here."

If all of this sounds complicated—well, it is, but it's not so complicated that you can't learn it fairly quickly if it really matters. If you're just capturing images as an aide-memoire, then the slight aberrations might not be at all critical and you might very well put your attention on things that matter more. But if the photographs are going to be used in an exhibition, then you want the color they report to be as true as possible to the colors that were there, and in that case you should be cognizant of the quality of the light and the characteristics of your film. (Several good introductory books cover all of this in detail. I'd recommend Pincus and Ascher, 1984, and Sussman, 1973.)

Metering Light

Delmer Daves, who directed *Broken Arrow, Cowboy, 3:10 to Yuma,* and many other notable films, watched while I made some photographs of Tim McCoy, Iron Eyes Cody, and Blanche Sweet. He asked to see the camera I was using, a Leica M-4, then said that years ago he had an earlier model Leica he used for taking stills on the sets of his films. "That one didn't have a built-in meter either," he said. He looked at the Leica again. "Neither does this one. How come you don't use a camera with a built-in meter?" I told him that I had such cameras but preferred the Leica even though it meant I had to take readings with a separate meter, which was more accurate anyway. "I never used a meter," Daves said. "Didn't need one in those days." I asked what had changed. "The filmstock. You have all kinds of filmstock now. Back then we had just one filmstock, so you got to know what it needed in different kinds of light. And one of my cameramen told me a trick he used. He said, when you know what setting you need and you want to shoot in a place that's brighter or darker, you just squint down your eye to keep the lighting level about the same or open up your eye to keep the lighting level about the same, and then you do the same thing with the diaphragm on the lens. That's what I did"—he squinted then went wide-eyed—"and it always worked just fine."

I thought that was just a terrific idea. I went around the rest of the day squinting and wide-eyeing, comparing what I sensed to the changes my meter told me the film needed. Sometimes Delmer's trick worked, sometimes it didn't. I think I would've had about the same success just figuring, "It's a lot brighter now, so let's close down two stops" or, "It's a little closer to dusk, let's open up a stop or two." The filmstock Daves had been using in the old days was slow, which meant he was shooting outside in daylight. He was shooting in the desert and in Southern California, which meant there wasn't much lighting variation from moment to moment or from day to day. He'd shot enough movie film to have a good idea what apertures the stock needed. And he was shooting B&W, which is the most forgiving of all of under- and overexposure. I decided I would continue using my meter.

It's possible, of course, to take decent pictures without using a meter. Most film comes with a little sheet suggesting speeds and apertures for different kinds of lighting situations. One rule of thumb is: If you're working in bright or hazy sun, set the shutter speed at the film's EI and set the aperture at f/16; if it's a little brighter than that, double the shutter speed or close down an f/stop; if it's a little darker than that, halve the shutter speed or open up an f/stop. If you do this you have a chance of getting passable pictures; not a big chance, but better than what you'd get setting the dials randomly.

That's for when you don't have a meter or when your meter breaks down. You should always plan on having a meter, however, and if you're really interested in getting good photographic images you should have a backup meter so you don't have to guess if your main meter breaks down. (I've never had a meter break down in the field, by the way; I *have* had them go dead because I forgot to check the batteries.)

All light meters work on the same principle: light energy strikes the surface of a photovoltaic cell (another transducer, one that's capable of changing light energy to electrical energy). The tiny electric current activates a galvanometer needle. The position of the moved needle indicates (either directly or by reference to a scale) the appropriate camera setting. The scale across which the needle moves may be calibrated in footcandles, lux, lumens, or some relative set of numbers. The reading is set on a rotating scale elsewhere on the meter where the range of f/stops and shutter speeds are displayed. Some light meters give the reading directly in light-emitting diodes. Light meters made especially for film cameras, which generally operate at 1/50 second, may give readings directly in f/stops. Meters built into reflex cameras may be centered in a viewfinder notch when the camera thinks the right exposure has been set. The operating principle for all these meters is the same: the meter is told the speed of the film, it senses the amount of light, and it tells the photographer what settings the camera needs to provide the proper amount of light to the film's surface.

The range for error isn't wide. Black-and-white film is more forgiving of sloppy metering than is color film, and negative color film is more forgiving than reversal color film. If you underexpose or overexpose B&W or color negative more than 1 f/stop you lose shadow detail or brightness detail. If you're off more than 1/2 f/stop in color reversal you not only lose detail but you begin to wash out or burn in colors inappropriately.

Light meters are used in two ways: to read *incident* light (the amount of light falling on an object) and *reflected* light (the amount of light bounced off an object). Reflected light meters use a flat surface to gather light; incident meters incorporate a hemispherical light-gathering device, which takes into account not only the amount of light falling on an object but also the geometry of the light. A *spotmeter* is a special kind of reflected light meter; it has a very narrow angle of acceptance—sometimes just 1°—which permits the photographer to take readings from parts of a scene—a person's cheekbone, eye, shirt collar, the hubcap on a car, and so on.

Reflected light readings give the average amount of light reflected by the objects within the meter's field of vision, while incident meter readings indicate the amount of light falling on all objects within the scene. The meters built into most 35mm reflex cameras are an enormous convenience; they are, unfortunately, the least accurate kind of meter of all, since they read reflected light only and most read it over the entire image area.

Reflected readings are easier and faster, which is why they're preferred by most 35mm still photographers. That's because the incident technique requires you to put the meter's surface in the position of the object being photographed and point the meter's cone at the camera position. Walking back and forth can be a bother; sometimes it's impossible. One compromise is to stand in a position getting the same light as the object and point the hemisphere in a parallel direction. That works well enough in outdoor scenes lighted by the sky; it doesn't work in indoor scenes lighted by uneven artificial light or on nighttime streets.

One reflected light technique that permits very accurate settings is to use a spotmeter to take readings from the darkest and brightest parts of the scene in which detail matters and set the lens and shutter somewhere between those extremes. This is the basis of the "zone system" developed by photographer Ansel Adams.

Incident readings are generally used in filming applications. Motion picture photography must have greater image consistency than still photography if scenes of the same person will intercut without annoying shifts in apparent skin tones. (A few cinematographers, such as Nestor Almendros, use incident level meters and trust their eye to balance the scene properly. This requires a very experienced eye, which Almendros surely has: he was cinematographer for *Claire's Knee, Days of Heaven, Kramer vs. Kramer,* and *Sophie's Choice.* See Almendros, 1984:11.) Incident readings are also preferred in critical still applications, such as photographing small objects close up or duplicating documents such as letters or photographs.

If you don't have a separate meter and if you're taking photographs of important documents or images with a 35mm camera, protect yourself by bracketing with two stops in either direction. Some people suggest always bracketing everything, meter or no. That means you take three shots of everything. There's nothing wrong with bracketing, though it does waste film, but I find it impractical. If you're shooting people in action there usually isn't time to photograph everything three times. My advice is to learn how to expose properly.

(A friend in Paris told me that when Giscard d'Estaing became premier, he asked the famous photographer Jacques Lartigue to take his official portrait photograph. Lartigue was reluctant: he didn't do portraits. The premier was insistent: Lartigue was, he said, France's greatest living photographer, so who else should take the official picture? Lartigue agreed. He arrived at the premier's office one day carrying a single 35mm camera and his exposure meter. The premier was puzzled. Other portrait photographers had lots of cameras, lots of gadgets. Lartigue shrugged. He took his meter reading, focused, snapped off a single frame, then headed for the door. The premier asked if he weren't going to take more pictures. "Why?" Lartigue said. "I already took the picture.")

A hand-held reflected light meter reads the total light in its field of view. This angle will rarely be the same as is seen by the camera lens. The behind-the-lens meters built into most 35mm reflex cameras have the advantage of always seeing what the lens is seeing. They make zoom photography possible. If a zoom lens is on the camera and you move it in and out, you'll see the meter indicator in the viewfinder shift as the average light in the frame becomes lighter or darker.

Most behind-the-lens meters are averaging meters: they take light readings in several parts of the frame and give you an overall reading. That works fine for average subjects, but it can be disastrous if there's significant variation. A dark person against a bright background will have little facial detail in the photograph. Some meters are center-weighted: they count more heavily the reading in a small circle in the center of the frame. The best technique with those is to center the small circle on the part of the scene that matters most, set your camera for that, then recompose the photograph and ignore the shifting indicator. If you have a zoom lens mounted on the camera, zoom in and take the reading from the objects of primary interest, then zoom out and recompose the image but don't change the aperture setting. If your camera is fully automatic—good luck.

However automated your SLR's meter, you must sometimes take charge. If you've ever done exactly what the camera's meter told you to do at the beach or in the snow, or if you've tried to photograph a performer on stage, you've probably learned that automation doesn't solve all your problems. Meters are built to render the world in a shade called *18 percent grey*. If you use the reflected light reading taken off a black card and set your camera as the meter tells you, the card will appear grey on a normally developed print; if you take the reading off a white card and do what the meter tells you, the white card will appear the same color of grey in a normally developed print. When you try to take a picture in snow or at the beach, the meter sees all that glare and it heads for 18 percent grey; when the sand or snow is grey, skin tones are nearly black. When you try to take a picture of the performer on the stage, the meter sees all the black areas not in the spotlight and tries to turn them 18 percent grey; when they come up to grey, your performer bleaches out.

Whenever your subject doesn't consist of an average range of light values, make an adjustment. If your subject is predominantly dark, close down a stop, which will keep the camera from overexposing it; if your subject is predominantly light, open up a stop, which will keep the camera from underexposing it. If you're taking a portrait, move in close and take the meter reading from the skin. If the subject is Caucasian, open up one stop from what the 18 percent of grey–seeking meter tells you to do (since average Caucasian skin is about 35 percent reflectance); if the subject is dark-skinned, close down one stop, and if the subject is extremely dark-skinned close down two stops.

Some cameras with built-in meters have a *back light adjustment.* This attempts to correct exposure when bright light is behind a subject, which means the surface of the subject facing you is in shadow and therefore needs more exposure than the meter thinks. Back-lighted subjects generally need at least one stop of additional exposure, sometimes more. If you don't increase exposure, the film will render them in silhouette.

Some meters give their readings directly in f/stops. You set them for the speed of the film you're using and the shutter speed you want and they read out directly with the lens aperture number. Since film cameras at sync speed have a shutter speed of about 1/50 per second, some light meters made specifically for filmmakers (such as the Spectra Pro) are designed to give this kind of readout. Most meter users are exposing film in still cameras, and those have a range of possible f/stops and shutter combinations. With the same amount of available light, the same light will reach the lens with any of these settings: 1/30 second and f/3.5, 1/60 second and f/2.8, 1/120 second and f/2, and so on. Double the speed of the shutter, halve the light passing through the lens.

Most hand-held light meters have concentric scales from which the aperture/shutter combination is selected. The meter is first adjusted for the EI of the film being used. Then the moving dial is turned to whatever exposure level is indicated by the meter needle. One of the concentric scales is stationary, the other moves when the exposure level is set. One scale is calibrated in f/stops, the other in apertures. If the camera is set at any of the combinations the film will, in theory, be properly exposed.

Some meters, such as the Weston Master V (which is no longer available, alas) and the Spectra Pro draw all their power from the light hitting their selenium cell. Such meters are wonderful for general use and have the virtue of one less battery to worry about, but they're not very good in extremely low light levels, and with the great speed of modern films and lenses, you might very well find yourself shooting in such levels without a flash. In such cases you need a meter with an amplifier to magnify the small amount of energy reaching the cadmium sulfide photovoltaic cell. That's what the meter battery in your 35mm camera is for—only a tiny amount of light actually reaches the cell, and the cell itself is tiny, so the signal must be amplified in order to give you an accurate reading and move the indicator in the viewfinder.

You choose on the basis of what you want or need. If you want a sharp image of a moving object, you determine how fast a shutter speed you need to capture it sharply, then see what f/stop is opposite that shutter speed on the ring. If you know you need a certain f/stop to get depth of field, see what shutter speed is opposite that f/stop on the ring.

Like every other piece of equipment, the meter you select should depend on the kind of work you're going to do. If you have to work fast and don't want to think about photographs much, trust the meter built into your camera (but take care to stop down or open up in those beach, snow, or stage scenes, and to compensate for light and dark skin tones). If you're going to use an internal meter, take some time to experiment with it before you go out in the field.

When I write "experiment" I don't mean shoot a roll of film and see how it turns out. I mean deliberately shoot pictures of several different kinds of scenes, such as light subjects against dark backgrounds, dark subjects against light backgrounds, light subjects against slightly lighter or darker backgrounds, front-lighted subjects, back-lighted subjects, and so on. Bracket each shot by at least one setting in either direction, and—most important if this is to be of any use—write down the setting and lighting situation for each frame. Be sure to indicate in your notes which setting was given to you by your meter. Then have the roll printed and get not only prints but a good contact sheet. Prints alone won't tell you where you're going wrong and where you're going right because a lab may compensate in the printing for a too-dense or too-thin negative and give you a better print than you deserve. The contact sheet will let you know which settings give you the best negative to start out with, hence which negatives will give you the best enlargements later.

Photographing Documents

To photograph documents—photographs, letters, certificates, and such—the light should be evenly balanced across the document and should strike the document in a way that it doesn't bounce up into the lens barrel causing unwanted glare. The usual way to handle this is by using two lights, one on either side, pointing down at the document from a 45° angle. If you're shooting black and white, you can use any kind of lamps; if you're shooting color, make sure that the lamp temperature matches the color temperature of the film (white lights for tungsten, blue lights for daylight) or you may change the color of the document in your photograph.

The best way to check for even illumination is by sliding an incident light meter with a flat light collector across the area to be photographed. If the light level doesn't change by more than 1/2 f/stop you'll be all right, though it would be better if there were no change at all. If one side is brighter than the other, you can even things out by moving one of the lights closer to or farther from the object.

If you're relying on the camera's meter to set the exposure, you'll have to check the balance by eye. Because the eye is capable of handling such a wide range of light levels at once, that's not easy. The best thing to do in such circumstances is try to have both lamps in the same kind of reflector, the same wattage, and the same distance from the object plane.

If there's a lot of black or white in the document being photographed (a photo album page, say, or a letter) the camera's meter will give you a distorted reading. If the page is predominantly white, open up one or two stops from what the meter tells you (if the meter says f/16, shoot at f/11 or f/8); if the page is predominantly dark, stop down one or two stops from what the meter tells you (if the meter says f/8, shoot at f/11 or f/16). In any case, bracket all your exposures at least 1 f/stop on either side, preferably 2 f/stops. A two-stop bracket means you'll shoot each document five times. Bracketing is a bother, but a greater bother is better than getting a photograph of a wonderful letter that prints up as being written on dull grey paper, or a photograph of a family photograph that has none of the original detail. Film is cheap; getting back to the field to do it again isn't.

Weather

You can take pictures in any kind of weather. Modern cameras are built to function in extreme heat and extreme cold. There are only three things you should watch out for.

—Extreme cold weakens batteries and may make film brittle. If you're going to be filming outdoors in the cold, keep your extra film and an extra set of meter batteries in an inside pocket, and carry your camera inside your jacket whenever possible. Some meters read a little low in extreme cold. If you're going to be doing a lot of work outdoors in the winter, find out about your meter's special responses to cold.

—Static electricity sometimes develops when it's cold and very dry. In such conditions, wind your film slowly, otherwise you may get streaks on the negative from static discharge.

—Coming from a cold place to a warm place may result in condensation on your equipment. The problem doesn't happen in the winter, when the indoors tends to be dry however warm it is, and the problem doesn't much matter with a tape recorder, but it can cause serious problems with a camera. Condensation usually occurs in the summer when you go from an air-conditioned environment to an environment that isn't air-conditioned. Your lens and viewfinder will fog up and you may even get internal condensation on one or two frames of film and on the reflex mirror. Don't change lenses before the camera body warms up. I sometimes carry with me Ziplock plastic bags. If I'm in an air-conditioned building and my cameras have gotten cold, I'll put them in a Ziplock and squeeze out as much air as possible. When I go outside again, I try not to take them out until they've warmed up to the ambient conditions. If I didn't use the plastic bag I'd risk internal condensation even if I weren't taking pictures right away.

13/Stills

Camera Types

Still cameras are generally classified in terms of their viewing and focusing systems, as follows.

Single-lens reflex: the same lens is used for focusing as for exposing the film. A mirror directs the image to the eyepiece during focusing, then is moved out of the way during exposure, which is why these cameras are so bulky and noisy. SLR cameras, such as the Nikon F3, can use zoom or variable focus lenses and there's no problem with parallax. The principal reason for the great popularity of SLRs is their ability to use a built-in light meter (behind-the-lens meter, or BTL) that takes reflected light readings from exactly the area being seen by the lens.

Rangefinder: a separate optical system is used for focusing. If the camera accepts interchangeable lenses, different frames come into view within the viewfinder when lenses of different focal lengths are in place. Rangefinder cameras are extremely quiet (they don't have the SLR's mirror slamming up and down), light (they don't need the mechanism for moving that mirror), and easy to focus (especially in dim light). Because the picture-taking lens and the viewing lens are slightly separated, there may be problems in exact framing at very close distances, a discrepancy called *parallax*. More expensive viewfinder cameras, such as the Leica M-4, shift the location of the viewfinder image slightly to compensate when the lens is focused at short distances. Rangefinder cameras cannot easily accommodate BTL meters, nor can they utilize zoom lenses or permit preview of depth of field. The Leica M-4 is the best 35mm viewfinder camera available. Many inexpensive pocket cameras are rangefinder cameras. Most of these have built-in meters and most have automated exposure or speed settings. Even when I'm taking my good cameras along, I often carry one of these because they permit me to point and shoot, which is nice when there isn't time to do any metering. Their greatest advantages are their speed and their size and weight—they fit easily into a jacket pocket. Also, they're cheap enough so it's not a major loss if one is broken or stolen.

Twin-lens reflex: uses one lens for exposing the film and another lens with a reflex mirror for focusing. TLRs such as the Rolleiflex and the Mamiya 330 use negatives several times the size of 35mm negatives (their normal lens is 80mm). The ones that support interchangeable lenses are built so the shooting and the viewing lenses are removed and inserted at the same time.

View: the image is viewed on a ground glass that's located in the film plane itself. These cameras use sheet film in holders. After focusing is completed, the film holder is inserted, the film covering sheet is taken out, the exposure is made, the sheet is reinserted in the frame, then the frame is removed from the camera. (SLRs also focus on a ground glass, but not in the film's actual position.) These cameras tend to be slow, bulky, and heavy. Because they can use larger negatives (4 × 5-inch view cameras are common; 8 × 10-inch view cameras are available; in theory any size view camera can be made), they can make the sharpest prints.

Automated Cameras

Some SLRs are fully or partly automated—you set the aperture, they set the shutter speed; you set the shutter speed, they set the aperture—and some just do the whole thing themselves unless you tell them not to. Most better cameras, whatever their automation, let you take over when you're not photographing the "average" situation the camera's computer is designed to handle. Some cameras even have autofocus: just point and shoot. (Be careful with that gadget: if you're taking a picture of a dancer and there's a mountain in the background, the dancer must be in the part of the viewing frame that sets the focus, else the mountain will be in focus and the dancer will be a blur. It doesn't take a dancer and a mountain: things can get screwed up with other pairs of objects as well.)

The advertisements for automated cameras promise so much I half expect that the next generation won't even need photographers. Nikon, for example:

Until recently . . . to use a Nikon you had to focus it yourself. . . . With the Nikon One-Touch and Nice-Touch you can now get Nikon 35mm picture quality without focusing. These Nikons also do a lot of other things that may surprise you.

For instance, you don't have to thread the film, advance the film, set the exposure, or rewind the film with the One-Touch or Nice-Touch. It's all done automatically.

. . . Both Nikons have a built-in flash. So you don't have to worry about missing a great picture when shooting indoors. The One-Touch even has a flash that pops up automatically under low- light conditions. (*Newsweek,* 21 May 1984, p. 34)

And Olympus:

It *automatically* loads the film, *automatically* advances to the first frame, *automatically* sets the exposure, and *automatically* winds to the next frame. In fact, when you're finished shooting a roll of film, the Quick Flash even rewinds it, *automatically.* (*Newsweek,* 21 May 1984, p. 44)

And Vivitar:

The smart camera for no-think photography. The micro-computer that loves to take pictures. Decision-free. Worry-free. The snapshot-simple way to great 35mm pictures.

Autofocus and auto-exposure, of course. But that's just the beginning. TEC35 has Smart Flash. . . . Smart Flash knows when it's needed, knows when it's not. Try to take an under-exposed picture. You can't. Smart Flash motors up, does its job and drops back into the camera. Beautifully. Automatically.

. . . TEC35 makes film loading a pleasure. It feeds the film and rewinds it at the end—all automatically. (*New York Times,* 9 May 1984)

Fully automatic cameras are nice if you're shooting from the hip or if things will happen so fast you won't have time to think about what settings you'll want or need. All the automatic cameras have one problem: if the batteries go dead you're out of business. Cameras with built-in meters but manual settings will still work when the meter battery dies (I change mine about once a year). If you're using an automatic camera, change the batteries before you go off on a field trip and be sure to carry spares at all times.

Not only is the operation of instant print cameras—currently made only by Polaroid—partly or fully automated, but so is the processing: you have finished prints within a few minutes. That means you know whether you've gotten the shot. You don't get very much else: a pretty picture, but you can't shoot very close (the lenses are wide-angle, so they're not good for portraits or close-ups) or very far away (the field of view is so wide you can't get much detail in distant objects); and you don't control the process as you do when printing from negatives or transparencies. But Polaroids are all right for what they do. (Sometimes Polaroids are just dandy. One of my favorite photographs in my personal collection is a Polaroid of my son taken by Walker Evans. Evans took three photographs in that sequence and they were like the porridge bowls at the house of the three bears: the picture of me was out of focus, the picture of Diane was distorted because he was too close for the lens, and the picture of Michael was just right.) When I'm doing a lot of photography I often bring along a Polaroid so I immediately can give pictures to the people I'm photographing and also make reference prints. I'll shoot Polaroids of everyone and write names on the set of prints I'm keeping, then I won't confuse names later on.

Motor Drives

Almost all quality 35mm SLRs accept motor drives, devices which advance the film and cock the shutter automatically after each shot and permit very rapid rewinding after the roll is completed. Most motor drives permit the photographer to shoot a rapid sequence of frames simply by holding the shutter release down. The Nikon motor drive, for example, goes up to six frames per second: it will expose a thirty-six-exposure roll in about six seconds.

Motor drives are great for sports photography (if you want to capture the moment a diver slices into the water, say) but they're rarely necessary for the kind of photography fieldworkers do. They have two significant disadvantages: they add weight to the camera and they make a great deal of noise. SLRs are already heavy and noisy enough.

Motor drives are useful for some left-eyed photographers who want to be able to shoot quickly. Most people are right-eyed, so 35mm SLRs are designed with right-eyed people in mind. If you use your right eye to focus and you hold the camera properly, you won't have to move the camera away from your eye between shots. Left-eyed persons do have to move the camera away from their faces when advancing the film; if they don't, they risk jabbing their right thumb and the film advance lever into their right eye. Try it and you'll see what I mean. Because of this right-eye bias in camera design, many left-eyed photographers use a motor drive so they don't have to lose continuity in their shooting.

I'm left-eyed, so when I saw *Rolling Stone* photographer Annie Liebovitz quoted as saying she'd bought a motor drive because she was left-eyed and was tired of sticking her thumb in her eye, that was all the justification I needed. I went out and bought one for my Nikons. For a little while it was great fun: I fired off rolls of film like I was shooting a machine gun. Then I realized I was creating contact sheets with thirty-six nearly identical frames, and the likelihood of finding any good frames on those contacts was no greater (and probably a little less) than when I had to work and compose more slowly. The advantage in speed and continuity and freedom from occasional eye jabs didn't compensate for the increase in bulk, weight, and noise. I haven't used the motor drive in years.

Supporting the Camera

The proper way to hold an SLR is with the body of the camera resting on the palm and last three fingers of the left hand. Focus and adjust the aperture with the left thumb and forefinger; use your right thumb to advance the film, your right index finger to push the shutter release, and the rest of the right hand for lateral balance. This provides the most stable support and lets you take a sequence of pictures without having to move the camera from your eye (if you're right-eyed) or change the positions of your hands. If you hold the camera by the sides (the way most amateurs do), you risk blurry pictures if you're shooting at 1/60 second or slower, and you have to shift your hands to focus. Holding the camera the correct way isn't only easier, it's faster.

Sometimes a tripod can be a great help. Tripods let you get into the picture (using the automatic shutter release many 35mm cameras have) and, more important, they let you shoot at very slow shutter speeds, which means you can often photograph in natural light objects that would otherwise require either electronic flash or floodlights.

Artificial Light

I almost never use a flash in my work. Many photographers use them and they do very well. For the kind of photography I do, flash is just too intrusive. I'd rather forgo the light advantage in favor of lack of intrusion. (For the same reason I've shifted from Nikon reflex cameras to Leica M-4s in recent years: the Leica is far quieter, smaller, and lighter.)

Flash interferes with the fieldwork situation in three ways. First, flash intrudes on whatever is going on. The sudden brilliant light may temporarily blind anyone looking at it, and the use of the light calls immediate attention to the photographer. Second, unless you're very experienced you never know with flash what you're getting until you see the printed photograph. That's because for a microsecond flash alters the scene's balance of light. Someone standing near a window may be lighted by a mixture of room light, direct window light, and window light reflected off a wall or the floor. Flash is so powerful that it overwhelms some of those light sources, so the shadows and shadings created by the other kinds of light are all washed out. Even if you bounce flash off the ceiling or use a diffuser, you can't know before you see the print what your image will look like. (With a rangefinder camera you might get a brief glimpse of the washing out, but you never see it at all with an SLR because the flash goes off at the same time the mirror is up.) And third, flash is one more technical thing you have to worry about doing properly.

There's one situation in which I've found flash useful: outdoors in direct sunlight. Indoors, flash takes away shadows that give faces and objects their three-dimensional quality; outdoors, it takes away the sharp shadows in eye-sockets, under noses, and under lips caused by sunlight, and it's so weak, relative to the sun, that it doesn't destroy what shaping shadows exist. Ellen Stekert tells me she finds flash useful in photographing material objects such as gravestones because the light helps make the letters more visible on film. If I were using a flash for that purpose I would try to have it off the camera, pointing across the object at an angle in order to create shadows in the cuts and make the letters stand out clearly; shooting straight in with a flash might just wash the lettering out.

With a good lens and fast film you can get an image in just about any light you can see in. If you do use flash, remember that it always calls attention to you, and not just from the persons you're photographing but from anyone in the area. Consider the situation carefully and decide if the flash will really help as much as it might hinder. Be particularly careful about background: if someone photographed with a flash is anywhere near a wall, you may get an ugly black shadow hovering like an aura around your subject and you'll never know it until you get your prints from the lab. The only camera I always use a flash with is my Polaroid. That camera is designed to be used with its built-in flash and the film Polaroid makes is designed to see in terms of that flash.

The least disruptive way of shooting flash is by bouncing it. Vivitar and some other flash manufacturers have a bounce card attachment for their flash units. The unit holds a white card, the flash shoots up at the card, the card is angled at 45° so it sends the more diffused light forward in a horizontal plane. Unless you're in a room with very high ceilings, you can often get satisfactory results by angling the flash at a point on the ceiling about halfway between the subject and you. That can give you a diffused light that won't cause harsh shadows; neither will it cause the plane-flattening common to horizontal flash. It's almost always better to have the dominant light coming from a place higher than your subject anyway. That's how people are lighted by the sky and in most rooms during the day.

If you're bouncing flash off the ceiling and you're shooting in black and white, all you need concern yourself with is the amount of light reaching your subject. Some flash units have a sensor that points in the direction of the camera lens no matter what direction the flash unit is pointed in; others require you to compensate for the longer path of travel for the bounce. (For the settings, see the instructions that come with the flash unit.) Whenever you use bounce flash and you're shooting color film, be sure that the surface you're bouncing it off is white. If the color isn't white, your subject will pick up coloration from the reflected light.

Color negative and slide films for 35mm cameras are now available with EIs of 1,000—more than five stops faster than good old Kodachrome 25, nearly three stops faster than High Speed Ektachrome, and more than a full stop faster than black and white Tri-X. If the room light required you to shoot at f/1.4 and 1/15 second to make a shot with Ektachrome (which meant you couldn't do it without a tripod and a stationary subject), you can now make the shot at f/1.8 and 1/60 second—which you can do without a tripod and without a frozen subject. With the color negative, color slide, and black-and-white emulsions now available, and with the availability of laboratory processing that can double the manufacturer's exposure indexes, a fieldworker can shoot by candlelight and know printable negatives and projectable slides will result.

Sometimes what's attractive to the eye—the way people look at a candlit table, for example, or the tones of light in a room at dusk—may not be what the fieldworker needs. The fieldworker, presumably, isn't after photographs that will make for an art exhibition; rather, the fieldworker wants photographs that contain as much information as possible. If you feel the need for more light and want to be as unobtrusive about it as possible, think about raising the wattage of the "practicals," what filmmakers call light sources that are part of the scene—table lamps, overhead fluorescents, and such. If table lamps have in them 60-watt bulbs, try replacing them with 100- or 150-watt bulbs. You might even bring some floodlights of your own if you'll be photographing objects, or lights you can bounce off the walls and ceilings if you're going to be documenting people. (If you're going to be adding more than one 500-watt bulb to a line, be sure the circuit will handle it. And carry some replacement fuses in your camera bag just in case you blow your host's fuses.) The advantage of lights that are left in place and left on is that people quickly become used to the light level and ignore it, and the photographer can know exactly what the film is recording.

Taking Pictures

Old-time Hollywood directors used to introduce all scene changes with an "establishing shot"—a wide-angle shot of the entire scene that was shown before any of the close-ups or point-of-view shots. The wide-angle establishing shot gave the audience the information necessary to understand the physical relationships in the close-ups.

When you're working with a camera—still or movie or video—it's usually a good idea to do the same thing. If nothing else, the wide shot will later help you remember the relationship of objects and the relative sizes of objects. With film or videotape, and if I'm using a zoom lens, I set the lens as wide as it will go without distorting the image and do a slow 360° pan. I usually also do a longer, static, wide-angle shot of the area where most of my action will take place or where it has taken place. When I'm shooting 35mm stills, I try to shoot a sequence of overlapping pictures with a 35mm lens. That's not for showing anybody—it's for me, so I can reconstruct where I was a few years later when the memories aren't so fresh or reliable.

Taking good pictures requires thinking about what you're doing. I have a hard time audiotaping and photographing at the same time; I tend to screw up one or the other. If I'm working alone, I try to separate the two kinds of work, which is easier on me and easier on the people whose lives and property I'm trying to document.

Cameras are more intrusive than tape recorders for two reasons. First, they make more noise. Second, and more important, they get between you and everyone else. Every time you lift that camera to your eye your face disappears and that glass cyclops is facing whomever you were talking to. Most people don't mind your taking pictures, but they mind being taken over by the picture-taking event. So be tactful about it. Don't whip out a camera and start clicking away. If you're going to be taking pictures later, have the camera out so people know it's there and that you'll be using it. Don't interrupt your interviews to take pictures of the informant and don't wreck your interview by taking pictures of something else while your informant is talking to you. If you're doing a filmed interview, move the camera as little as possible. Few things are so distracting as seeing that lens wave back and forth while a conversation is going on. It's just like having a conversation with someone and having that person turn away and stare at someone elsewhere in the room. If you're shooting film or video, and if you're not certain where you want your transitions to come, it's probably better to keep the camera on the subject during the interview and pick up the other stuff later. The objects aren't going anywhere.

Whatever kind of camera I'm using, in addition to the photographs of people doing what they're doing and showing who they are, I do close-ups and extreme close-ups of objects—things that were made, doorknobs, photographs, hands, anything of possible interest. These shots provide detail not apparent in the wider shots, and in film and video they can provide valuable transition scenes useful in editing. I do more of those now than I used to. I used to photograph just the important objects or samples of classes of objects, then I realized that I couldn't know what was important in those brief and busy moments in the field, and I probably couldn't know what were the real classes of things until I'd had time to give the facts some thought.

I started taking more detailed pictures because of something Walker Evans said. Evans looked at a group of my photographs scheduled to go up in a show at the University of Texas. One image was of a young Arkansas convict sitting on a bed next to his lockerbox. The inside of the lockerbox top was a collage of photographs of the man's family, pictures clipped from magazines, and drawings.

"Was he the only one who did this?" Evans asked.

"No," I said. "Most of them decorate the lockerboxes like that."

"And you have other photographs of the lockerboxes?"

"Sure," I said. "I took several."

"I would have taken them *all*," Evans said.

14/Movies

Film and Video Equipment

Modern 16mm movie cameras produce far better images than the most sophisticated video equipment presently available. Sixteen-millimeter film can handle a wider range of light than any videotape; a film projected on a screen will deliver a wider tonal range than any television monitor. But that doesn't mean 16mm is always better than portable video for documenting a field situation. Sometimes a home video rig, the kind of VHS or Beta unit that has replaced Super-8 (or the 8mm equipment that will soon replace VHS and Beta) might be far preferable to 16mm. The maximum load a hand-carried 16mm camera can manage is 400 feet, or twelve minutes (there are 1,200-foot magazines for these cameras, but that makes them too heavy to hand-hold); home video equipment can record two hours without changing the tape. Unless you use magnetically striped film, which has its own problems, the sound and picture in 16mm are recorded separately, so editing and maintaining synchronization are a complicated affair. Video has the sound and picture on the same tape and can be operated by one person with ease. Quality editing for video, on the other hand, is far more expensive than for film. The basic machine for editing a documentary film is a six-plate flatbed; good ones can be purchased for $14,000 to $25,000 brand new. They last a long time—I was in a studio in Munich not long ago where twenty-year-old Steenbecks were still in daily use. No television studio uses twenty-year-old video equipment—it doesn't hold up that long and the technology doesn't remain in place that long. Tapes made on the best video equipment twenty years ago can't be played on any modern equipment, but Super-8 or 16mm or 35mm film shot on any film equipment twenty years ago can be projected by and edited on any modern equipment.

In the 1960s, portable audio recorders revolutionized the options open to the fieldworker. Instead of being dependent on heavy machinery with limited recording time, fieldworkers could document long performances in high-fidelity. In the 1980s, portable video recorders are having the same effect. For the first time fieldworkers can, with relatively little money or training, document whole events. Working alone or with one partner, they can make moving and sound records of almost any kind of behavior or event.

The technical quality of nonprofessional video equipment in the past decade has increased dramatically, and the weight and cost have declined equally dramatically. In 1973, $1,500 purchased a Sony Portapak, which recorded black-and-white sound videotape on 5-inch open reels of 1/2-inch tape; the camera came with a Canon manual zoom lens. In 1985, $1,500 purchased a VHS or Beta camera and deck capable of recording and playing color videotapes on 1/2-inch cassettes, with far better image, sound quality, and optics than the Portapak, and also with automatic focus (you can turn it off if you don't want to use it), power zoom, titling, and the ability to function as a video tuner as well. The new machines are capable of producing excellent color images in ordinary room light. They use cassette tapes which cost as little as $5 for two hours of recording time at their highest operating speed; the open-reel black-and-white Portapaks of a few years earlier used tapes that cost about $20 for thirty minutes of recording time—and keep in mind that 1986 dollars were worth less than half 1973 dollars. (A two-hour cassette contains the same amount of tape as a thirty-minute reel.)

By early 1986, several firms were manufacturing portable video *camcorders*—recorders built with the recording optics and electronics and the tape transport housed in one small, light unit. Some of these use 1/2-inch VHS tape cassettes; others use the new sophisticated 8mm videocassettes; excellent machines can be purchased for less than $1,500. Separates (cameras connected to recording decks) offer more options— such as titling and fading controls—but it's clear that within a few years camcorders will dominate the market. These very lightweight units are generally capable of working in very low light levels. Many of them weigh less than five pounds and perform in only one or two footcandles of illumination. With advances in digital recording technology and circuit miniaturization, the options for the fieldworker in the next decade should be spectacular. The 8mm video equipment (which uses Sony's Beta format) now available provides far better sound and video performance than the best of the 1/2-inch VHS and Beta equipment, and prices of 8mm equipment are already competitive. Many industry analysts predict that within a few years 8mm video will displace 1/2-inch VHS and Beta entirely. (The three formats can copy to and from one another without difficulty, so it's possible to transfer a tape made in one format to any of the others.)

The decision about what medium to use is based on the amount of money available, the technical skills available, and what's wanted. It may make economic and other kinds of sense to spend time making a good VHS, Beta, or 8mm videotape about a folklore event or performance when it's madness to spend the money, time, and energy documenting the same thing on film. Documenting an event on video may so restrict the ultimate applicability of the field recordings that it might be worth the time and effort to find the money and put together the team needed to record the event on film. Like all other decisions having to do with fieldwork, these choices are never made in the abstract.

The Nature of Videotape Information

Studio open-reel video equipment moves very fast and therefore consumes a great deal of tape. Such equipment is designed much like audio recorders: the tape moves across a stationary recording head and the information is encoded linearly. That studio technology was impractical for field video recording: news gatherers (the primary market for which video technology is designed) couldn't lug around the necessary bulky reels of tape and neither could they conveniently carry the large tape transports necessary to handle those reels. Studio video is still done on 1-inch and 2-inch open-reel machines, so another technology was developed for the needs of field units.

This technology was possible because of a simple fact: the quality of the electronic signal on a tape is determined by how much tape is "seen" by a recording or playback head for any unit of time. One way to increase the amount of information is by making the tape go faster (which is why in open-reel audio, 15-ips recorders give better fidelity than 7.5-ips recorders); another way is to widen the track (which is why studio video recording was for a long time done on 2-inch tape); another way is to control the tape path (which is why some cassette recorders are capable of performing so well). A fourth way, the one developed for portable video equipment, is to change the nature of the tape-to-head relationship. Portable video recorders—3/4-inch U-Matic professional decks, 1/2-inch VHS and Beta decks, and 8mm

Beta decks—use a principle of recording in which not only the tape moves but so do the recording and playback heads. The tape, instead of moving horizontally across the heads, moves around a drum within which the heads rotate rapidly; the tape path is inclined at a slight horizontal angle. The geometry engenders a method of recording called "helical scanning." The signal for any moment extends across a long diagonal line.

If you cut an audiotape vertically you get information for just one moment in time; if you make a vertical cut across a tape that has been scanned helically, you cut into the information for several moments in time (which is why such recordings cannot be edited by the cut-and-tape method common in audio).

Because of that long diagonal signal path, slowly moving videotape can contain an enormous amount of information. A VHS T120 videocassette, for example, which produces a two-hour recording in the standard play mode, moves at 1.345 ips—slower than an audiocassette which contains far less electronic information. In the four-hour mode, the VHS tape moves at 0.672 ips, and in the six-hour mode it moves at 0.448 ips. The Beta L750 tape moves at 0.80 ips in the standard three-hour mode and 0.0053 ips in the 4 1/2-hour mode. But because of the helical scan, which produces that long diagonal signal, the effective speed for both VHS and Beta is far greater. The Beta tape at standard speed, for example, has an effective head-to-tape speed that is much faster than any audio recorder made. A home videocassette deck, therefore, has the potential of recording audio sound with far greater fidelity than most audio recorders now available; it's possible that within a few years a single tape transport will serve as home audio and video recorder and playback machine, and will also be capable of storing massive amounts of computer programs and files. Right now those devices provide us the option of documenting an enormous range of events in great detail and at little cost.

Seeing

What you see in the viewfinder of a film or video camera and what the viewer sees on a screen aren't the same thing. If, say, you want to show a letter, your camera starts at the top and moves down across the lines, stopping at the bottom. When that footage is projected, the viewer will have no sense that the camera is moving down; rather, it will seem that the letter is moving up toward the top of the screen. This is easy enough to check and you don't have to expose film to do it. Just do the shot with no film or tape moving, and when you see

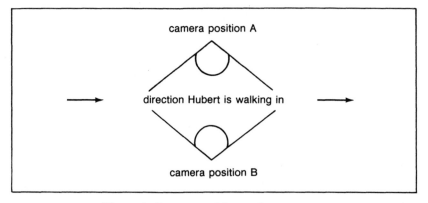

Figure 4. Camera position and movement.

the image moving across the viewfinder think of a *screen* rather than what you *know* is happening. If you want the viewer to know it's the camera moving, you must include in the shot something the viewer knows isn't moving—such as a desk top or some other object. The viewer, in fact, can't even tell in what direction something on the screen is moving unless other information is provided.

Imagine a man entering a room on your left, crossing the room, and exiting to the right. On film, he seems to move from left to right. If you were to film him from either door, you would know he was moving toward or away from you, but you wouldn't know which side of the room he was coming from or moving toward. If you were to film him from the other side of the room, he would be moving from right to left even though he was walking in exactly the same direction as before. That's because the notion of "right" and "left" are meaningful only in relation to something else. In film, they're meaningful from the position of the viewer. In real life, if you move to the other side of someone's path of action, you're not disturbed about the reversal of left and right because you know why that relationship has changed. In film, if the movement of the camera isn't clear, the change in direction is often confusing and annoying to a viewer.

The problem of consistency in movement is easily enough handled once you're aware of it. As long as the camera doesn't cross the line in which action is happening, the action will proceed normally. If the camera does cross that line, the action will reverse itself. In the scene depicted in Figure 4, a camera at position A will indicate Hubert is walking from right to left; a camera at position B will indicate he's walking from left to right. The trick is, always think in terms of a screen rather than in terms of what you're filming or even what you think you're seeing in the viewfinder. Video equipment now available permits you to just point and shoot; but if that's all you're doing, you'll make moving images that are perhaps amusing and perhaps interesting but not awfully useful. You always know more than the camera knows and you always see more than the camera sees. Be sure that what you put on film or videotape gives the viewer who comes along later enough information to understand what's going on.

Movement

Because you're making a moving picture, there's a great temptation to move the camera or zoom the lens. Resist the urge whenever you can; move the camera only when you have a reason for moving it. Pans and zooms and tilts are annoying unless there's a logical reason for them. The eye doesn't zoom, it selects. The telephoto capacity merely attempts to mimic the brain's ability to focus its attention on certain aspects of field of vision which are always the same width and height.

These are the ways film records motion:

—the subject can move across a stationary field of view (the camera doesn't move and the focal length of the lens doesn't change);

—the stationary camera can turn to follow the object as it moves across a horizontal field (*panning*);

—the stationary camera can follow the object as it moves across a vertical field (*tilting*);

—the focal length can be changed to longer or shorter settings (*zooming*);

—the càmera can move in relation to a stationary object or along with a moving object (*tracking*);

—neither the camera nor the subject move in the course of a single shot, but the juxtaposition of shots showing the subject in different positions implies movement (*editing*).

The best filmwork is the most transparent. That is, the viewer is conscious of *what* is filmed but not of the filming itself. A lot of unnecessary camera movement, a lot of unmotivated zooming in and out, merely calls attention to the camera operator; it detracts enormously from the attention a viewer can give to the real subject. (This isn't the same as saying you should hide your presence from the film; I'm speaking here of camera business that interferes with viewer understanding. I'll say more about revealing your own presence later.)

Every time you move the camera you should have a reason for moving it. Every time you change the focal length you should have a reason for changing it. The temptation to push those buttons is great, but remind yourself that zooming is always at least ten times more interesting in the viewfinder than it ever is on the playback screen. Look carefully at any movie you like. How many zoom shots do you see in it?

Professional camera operators who use zoom lenses use them because they're efficient: they're time-, labor-, and space-saving devices. The zoom lens means the camera operator doesn't have to carry a bunch of expensive prime lenses and doesn't have to spend time switching them for different shots. It's not the zoom that matters but what the lens is seeing after the zoom is completed. (Hollywood films are rarely made with zoom lenses, except for shots in which a zoom is required, and there aren't many of those. But Hollywood films are made with a lot of crew members and people to fetch and carry and load. Fieldworkers in folklore often work alone, or at best in small groups, so fieldworkers who use film or video cameras usually prefer the flexibility afforded by a good zoom lens.) There's little pleasure for a viewer in watching the scene get larger or smaller for no logical reason. Zoom only when you have a very good reason for it; otherwise, think of and use the zoom lens as several nonzoom lenses in one box.

Camera Supports

One kind of image movement is nearly always unwanted: movement caused by accidental shifting of the camera. This occurs most at long focal lengths when a slight movement of the front lens element results in a massive jump of the image recorded.

Most portable video cameras now available have zoom lenses with a 6:1 zoom ratio; a few have a 12:1 ratio. That means they go from wide-angle to telephoto. Having all those focal lengths available is a great convenience. It's also the source of great problems for inexperienced photographers, because the greater the focal length the more your body movements affect the image that reaches the tape or film. You won't notice any but the most violent shakes and jiggles in the viewfinder, but you'll notice them later when your subject bobs and weaves on and off the screen.

Here's why. Long focal lengths have very narrow fields of view, so slight movements of the front element of the lens are multiplied enormously. Moving 2° or 3° is no big deal when your lens is seeing a field 45° wide, but it's a massive dislocation when your lens is seeing a field 10° wide. Anyone who's ever fired a pistol knows that if the front sight moves only a fraction of an inch the bullet will miss by several feet a large target only twenty-five feet away. Rifles are more forgiving: move the muzzle of the rifle the same amount and you'll still hit the target. The fraction of an inch creates a much larger angle with the short pistol barrel than it does with the long rifle barrel. With a lens, telephoto has the problems of aiming a pistol and wide-angle has the accuracy of aiming a rifle. A wide-angle shot in which you move the camera 1/4 inch will produce a mildly annoying but not critically destroying bobble on the screen; a telephoto shot with the same shake will send the subject completely off the screen.

Professional camera operators use a support of some kind whenever they can. But, except at formal interviews and press conferences, news people don't have that luxury, so they rarely shoot telephoto when they're hand-holding their cameras. They're far more likely to move in close and shoot wide-angle if they want a close-up than they are to stand back and zoom in at 10:1. (That's why they appear so ghoulish when filming an accident.) Some camera operators are very good at hand-holding heavy cameras steadily for long periods of time; that takes a lot of practice and good physical conditioning.

If you use a video or film camera a fair amount, you'll get better and better at keeping it steady, but you'll always have difficulty shooting watchable film when you're using the longer focal lengths. That's not a fault of yours; as I said, even experienced camera operators can't always do it well. If you're going to do a lot of video or film shooting requiring long telephoto shots, use a support. There are several kinds: the shoulder of another person (not bad in an emergency if your friend doesn't twitch), monopod, shoulder pod, still camera tripod (terrible), spring-damped video tripod (better), fluid-head tripod (best).

Some camera operators prefer not to use any device at all when they use the camera on their shoulder because that slows the shift to and from a tripod—you have to lock in the shoulder device and take it off again. Sometimes the choice is based on characteristics of the camera operator's body or the camera being used. An operator using the Äaton 16mm camera, for example, needs no special shoulder support because the Äaton is designed so there's a natural and comfortable notch made by the way the magazine joins the camera body. Many 16mm cameras used for documentary work, such as the CP-16RA, have flat bottoms and can rest directly on a shoulder if the operator is strong (and has a slightly fleshy or muscular shoulder; thin camera operators with bony shoulders can experience a great deal of discomfort after several hours spent shouldering that seventeen-pound metal machine). Frenzel makes a double body brace for hand-held filming: large curved hooks fit over each shoulder and the camera rests on a bracket on the operator's chest. The device provides a great deal of stability, but men who are overweight (like me) find it moves up and down with their breathing (which makes for a lousy film image: the horizon moves as if you were on a boat slowly rocking at sea) and women with large breasts often find the vertical front bars extremely uncomfortable. The most common shoulder support is a C-shaped piece of metal with padding on the shoulder side and a bracket for the camera on the other side; this type is made by several manufacturers. Victor Duncan manufactures what is probably the simplest shoulder pod: a beanbag that attaches to the underside of the camera. It cushions the shoulder and provides far more stability than the plain camera bottom, and it takes up little room and adds little weight to the equipment box.

If you're going to be doing hand-held camerawork, practice without film first. Learn how to move your body rather than the camera. That makes for a smoother movement and doesn't get you into positions where your muscles start vibrating or get cramped. Pay attention to your breathing: hold the camera so that it doesn't move as your chest moves. As you're holding the camera don't think how well you're managing; think how the image you're seeing in the viewfinder will appear on a screen. You tend to think the camera is moving and the image is remaining still (which is the case), but when projected, that jiggly footage makes the image move—because the movie or video screen is always still.

You also have to worry about keeping the horizon level. If you tilt the camera just a few degrees it will make the world on your screen seem to be running uphill or downhill. Force yourself to check verticals now and then—trees, telephone poles, sides of buildings. And, again, think in terms of how they're going to look on the screen. Professional film camera tripods all have spirit levelers so the tripod's head can be perfectly oriented in vertical and horizontal planes. If the head isn't oriented, pan shots (when the camera moves horizontally) will make the image seem to be moving along an inclined plane. This problem doesn't exist with still photography because each shot has its own composition; in film the unit is the scene, not the shot. Movies are far prettier and far more informative, but they're far harder to do correctly.

Light Sources

In color photography windows present two problems: not only does the light coming through them change rapidly in intensity, but it also changes rapidly in color. Window light, as Vermeer taught us, can be beautiful, but Vermeer wasn't making movies. For people making movies window light can mean a lot of extra work. If someone is lighted entirely or primarily by window light, you can shoot film for a large portion of the day with only slight changes in aperture and much of the footage of the person will intercut. But the window will show dramatic changes in the lighting outside. Often, window light that permits you to shoot at f/2.8 inside will result from an outside level that requires f/16 or f/22, so if you expose properly for your indoor subject the outside world will burn out. Many filmmakers like to keep the outside about two stops brighter than the inside. That reduces detail enough so the outside doesn't intrude on the indoor scene and because outside should seem brighter than inside. But a difference of four or five stops will make the window an annoying and intrusive element.

If you're shooting video you can check what's happening immediately. If the outside is burning out and it's annoying, you might try reframing the shot so the window isn't in it. Be careful of shots that require you to pan across windows when you're using video cameras because the sudden brightness will kick up the automatic aperture settings and your image inside the room will momentarily go dark. Be especially careful of small bright light sources, such as lamps or very shiny surfaces, since these can produce *comet-tailing*—images that continue briefly on the screen when the camera pans past them.

If you're shooting color film and the sources of illumination are mixed (incandescent, daylight, fluorescent, etc.), you have two choices: go with the dominant source and expect some weirdness here and there, or filter the light sources so they all emit the right color temperature. B&W incurs none of this busywork. You just take the reading, set the aperture, and take the picture. Almost all portable video cameras have a "white balancing" function: they generate internally a signal that would produce white, compare it to the dominant light source, and adjust the electronics accordingly. The basis for this is the fact that white is composed of all other colors; if white is recorded correctly, the component colors will likewise be recorded correctly. It may be that the dominant light in the main part of the shot is from a different kind of source than light in another part of the shot. You might have, for example, a scene in a room lighted by tungsten lights and a corridor lighted by fluorescent is visible in the background. If, while the white balance is set for tungsten, someone moves through the fluorescent area, that person's skin will take on a greenish tint. There's no way around it, short of filtering the lights, just as you might when shooting in color film. Minor distortions of this type rarely bother a viewer anyway.

Most manipulation of light source takes place when the documentation is being done with color film. If, for example, you're working in a small room with one or two windows, you might gel the windows (cover them with transparent 85 filter sheets) to bring the outdoor light down to 3,200°; this will permit you to use tungsten or quartz lights without filtering the lights or the camera. If you use the windows unfiltered and have to filter the lights, you lose a great deal of light because those blue gels cut output by the equivalent of two stops, and in addition you must use an 85 filter on the lens, which reduces the effective speed of the film. (If you had film rated at EI 100 in the camera, the 85 filter brings that EI down to 64. If the lights let you shoot at f/5.6 unfiltered, covering them with blue gels will force you to open up to f/2.8, which means significant loss in depth of field.)

There's another reason for going with 3,200° when possible: the color and brightness of outside illumination change rapidly, not just from passing clouds but from the passage of the sun in the sky. If you're filming in a room for several hours, your eye probably won't notice any significant changes, but the differences will be striking if you have to intercut footage from different parts of the day, or if you try to intercut footage from different days. If you've been shooting with 3,200° as your primary light source, the slight changes outside the filtered window won't be obtrusive. Some photographers and cinematographers like the difference between the cool outside light and the warmer tungsten light indoors, but if the difference in intensity is very great, the outside will just seem washed out.

When using lights remember the inverse square law mentioned earlier in connection with sound, because the same relationship between intensity and distance obtains with light. Move a light from four feet to eight feet away and the amount of light hitting any area of your subject becomes a quarter of what it was; cut the distance from the light in half and the amount of light hitting the same area of your subject increases by a factor of four. That means you can often get the light you need simply by moving lights already in place a little closer (or moving what you're photographing a little closer to the light source), and you can correct an imbalance in light by moving the subject away from the strong light and closer to the weak light. If your subject will be moving about, don't have the lights too close or you'll get changes in illumination level great enough to range from under- to overexposure.

Sync

Sound for film soundtracks is recorded in one of two ways: on magnetic stripes that are part of the film (called *single-system*) or on separate tape recorders (*double-system*). Double-system generally produces better sound and gives more options in editing; single-system offers the advantage of always being perfectly in synchronization, since the sound is placed on the film at the exact moment it's being recorded. Because two objects can't occupy the same space at the same time, the picture in the film gate (the frame being exposed) is twenty-six frames behind the frame going past the camera's recording head. If you want to cut that film, you lose sound twenty-six frames (slightly over a full second) ahead of where you make the cut. If you want to edit it, the usual practice is to transfer the soundtrack to a separate magnetic track and edit the two in the usual fashion.

Not all 16mm sound films are made in sync (when the sound you hear and the event you see represent the same event and occur simultaneously). Many earlier documentaries were shot silent and sound was added later. Sometimes soundtracks consist of *wild sound*—sound recorded at the event filmed (or one like it) but not synchronized to the picture. The combat sections of the excellent British film series narrated by Lawrence Olivier, *The World at War,* for example, consist almost entirely of silent film to which wild sound, sound effects, and narration were added. Most World War II combat footage was silent because the technology at that time didn't permit easy recording of sound and picture simultaneously. Most combat footage of Vietnam, on the other hand, is sync, because it was done on film cameras with mag stripe (single-system) or on video (where sound is part of the same signal). Fieldworkers making films may do some of their work in sync (interviews, performances) and some of it without sound (shots of objects, close-ups of performers, etc.).

Single-system cameras were common in Super-8 equipment and in 16mm news cameras. News stations liked them because a single operator could capture sound and picture at the same time; the film could be developed and then shown on the air as soon as it dried since the developing process didn't hurt the magnetic track. Both are pretty much obsolete now. Super-8 has been replaced by portable 1/2-inch and 8mm video equipment (which doesn't give as good an image but is far easier and cheaper to use), and the 16mm camera has been replaced by various kinds of electronic news-gathering (ENG) equipment.

Before the mid-1970s, the movie cameras and tape recorders of filmmakers working in double-system had to be physically connected by an electronic cable so the same pulse signal regulated the speed of both machines. For the past decade location work has been done with crystal-controlled cameras, which run sync film at exactly twenty-four

frames per second, and audio tape recorders with a special synchronizing signal recorded so the tape can later be played back at exactly
the speed of the original recording. Getting rid of the umbilical hookup
greatly increased filmmakers' flexibility, but it meant that there always
had to be some mechanical way of putting a signal on the film and
the tape showing where each began for a particular scene. (When they
were hooked up, the camera operator could push a button that put a
beep on the soundtrack and also flashed a frame of film.)

The familiar slateboard or clapstick does just that: the clapstick is
held in front of the camera and the upper blade brought down sharply.
The editor later marks on the soundtrack the point where the sound
is first heard and lines that up with the frame of the film where the
blade stops being blurry; the rest of the shot (assuming the equipment
worked properly) is then in sync. There are small electronic devices
that can accomplish the same ends. The one I use plugs into the microphone jack on the tape recorder and the microphone plugs into it.
At the start of a scene, Diane points the beeper at the camera and
pushes a button, which causes a strobe on the beeper to fire at the
same moment that a brief beeping sound is fed into the recorder. The
device is passive throughout the rest of the shot; the microphone's
signal just passes through it as if it weren't there. (The disadvantage
of the beeper is that the camera operator must be able to see the
recordist. The mike and the recordist are not always in the same place
at the same time, or it may be inconvenient to swing the camera to
where the recorder happens to be. In such cases it may be easier to
find the mike in the viewer and use one of the other methods—such
as the clapstick or the tapping or clapping techniques noted below.)

Recent equipment innovation simplifies syncing even more. Users
of the Äaton 16mm camera can have their camera and Nagra fitted
with *clear time coding* devices so that after the film is processed and
the mag track run through a special head, both have along their edges
exact real time markings. That means the tape recorder and the camera
can start, stop and run entirely independently of each other. The photographer can start and stop whenever he or she wishes and the footage
can be easily and accurately synced later. The method is especially
useful for multiple camera applications, which previously required
separate slating of each camera, and for location situations where the
sound recordist and camera operator cannot maintain eye contact with
one another, or for situations in which the filmmaker cannot afford
to intrude on the action.

In the field, any slating can do. The simplest is to hold the mike in
camera view and tap it with a pencil. If you're going to do that, be

sure your tape recorder's automatic limiter is off, or else you may not even hear the tap, and be sure that you have the pencil going in a plane *perpendicular* to the front-to-back axis of the camera, since that gives the camera the longest view of the pencil's movement. If you're not holding the microphone, you can have someone who is in the shot and within hearing range of the mike clap hands once or twice.

The camera at sync speed goes at exactly twenty-four frames per second. Within certain limits the actual speed of the tape recorder doesn't matter, so long as a sync signal is recorded on it. There are various systems for recording sync signals, but they all have the same function: to indicate to a device called a *resolver* the speeds at which the tape should move on playback to reproduce exactly what it heard when it was recording. If that's done, it will produce a signal that exactly parallels the fixed twenty-four frames per second of the film, and the combined picture and sound tracks will be in synchronization.

The process goes like this. In the field you shoot your film and record on your tape recorder. The audiotape has on it whatever sync signal your system utilizes. Back in the lab that tape is fed to the recording head of a tape recorder that uses 16mm fullcoat—16mm film that has a coating of magnetic oxide rather than film emulsion. The fullcoat is transported by a recorder with sprockets, like movie film, rather than a recorder with capstans, as is the case with ordinary sound recorders. The resolver is hooked up to one of the output channels of the tape recorder and it feeds a signal back into that same tape recorder. The resolver reads the signal it's receiving and adjusts the speed of the playback recorder so that signal fits a certain pattern. If in the field the recorder sped up slightly at one point, the resolver will make it speed up slightly at exactly the same point in playback; if in the field the recorder slowed down for two minutes, the resolver will slow it down for two minutes. The sprocketed tape recorder carrying the fullcoat moves at constant speed. It hears the signal corrected by the resolver, a signal that matches in real time what happened on location.

The original tape is now placed in storage and the rest of the process uses the tape produced on the sprocketed recorder. That tape moves, on record and in playback, at exactly the same speed as the camera at normal sync speed—twenty-four frames per second, forty feet per minute. In 16mm there's a sprocket hole in the film for each frame of film. One frame cut out of the film is equal to one frame (the space from one sprocket hole to the next) cut out of the sound tape. If the mag tape and the picture roll are placed in a Moviola upright editing machine or on a flatbed editor, and if the clapper sync point on the film is put into the frame showing on the screen and the frame of the sound tape with the sync signal on it is placed at the sound head, then the two transports can be electronically locked together so each moves forward or backward in frame-by-frame parallel and the two will be in perfect synchronization for the remainder of the shot. The editing machine can run one frame at a time or at high speed or at sync speed, and it can run forward or backward; so long as it's working properly, those two rolls will remain in sync.

If all this sounds terribly complicated—well, it is, at least until you've done it a few times. More of a problem is the sheer cost of equipment and labs and editing, and those costs are coming down rapidly. The great advantage of the new video technology is that it offers us the ability to preserve color moving images with high-quality soundtracks at relatively low cost with machines that are relatively easy to use. It will, I suspect, be decades before our imagination catches up with the opportunities provided by the available equipment. Recording technology has, at every phase, changed radically the ways folklorists and anthropologists have defined their work. That process will continue, but at an ever-accelerating rate.

The Pace of Images

My colleague Leslie Fiedler told a Sun Valley conference audience a few years ago that younger people now watch so many movies and so much television they have eyes that are far more educated than the eyes of people of his generation. Fiedler at the time was in his early sixties.

I agreed with him for a few minutes then decided I didn't agree at all. People who have grown up in the past thirty years have watched film more than people of Fiedler's generation and they've watched film and video more than people of my generation (I was born in 1936; you had to leave the house to see a movie). But having watched and being educated to see are two very different things. I think that television teaches us *not* to see well at all. It also does something else; I'm not sure what, but seeing well isn't it.

The operator of a movie camera has the power to direct your eye. The operator can focus on a narrow plane, zoom in on a specific detail, follow one object to the exclusion of all others. You can do this too; in fact, you do it all the time: if you follow a person moving toward you through a crowd or moving away from you across a field, you're concentrating on that person even though the mass of detail in your vision includes thousands of other objects and movements. The difference in the video or film situation is that movement and selection are done for you; you see through someone else's eyes (the camera operator's) and at someone else's pace (the editor's). You're a passenger, not an observer. And that's not necessarily bad. Some filmmakers see very well and you can learn a lot joining in their looks. But you should know what's happening, and you should be aware of the process and control it when you're making images for the later use of others.

The chances are very good that television has trained you never to look at anything for very long. Learning the pace of images from television is like learning how to design a meal by eating at McDonald's or Burger King. Nothing on commercial television is there for more than a few seconds. Watch a commercial or music video and count the number of image cuts and figure out how long each one lasted. Watch a television drama and count the number of times an image is held for even a full minute. Watch a football game and count the cuts in the coverage of a single play. Modern American films have much faster cutting than films of even a decade ago—one impact of catering to a television-trained audience. People seem to need it fast and quick; they seem to get bored if several balls aren't in the air at once.

I recently showed a group of people Leni Riefenstahl's *Triumph of the Will*. The film begins almost leisurely: an airplane's slow passage and slower descent through the clouds. The rhythm is powerful and compelling, but you must submit to it if it's to work. Audiences of the 1930s did that easily (look at a movie made in that decade on late-night TV sometime; they have many shots lasting more than a minute). If a film like *Triumph of the Will* were made now, the opening plane sequence would probably take no more than thirty seconds.

I mention all this here because that incredible boredom with anything that hangs in vision for more than a few seconds has a tremendous influence on the kind of filming done by young filmmakers and videographers. That rapid pace is perfectly appropriate if you're making a dramatic film or music video; but if you're doing folklore or ethnology, it's perfectly wrong.

You may have to force yourself to keep your hands off the camera once it's started. Sometimes the most useful footage from a field situation isn't the prettiest (what would go on television) but the longest— the shot that shows an entire event: an entire song from beginning to end, the making of a whole pot, the telling of a whole story, with the camera trained on the performer the entire time. Audience reactions are important, but every time you cut away from the performer to the audience you're changing the story being told by your film. Time through the lens passes much more quickly than time watching the footage later. Until you've had a great deal of experience working with field videotapes or field film, always let the camera roll longer than you think it should; excess footage can be cut or ignored later.

Film and video equipment take the fieldworker out of the scene. They require so much attention that you can be nothing but full observer and outsider when you're using them. When you're filming, it's terribly difficult to pay attention to anything but the subject and the operation of your camera. That means you can't, when filming, do much subtle observation or much deep thinking. Film and video are wonderful tools for the fieldworker, permitting us to preserve kinds and quantities of information we could never before preserve, but they also make us more distant from what we're watching than any other kind of instrument we've ever had at our disposal.

Use them, but use them with care and caution. I said earlier that it's best to work with the simplest method of documentation you can manage. Each stage of documentation complexity provides more information for later examination and simultaneously draws the fieldworker further from the world he or she is trying to understand. Nothing comes free.

15/Records

The Logic of Record-keeping

Fieldwork has one purpose: to gather information from one place in a form capable of being moved to another place. The field information is recorded and preserved in various ways. Fieldwork done without the express goal of capturing and preserving information is a vacation. Vacations are swell, but it's good to understand the difference between them and fieldwork, if only so you won't confuse yourself about the amount of work required.

The least reliable field data preservation mechanism is memory. Some memories are very good; some aren't good at all. And they all suffer the same problem: unsupported by hard evidence, there's no way to evaluate the accuracy of memory. The mind does its own creative recomposition, as anyone who has fond memories of a long-ago event and who finds one's own diary notes of the same time learns all too well. Memory can't help you know about what it's lost: the moments you've forgotten don't always leave obvious holes. The sand closes in and you think you've got it all in mind.

That doesn't mean the other techniques are pure or objective or wholly reliable either. Each form of information capture or preservation—notes, photographs, film, recordings—has its own very real limitations. No fieldwork technique is entirely objective or completely reliable. All renditions of the world are compromises of some order.

You go to the field to get information. You come back from the field with information stored in mind, notes, film, or tape. Unless you also have a system of identification and cataloging, the information will grow less useful with every passing day. Listen to a tape made ten years ago: what were the instruments? how many? what speed was the recording? how many people were in the room? what time of day was it? why was the performance going on at all?

You make notes on the fieldwork in order to make the information you've worked so hard to capture be available to you and to other people. It's difficult, when in the field, to know what will be useful later, or to whom it will be useful. The process of analyzing your own field information often reveals unexpected avenues worthy of exploration and analysis. The notes you make while you're there become both sources of basic information and the collateral information necessary to make the information in other media useful and meaningful. The catalogs you make after you come home are the maps that let you or anyone else travel through your collection. Both are necessary if the fieldwork is to be of any value.

Your field notes and logs should include as much information as you can manage to put down on paper or dictate on audiotape. There's *never* too much collateral information. If you need help deciding what to put down, imagine a complete stranger coming upon your collection, someone to whom the material might be important if only he or she knew how to unlock its secrets. What would that person need to know in order to be able to utilize fully the whole and the parts of your collection? Memory being what it is, and time going as fast as it does, that stranger may very well turn out to be you, coming back to the material several years from now for reasons you never expected or thought of back then when you were getting sore feet from all that walking.

Your notes should answer such questions as:

—When and where and by whom was the recording made?

—Who was there?

—What was going on?

—What were the conditions? (Were some participants drunk, particularly shy, curiously silent? What's that pinging noise—a problem with the tape or something in the room?)

—How did you *feel* about what was going on?

Your general notes, the overall notes accompanying the whole collection, should say why you were there, what you were trying to do, how you got there, how you made the access. Again, they should provide whatever is necessary to make it all sensible and accessible to a stranger.

A collection might have several different kinds of complementary logs. Ellen Stekert recommends that her students keep

[a] log of the chronological order of activities and with whom (who could have influenced whom?), including tape sessions. Then I ask them to

make a series of observations about the recording session itself, first, how they felt it went and their subjective reactions, and then include information on what happened, a sketch of the situation during and surrounding the recording (diagram), also including who was there, when they left, etc. Then there is the transcription, which they can do in an arbitrary summary form, just giving sections of the tape numbers and splitting the pages and writing opposite the recorded events what happened during the recording. These comments can be information about things heard but not explained on the tape; things that cannot be seen (the informant just lit his sixth cigarette in a row—two are still burning) but which tell us something about what is being recorded and brief interpretive comments or references to other parts of the collection or the tape. Now this is a bit much, but there are various levels of logs, all of which can be used with flexible "rules."

A collection done for an undergraduate class may consist of a few tapes and perhaps a few rolls of film and may involve a single event. A collection done for a complex professional project may involve scores of audio- and videotapes and hundreds of rolls of film and may involve many separate events. The need for documentation is far more critical for the larger project, but the reasons for doing adequate documentation are the same for all projects. Without documentation, the contents are never fully accessible.

Tagging and Labeling

Everything should be tagged or labeled: tapes, tape boxes, tape reels. Few things are more frustrating than finding a loose reel of tape and not knowing for sure when and where the tape was made. Rolls of film should be labeled too. The cans and boxes film comes in are often discarded when the film is developed, but there are ways to label the rolls of film themselves.

Whatever cataloging system you ultimately use, it's a good idea to number everything in the field serially: the first tape you make is number 1, the next tape is number 2, and so on. If you're shooting rolls of film, try to have something identifiable in the first frame or two to set the scene so you won't have any trouble ordering the negative and contact sheets later. If you're shooting 16mm film and haven't used a slater with sequential roll numbers, number the cans carefully and tell the lab to make workprints in the order of your numbers. You might think it will be obvious to you later which tapes came first and last, which pictures were made at what time of day. Sometimes, but not always. You might, for example, record Henry on Tuesday morning, Tuesday afternoon, Thursday afternoon, and Sunday morning; you might take photos of him at all those sessions. The rest of the week you might record and photograph a dozen other people, some of them two or three times. A year later or five years later you might not have the faintest idea which session came before or after which other sessions. You might want to know the order in which certain stories were told; you might want to know the order in which you posed certain questions. If you don't know the order in which the materials were obtained, you won't be able to obtain the answers. You might later decide to group all of your tapes of Henry together and to group the other tapes separately. Having serial field numbers means you'll always be able to reconstruct your original recording sequence. (Ellen Stekert labels tapes with the name of the informant, date, and number of the tape for that day: Ben Dobbs, 12 July 83-1; I label with the name of the informant or the general subject, place, date, and number of the tape in that project: River songs, Ramsey, 7/3/64, #44.)

Most folklore fieldwork manuals advise putting a tape announcement at the head of each tape: "This is Joe Smith, I'm recording Henry Farfel at his home, this is tape 22, the date is. . . ." I do something like that on all tapes if I'm recording an event, such as a concert or an interview involving several people in a formal situation, but I handle individual interviews a little differently. When I'm talking with one person, I use the moment of starting the first tape, as I said before, to get the interview going, but after that I like to downplay the machinery as much as possible. So what I do when changing tapes is run the tape fast forward a bit to leave me space to add the announcement later on. I try to get something on the head of the tape that relates to the tail of the last tape—a question, a comment, anything that will preserve the continuity and help me put the tapes in proper order even if I forget or can't write the tape number on the tape itself: "You were telling me about the time Beartracks caught you and Ten-Four making chock. . . ." Cassettes are marked for sides A and B, so assuming you haven't wound through one side without rewinding, you can tell later which side came first and which came second; open-reel tapes provide no such data, so if you're using an open-reel machine and if you're recording on two sides, try to let the tape know somehow which is side A and which is side B. In general, intrude as little on the recording session with your record-keeping business, but whenever you're not sure you'll be able to get things straightened out later on, by all means put a full announcement at the head of each tape.

Cassette tapes have leader that runs about five seconds before the magnetic oxide begins passing over the head; so be sure you don't start talking too soon, otherwise you'll lose your first few words. With open-reel tapes don't put anything important on the first few feet—those first feet are often lost in later use.

If you end a session when there's still a lot of space left on the side, let the tape (and whoever listens to it later) know there's nothing more coming. Say into the microphone, "End of side A; end of tape," which lets the listener know that there's nothing more on this first side and there's no need to bother searching through the second side which is blank. If you finish recording before the end of the first side but know you're going to use side B, say, "End of side A." And if you end somewhere before the tape runs out on side B say, "End of side B, end of tape." You can put these announcements on at the session or later when you're neatening things up. It's a simple housekeeping chore that will save you, your transcriber, and anyone else who uses your tapes a lot of time.

Location Logs

A location log is your record of what's recorded within the various media you're using. If you'll be depositing your tapes in an archive, check beforehand to see if their preferred cataloging and indexing forms are compatible with the way you plan to be working. Sometimes you can key your field logs to those forms and save yourself and the archive personnel a lot of work later. Even if you're not planning on giving your material away, you should always keep a detailed log. You never know when you might be talked out of your material by an enterprising archivist, when you might decide to give the stuff away because you're through with it and know someone else might get some good use out of it, or when you decide you can use the tax deduction you get for contributing those materials to a tax-exempt organization. In any event, if you're going to be writing up your findings you'll need the log to know what you've got to work with.

If you're working alone there's usually little time for logging while you're in the field: you may make brief notes on a pad or on a tape box, but it's hard to do more without breaking the rhythm of the event. In that case, plan on spending an hour or two at the end of each day doing catch-up work with the logs and notes. You'll be tired and perhaps even bored with the stuff, but you'll be glad for the effort later on. Your memory of the day's events will never be better than it is that day. Sometimes, rather than waiting for nighttime when I know I'm going to be tired, I go hide somewhere during the day and spend some time writing up notes and thinking over what's happened so far.

| Location tape # | 63 | Archive tape # | 221 |

Project *River Songs* _____ Recorded by *Jackson*

Date *7-12-67* _____ Location *Ramsey 2*

Equipment used *Uher, AKG D19E*

Comments *negatives 63/31-32 Group: Johnny Jackson, Houston Page, Joe Williams, T. D. Smith*

Item #	Performer	Title/Description	Comments
1	Tippett lead	Raise Em Up Higher	flatweeding
2	" lead	Rattler	"
3	"	story about the bear	
4	Jackson lead	Raise Em Up Higher	flatweeding

Figure 5. Sample location or field log.

I try to keep my location or field logs as simple as possible. Depending on the kind of material I expect to be getting, I make up a log sheet before a field trip and make plenty of copies. If I'm going to be recording musical and conversational material, for example, and if I expect the tapes will each have a number of distinct items, my log sheet might look like the one in Figure 5.

The "location tape number" is the serial number for that trip or that project. The "archive tape number" is the serial number for that tape in the archive at the Center for Studies in American Culture, where I presently deposit my tapes; it isn't filled in until the tape is accessioned in the archive, but I put the blank on my log sheet to make things easier for the archivist later and to be sure that in at least one place there's a notation indicating the two numbers assigned this specific tape.

"Project" is whatever my working title for the investigation is: the name of a town, a subject, a person. "Date" is the date on which that specific tape was recorded, and "location" is where that specific tape was recorded. I list the "equipment used" because I have at my disposal several recorders and microphones; and if I later want to know why something worked especially well or especially badly, knowing what equipment I used might help me establish the pattern. "Comments" are for general things about the session: who else was there as part of my team, who was hanging around, the nature of the high-pitched whine in the background. . . . I want to note who was there so proper credit can be given if something is done with the recorded materials later on. I want to note the nature of strange sounds so I don't blame the equipment and look for bugs that aren't there. I also note if photographs were taken while the recording was being made so I can key them to the transcriptions later.

"Item number" is simply a serial listing of discrete items on that tape. Some tapes won't have discrete items; they might consist of one person telling one story or the general sounds in a bar or at a rodeo. If so, fine. But if there are discrete stories, discrete songs, discrete events, discrete subjects of discussion, I try to indicate that. "Performer" is the person being recorded. If there are five musicians, I put down all the names and what each is doing and, if I'm recording in stereo, where each is located in relation to the others.

"Title/description" is for the performer's title for a song, story, whatever, or for my title or brief description of the item. It's often a good idea to ask, if the situation permits, what title the performer knows that song by and whether he or she has ever heard it called by any other title. If a title isn't offered and I don't know one for that song or story, I'll write, "song about drunk soldier," or "story about meeting four hackers at computer store," or something of that order. This line is primarily a mnemonic, merely to remind me when I'm working with the tapes later what was happening at that time. Adopt a format that will let you know when you're writing down their title or yours; you might write, "(his title)" after the entry. Whether I'm recording oral history or folklore, I try to use the column labeled "comments" for brief summaries of the items so I can find them later and so someone else can recognize something that might not have a familiar title.

If the audiotapes will consist of interview material rather than a number of discrete items, I adopt the slightly simpler format shown in Figure 6. This means I don't have a lot of pages for tapes that are described with one line: "Jones discusses unionization of the plant," or something of that order. Instead, my log sheet lets me keep track of the tapes, who is on them, and the general topics of discussion. Later on, either during long breaks in the fieldwork or back at home, there's time to work out descriptions of the tapes' contents. There's another reason for putting off the cataloging of discursive tapes until later: you often don't know the point of a part of the discussion until

Project __Death Row__ Recorded by __Christian__

Date __3-27-79__ Location __Ellis Prison   Huntsville__

Equipment used __TC 1585D,   Sennheiser lav.__

Comments _____

Tape #	ATN	Subject	Comments
12	2091	Hughes	
13	2092	Hughes	
14	2093	Hughes	
15	2094	Barefoot	
16	2095	Barefoot	
17	2096	Barefoot	break about halfway through; continues after lunch

Figure 6. Sample log for interview tapes.

it's over (what starts out as a personal anecdote about a work-related incident develops into a discussion of a religious attitude, say), so if you're trying to keep current while the person is talking, you're very likely to be continually revising your log and simultaneously dropping out of the discussion, or if you're not revising your log to reflect the changed direction of narration, then the log is inaccurate. The point of field logs is always to simplify your work when you get home, not to make it more confusing than it would be otherwise.

If I'm shooting 16mm film, my log sheet is designed to provide information about what's on the rolls of film and the accompanying audiotapes (see Figure 7). "Production" is the film's title or working title. "Director," "camera," "sound," and "crew" are the people working on that film that day. "Filmstock" is both the kind of film used and the batch number. It's not a good idea to mix brands of film on a single production, but you may use films made by a single manufacturer having different characteristics; this information may be important later when the lab and you try to match up shots or figure out why certain colors don't remain constant. If I'm working on a film that's being shot over a short period of time, I buy all the film at once

Production	Creeley		Director	BJ + DC	
Camera	Bruce		Sound	Diane	
Crew	Mike + Rachel		Filmstock	7291	
Recorder	TC D5		Date	8-21-85	

Roll #	Tape #	Scene #	Sound	MOS	Filter	Comments
71	32	1	X		85	Waldoboro Int. in study
72	32	1	X		85	" " " "
73	33	1	wild		85	cutting tree
		2	wild		85	in field with Maggie
		3	X			in kitchen w/ Willie + Peg
74		1		X	85	books + objects in study
						at Waldoboro Post Office

Figure 7. Sample location film log.

and it's almost always from the same batch number. If the film is a long time in production, then the film is from different batch numbers. It might be that different batches have significantly different performance characteristics, or even that film from one batch is somehow defective. Knowing what batch any roll is from can permit accurate prefield testing or at least help you avoid further problems after the first set of rolls is processed by the lab.

The "roll number" is my serial number for that roll in that film; the "tape number" is my serial number for that audiotape roll or cassette in that film. If the film involves a dozen shoots over a twelve-month period, I maintain the serial numbering from beginning to end. This is different from the way I handle soundtape numbering when no filming is involved, and it has to do with keeping straight the various workprints sent from the lab and being able to find the correct negative rolls when the time comes for making final cuts and assemblies.

"Scene" is the number of the scene on that particular roll. The sequence starts again from 1 with the next roll of film. "Sound" and "MOS" are to let me know whether or not the scene was recorded with sound; just one of the two boxes is checked. ("MOS," according to the folklore of the film business, comes from the days when many Hollywood technicians and directors were German immigrants: "Dis scene vill be mit out sound"—hence the abbreviation, MOS.) If I'm recording wild sound (sound without an accompanying synchronized image), I leave the "roll" and "scene" columns blank and note in the "comments" column what was recorded.

"Filter" indicates which filter I have on the lens for that shot (see the section on filters in chap. 12). This is important to record so I can later know what did or didn't work well. "Comments" is for anything I think matters. When I'm filming, this column contains mostly technical data. The entry always identifies what's going on, sources of sounds if they're not apparent, light sources if they're not obvious, filters I have on my own lights, if I think the scene is especially good or probably useless, and so on.

All of this may sound complicated and enormously time-consuming, but in fact it's neither. How much material goes in the "comments" column depends on how much time is available and why the work is being done and what kind of work is being done. If I'm filming, the logging is done by an assistant; if I'm doing tape interviews myself, I do the logging either as I go or as soon after the recording session as possible. Sometimes finding the time or energy to do the logging is difficult, but I've always been glad later that the work was done.

My several forms may seem like a lot of bother, but I do a lot of fieldwork and the forms help me control the information. They also make it possible for me to work with assistants sometimes and for other people to use my materials. All responsible fieldworkers develop ways of logging that make sense in terms of what they're doing and why they're doing it. The devices I describe above work for me; you may find some others far more comfortable. Bear in mind that the need for detailed logs increases exponentially with the complexity of the project. A simple class assignment may require very little—perhaps nothing more than running notes. An extended project of any kind, however, requires careful and continual management of information. Otherwise there's a real mess to be dealt with later.

Logging doesn't take the place of field notes, by the way. There are still many other things that should be written down, whatever medium you're using to capture your information. As I said earlier, imagine someone who knows nothing about what you're doing, what you saw, what you were thinking: what would that person need to make sense of the documents you've made? (If you want to see what can be done with really good field notes, look at Jean Malaurie's *The Last Kings of Thule,* a splendid ethnological work that not only gives you an enormous amount of facts about the Inuit he studied but also enough information about his relationships with the Inuit and his own feelings for the reader to evaluate the ethnological material.)

If you look at logging and archiving forms used by different programs and archives, you'll notice a great difference among them. That difference is usually less important than the archivists preparing them think. What's important is that the basic information be there so that you and a stranger can figure out later what went on. Five years from now, when you get around to doing that book or article, or just haul the stuff out to see if it's as you remembered, you may not recall the full name of the singer you were sure at the time you would never forget. Worse, you may think you remember it perfectly, publish it, and get a note saying, "My name is Fred; Frank was my cousin Alf's dog, the one that bit you the first time you came to the house."

Logging Photographs

Photos can be harder to keep track of than tapes. If you don't shoot many pictures, you can have an extra set of prints made and write on the back of that extra set all the reference data you might need. Then you can add to your field notes or logs references to the photos so you can find them later. If you shoot a lot of photos, that isn't good enough. I said above that I try to include something in most rolls to tie the shots to an event or a time. That's a starter, but it isn't enough either.

I shoot mostly in black and white. As soon as I get home from a field trip I develop the film and make contact sheets. Because I take a lot of pictures not connected with fieldwork, I maintain a separate numbering system for all my negatives. The system is chronological by year: 76/55 is the 55th roll in 1976. I write that number on the contact sheet and on the plastic negative holder. I keep a serial log of all my negatives and contact sheets and file them serially. If I'm looking for a photograph I took of Robert Creeley in North Carolina in 1982, I look through the serial log for that group of negatives, then I pull the appropriate contact sheets and find the image I want, and then I go to the negative holders for the appropriate negative. I also use this system when I'm shooting color negative film. If the photographs are part of a field trip, I enter the roll numbers, and sometimes the frame numbers as well, on the field log after I've made the contact sheets. An entry in the "comments" column reading "76/82:14–21" tells me that frames 14 through 21 of roll 82 in the 1976 group are connected with this item or event.

Color transparencies are more of a problem because it's so easy for them to be separated later and it can be difficult to decide, once they're separated, what sequence of shots they were part of. I usually write on the cardboard transparency holder enough information for me to identify the image: "Jack Clinton, Cedar Breaks, 1984." I keep my transparencies in sheets that hold twenty slides each; the sheets fit into a three-ring binder. Sometimes I write additional information about the slides on the margins of the holder. That isn't very efficient—every so often there's a slide I can't identify exactly. If I took fewer pictures when I was doing serious fieldwork I probably would number every acceptable slide when the processed film came back from the lab and I'd write up a page identifying each one.

There's another problem with transparencies: unlike prints pulled from a negative, transparencies are unique—they're the original. They can get scratched easily and they fade with repeated projecting. If I'm going to be using a particular transparency a lot, I have it copied and I use the copy for everything except making prints.

I recommend writing in your notes, on prints, or on contacts sheets the names of everyone in your field photographs. It seems a bother at the time, especially when you're certain that you'll always remember these people, but it saves you the embarrassing work later of writing someone to ask, "Who's that guy on your left?"

Archives

You've done fieldwork for a purpose—to fulfill a class requirement, to gather information for a book or article or record or film, to preserve information you thought deserved preservation. What do you do with the raw materials from the field trip after you've gotten from them what you want or need? You may destroy them, you may keep them on your own library shelf because you're going to be working with them again or because you want them to show to visitors, or you may deposit them in an archive.

Many archives around the country accept contributions from independent collectors. All universities with folklore programs maintain such archives, and there are regional archives and historical collections. Some archives are nothing more than a few file cabinets in a professor's office; others are elaborate affairs with their own staffs and publication series.

Most archives require depositors to sign a contract or agreement. This spells out (or should spell out) what rights the collector has and what rights are being assigned to the archive. You might, for example, want to deposit your materials in an archive so they'll be safe or so other scholars can consult them, but not so other scholars can publish them; the deposit agreement should make that restriction clear. You may have recorded material on the informant's condition that it be used for listening purposes only; again, the deposit agreement should state that explicitly, if only to protect you. The contract might also contain clauses stipulating that informants must be notified and their permission obtained before any publication is made using their names or materials. You might have all rights to the materials or you might deposit your collection with no restrictions whatsoever. The latter delights archivists, but think carefully before you give everything away. Your goal in depositing materials in archives should be to ensure that the material is physically protected and made as widely available as possible, without doing harm to your informants or interfering with your own use of the materials now or later. (You can get information on folklore archives in your area by writing to the American Folklife Center, Library of Congress, Washington, D.C. 20540.)

So that's it for doing fieldwork. I've told you what I know about talking to people and working with machines. Now we have to spend some time on the most important thing of all.

Part Four/Ethics

If you can do no good, at least do no harm.
Hippocrates

16/Being Fair

A Simple Definition

Ethics in this context have to do with the moral implications of the role you play while you're doing fieldwork and with the moral consequences of your decisions and actions after you're done with the fieldwork. Ethical questions arise in relation to who and what you tell people you are and why you tell them you're doing fieldwork and what you tell them you'll do with what you find. There are ethical implications in your decisions about what material you destroy and what material you deposit in archives, what conditions you impose on access to and use that can be made of archival materials, what field information you publish and tell other people about and what you keep secret forever. The answers to ethical questions define your relationships with and obligations to your informants, other collectors, and your sponsoring agencies.

Who Owns the Folklore?

Not you or me, that's for sure.

Ikkometubbe, the Chickasaw chief who figures in Faulkner's Yoknapatawpha stories, angered and puzzled some of his tribesmen when he sold Thomas Sutpen 100 square miles of land. It wasn't the size of the deal that got the Chickasaws riled but the fact of it. As far as they were concerned, you could no more sell land than you could sell air: both were there for anyone who wanted to use them. But the white settlers didn't want abstractions; they wanted clear title to the land so they could hack it up and make money on it.

259

In the case of folklore, it's been the collectors who confused the issue; the legal document has become the copyright notice rather than the deed. Most folklore collections are copyrighted in the name of the collector or publisher. A few authors stipulate that the texts in their published works are in the public domain or they assign copyright for texts to the individuals from whom the texts were taken. That assignment doesn't clarify things much; it would be like Ikkometubbe selling land to another Indian—the thing is still nailed down in a way it wasn't nailed down before, its use is still restricted in a way it wasn't restricted before, and ownership is asserted where ownership was not asserted before. The singer of "Barbara Allen" may have only marginally greater right to copyright that text and tune than the collector who taped the performance.

So what belongs to whom? No one argues that collectors "own" the rights to their comments and analyses—but what about the "rights" to a specific singer's versions of a traditional song? What about the "rights" to a specific performance?

The practice of not even sharing copyright developed in the early years of folklore research when the item was seen as having an existence and legitimacy distinct from the performer or performance. Scholars like Child were content to note the printed source, with no mention at all of the performing source; many would use a performer's name merely as a way of locating geographically the source (see Wilgus, 1959). The nineteenth- and early twentieth-century definition of folklore was far simpler than definitions used by folklorists now. Folklore texts were assumed to change little from performance to performance, authorship was always assumed to precede performance and performer, and communality of composition was often assumed as well. If the song or story was *really* folklore the performer had no more claim to it than someone had to a text from the Bible. The text belonged to everyone equally. That communal ownership was part of what made it folklore in the first place.

Modern folklorists tend to be far more respectful than their predecessors of individual redactions and far more sensitive to the adaptations and changes individual performers make. That's in part another result of the development of accurate recording technology. Before portable recording equipment, texts and tunes were taken down by hand, so a collector brought home from the field the collector's version of the performer's version of something from tradition. Modern collectors—with their high-fidelity audio equipment and portable video equipment—bring home a part of the performer's version itself. The nineteenth-century collector wanting people to know what a certain kind of song was like wrote an article or book in which that song was transcribed and the nature of performance was marginally, if at all, described. The twentieth-century collector makes a tape or record or video or film and lets people hear and see what was done. The technology frees the collector to talk about far more interesting things; it's no longer necessary merely to report or to spend most of the time doing the simple reporting. Simultaneously, that technology extends the collector's responsibilities to the sources of information. (For an excellent discussion of this, see Tedlock, 1983:3–19; see also Jackson, 1985.)

There are other important differences. In former days the stakes were not large. Except for Joel Chandler Harris, few authors of early folklore books earned significant royalties, so the notion of who owned what was largely academic. Once folklore books began selling well, however, things changed. When John A. and Alan Lomax tried to publish *Negro Folk Songs as Sung by Lead-Belly*, their publisher, Macmillan, learned that Lead-Belly might sue John Lomax over some postdated checks Lomax had given him when he left Lomax's employ and went home to Louisiana. Macmillan refused to go ahead with the publication until John Lomax produced a full release from Lead-Belly. Lomax paid up on the checks, Lead-Belly signed the release, and the book was published with all the songs copyrighted by Lomax.

If a folklore study contains 100 field-collected items and it earns for its author $1,000 after subtraction of field and preparation expenses (extremely rare, so far as I can tell), and if half the book is written by the author and the other half consists of the texts, then does the source for each individual item deserve $5? Maybe, but it would cost more than that to get the checks to them.

With phonograph recording of traditional materials the matter becomes even more complicated. Phonograph records sometimes make a lot of money—not records performed by the original folksingers, but covers performed by other artists. When the British group Cream included Skip James's "I'm So Glad" on one of its albums, the song earned more in royalties than James had earned from all the records he cut in the 1930s and the several records he made in the 1960s for Vanguard and Takoma. What did Cream owe James? James said "I'm So Glad" was a children's song he had learned many years ago; he never claimed he wrote it. The simple text derives from a nineteenth-century spiritual. But the style of performance, the complex guitar work, and the pacing of the lyrics were very much his contribution, and Cream copied those very closely. Cream paid up because anyone listening to James's early recording could hear the derivation.

Even fuzzier is what happens to materials deposited in archives and subsequently used by someone else. Most archives now have contracts with collectors stipulating the kinds of uses to which the materials might be put; some archives insist that collectors provide releases from informants. So who then owns the texts and tunes? If the answer is "No one, they're public property," who in the public gets whatever money is earned from them? Who owns the performances? What responsibilities does the informant have toward the tradition? What responsibilities does the collector have toward the informant? What responsibilities does the archive have toward the collector and the informant? Who decides?

I wish there were a simple, unambiguous answer for these thorny questions, but there isn't. The ethics have to be worked through anew every time.

Lying

Some folklorists don't tell the people they're studying what they're doing. They don't necessarily lie—they just don't say all they might. J. Mason Brewer, for example, wrote in the introduction to his collection of North Carolina black folklore, *Worser Days and Better Times:* "I think it advisable . . . to explain why no informants are listed in the work. Since most of the material was recorded without the knowledge of the contributors, I saw no reason to list some of them if I could not list them all. Most of the items included in the book were gathered while I was a passenger on a bus or train, or seated in cafés or drugstores or barber shops, or standing on street corners. The only exceptions are the autograph album rhymes. I believe a more authentic and natural product can be obtained when the informant is unaware that what he says is being collected" (1965:25). The book suffers from the secrecy: it consists of floating texts with no collateral information at all. Since Brewer presumably didn't set out to misrepresent himself, the cost is to his study and the ethical problems aren't great. Deliberately misrepresenting your aim and your role is quite another matter, however.

In his manual on folklore fieldwork, Kenneth S. Goldstein recommends what he calls the "induced natural context" for collecting folklore:

> The collector chooses his accomplice from that group of people who would normally be participants in the natural context being re-created. Ideally, that person should himself be a performer, but of the type which may be designated as average or typical, rather than a star performer (the aesthetic

evaluation to be used in such a choice should be that of the community involved). The accomplice's major role is to bring about the context in which he and others will perform. This he achieves by calling together a group of his cronies or friends for an evening of storytelling, singing, riddling, or any other lore normally performed in such a context. And he must do so with as little fanfare as possible and without informing the participants that the purpose of the session is to allow a collector to observe them in action. When the participants arrive at the place selected for the session (usually the home of one of them), the collector is introduced casually as if he had dropped in unexpectedly. . . . (1964:88)

Perhaps this sort of deception and manipulation seemed to make sense back when folklorists assumed that what they did had nothing to do with what went on in the community after they left and that they owed nothing to the people who provided them the information they sought. I don't know any serious collector nowadays who would make such an assumption, nor can I think of any situation in which the need to collect folklore justifies lying about who or what the folklorist is and is doing. If you're working for the CIA or if you're an investigative reporter seeking out corrupt officials, perhaps your job justifies a measure of indirection. But folklore isn't that important. It's interesting, it can tell us a great deal about the way people live and what matters to them, but getting the information isn't important enough to warrant going undercover and lying to people and compounding the lying by getting a friend of the people lied to to do some lying as well.

What happens to that accomplice when the collector's work is published and the local people find out what the stranger in their midst was really up to? What happens to the *next* stranger who visits that place, one who perhaps has nothing to hide, who is exactly what he or she seems? How will those people deal with the new visitor after their experience with the undercover folklorist and the co-opted neighbor?

Bruce Nickerson studied the folklife of factory workers without telling any of the workers in the factory his real reasons for being there. He pretended he was simply one of them. He wrote of his study: "The participant-observer technique was an excellent and obvious way for me to collect materials. By working as a piece-work machinist in a large urban plant where I had worked before, I also had the collateral but important benefit of receiving a decent paycheck. During my eighteen months at the plant, my fellow workers accepted me as another 'working stiff' and had no idea of my eventual goals. During my last week on the job, I told my friends that I had been working with them to gather material for my dissertation. They were pleased to learn that 'one of us' would be telling their story" (in Dorson, 1983:122).

But Nickerson was *not* "one of us"—he was a graduate student working on his Ph.D. thesis and using the factory as a place to provide the information he needed. The paycheck, as he says, was only a "collateral benefit." Nickerson, so far as I know, meant no one any harm by concealing his real identity and purpose, but does that justify the deception? What about those factory workers who were observed in Nickerson's study and who were reported on who were not his friends? Were they as pleased about the telling of the story? Even if no one was harmed, what about the idea of working with people for eighteen months and having them assume you're there for the same reasons they are when in fact you're there to examine them, study them, objectify them?

A friend of mine some years ago was collecting data in rural Arkansas. Someone took her to visit a woman well known locally as a fine singer of religious songs. Even though my friend was brought by a person the singer knew well and liked, the reception was icy. People in the Ozarks are often suspicious of strangers, but when you come with a good introduction they tend to take you at face value until you give them reason to think otherwise. The chill was inconsonant with my friend's usual experience in the area. After a long time she learned that the singer had previously had an experience that turned her against anyone carrying a recording device of any kind. Another folklorist had visited the woman's house and had asked her to sing some old ballads, which she formerly had sung frequently and well. She refused, telling him that she had some years earlier married a man who was a member of a religious group that didn't approve of the singing of secular songs and she had joined his church and had promised her husband she would accept his church's dictates on such matters. The folklorist pressed her to sing; he said the material was of great value to researchers and he promised that he and only he would hear the records, that they would be used for research only. She finally agreed, but only after he promised that not only would the recordings not be used for anything but his research, but that he wouldn't even tell people she'd been singing secular songs. She told the folklorist that her husband was more passionately reborn than she was, that he'd be furious if he knew she'd sung these songs, scholarship or no. Absolute confidentiality would be maintained, the folklorist said. Two years later, the woman heard herself singing on the radio. So did her husband and her friends in the church.

I had an experience similar to my friend's, though the informant in this case was just disgraced, not injured. Near Saltville, Virginia, in 1965 a seventy-year-old man said, "You're from New York. You know that —— feller?" I said I knew the man. The old man's eyes narrowed. "You a *friend* o' his?" I said that I *knew* him, nothing more. We weren't friends, we weren't enemies. The man relaxed a little. "You ever run into him, you tell him I'm still waiting for that money he promised me." Fifteen years earlier the collector had promised this man that if ever a record were released incorporating any of the songs collected from him or his family, they would be paid. The collector told the man he wouldn't think of issuing a record without discussing it with the man and his family first. The man learned about the record via a phone call from a cousin who had just heard the record on the radio in Bristol.

No folklore project justifies that kind of violation of trust. No collector's mission legitimizes that kind of exploitation of other people. We have a responsibility to the people whose traditions we're exploring, and we have a responsibility to the explorers of tradition who will come after us. It's very easy to poison the well.

Lying about what you're doing is bad ethics. It might also be bad fieldwork, because if people suspect the truth they may find subtle ways to take revenge. "If, like some misguided field workers," wrote Rosalie Wax,

> I play a false role or deliberately mislead the informant about my activities and intentions, I can expect to be repaid in kind. One particularly discourteous field worker of my acquaintance, who makes a practice of trying to deceive informants, has some very inaccurate data in his possession. Determined to get information on the sexual behavior of one informant, he falsely promised that he would keep the information to himself. The informant saw through this attempt at deception and repaid falsehood with falsehood, giving the interviewer an ingenious but quite fictitious account of her erotic activity. So far as I know, the interviewer still thinks he has accurate factual data. (1960a:93–94)

"Telling the truth" doesn't necessarily mean telling everything you know or think. You're out there to observe, not to judge. Most extended projects change in design as the fieldwork goes on. Information coming in redefines the movement. For most people, a simple statement of your plan or activity is enough, so long as you don't give them the feeling that you look upon them as experimental animals ("I want to determine the effect of increased unemployment on narrative performance and since you've been laid off for eight months now. . . .")

When Diane Christian and I worked on death row in Texas we said we wanted to make a film and write a book about what living on the row was like. We said nothing more about our plans, though at the time we had several specific ideas about the film and the book (most of which changed as the work progressed). No one asked us for more.

Saying "I don't know" is permissible. If something interesting comes up and you don't know what you might do with it but you don't want to lose the chance of getting it down, go ahead and get it down. If you're asked, "Why do you want that?" you can say, "I don't know now but I might later." People understand that and accept it. They understand—but don't accept—people who deliberately tell them lies.

You don't have to agree with everything you hear or approve of everything you see when you're doing fieldwork. Like the work done by doctors or lawyers or ministers or accountants, the fieldwork involves a suspension of moral evaluation while you're on the job. The fieldworker's task isn't to decide whether or not people *should* be doing what they do, it's to find out what they do and what it means.

A fellow I met on death row had killed three people; he's a member of a racist organization. I knew those things about him and didn't ignore them, but I did put in escrow my moral reactions to them. He knew I was a Jew and he knew my politics were far to the left of his (even Barry Goldwater and Ronald Reagan were to the left of this man), and he put that knowledge wherever he puts such things. With those qualifications we held several conversations of interest to both of us. I can't imagine any situation in normal life, in nonworking normal life, where I would comfortably sit down and chat with such a person, and I'm sure he would say the same thing about me. He didn't apologize for his positions and I didn't apologize for mine; he understood that the point of the interview was to document what he had to say, not so one of us might judge or convert the other. But if he'd asked me what I thought about his opinions I would've told him the truth.

Sometimes a measure of pretense seems justified: "I do fieldwork," writes Robert Byington, "among men who are virulently racist/sexist and who express those values in a never-ending stream of jokes, many of which are told for my benefit. Were I to indicate my disapproval for a second, my carefully nurtured rapport with them would be seriously eroded. So I pretend, as distasteful as it sometimes is. It's one of the things you have to do if you want the data. . ." (1978:xx).

Note that Byington doesn't say he pretends *he* is "virulently racist/sexist," he just puts his real disapproval on hold. I don't think my conversation with the multiple-murderer and Byington's with the racist joke-tellers vary much from the experiences of most sociologists or anthropologists or folklorists, nor do they vary from the conversations of many other professionals who deal with people in their own contexts. If in literature we follow Coleridge's dictum about suspending disbelief, in fieldwork we suspend moral judgment. We don't usually pretend we agree with things with which we don't agree, but neither do we argue points we might in other circumstances argue or contemn behaviors we might in other circumstances contemn. The point of fieldwork is to learn what people do and think; changing or judging what they do and think is a different task entirely. But if our learning requires us to pretend to believe things we don't believe or say things we don't want to say, we should examine the moral price the present fieldwork is exacting and ask if the trade is really worth the gain.

Paying

Should informants be paid? If yes, how much? If no, why not and what, if anything, should you do instead? What do you get when you do pay? The right to listen? The right to record? The right to play your recording for others? The right to sell or lease your recording?

The answers depend on several factors, the most important of which is local custom. In some places, payment isn't only expected but necessary; in others, payment would be insulting. The answer also depends on the resources of the collector, the uses to which the material will be put, and the relationship between the collector and the informant. "By pre-arrangement, I paid John $100 for as many stories as he wanted to give me," wrote Andrew Giarelli, who was studying Cheyenne narrative in the early 1980s. "This is consonant with the tradition of paying for stories or ceremonial instruction among Cheyennes. Important stories, Herman Bearcomesout tells me, traditionally call for the gift of a freshly killed deer to the narrator; Herman, his cousin Tom Rockroads and his Sioux friend Mike Running Wolf all recall bringing food to the homes of old people to hear stories when they were children. Ceremonial instruction is more expensive: I have been told about one Cheyenne who recently gave a $500 rifle to an instructor, and another who gave the instructor all his possessions" (1984:24).

No one expects a student collecting folklore from family or friends to pay for help, at least not when such material is being used for a class project or a thesis. But what if the material is being used for a project on which the student will subsequently make money? What if it's being used for a project on which someone else will make money?

A poll of several collector friends produced these responses to "Should informants be paid?":

—"If you can spare the money and you want to pay someone, why not?"

—"Scholars collecting folklore for scholarly purposes should never pay because that gets people started making things up for you."

—"If you get paid for it, they should get paid for it; if you don't, they shouldn't unless there's no other way you can get them to cooperate."

—"Only if they're losing money by helping you. If it's time sitting around and telling stories when someone might be sitting around and telling stories anyway, no, no payment is necessary, though I'll probably buy the beer or something like that. But if someone is missing out on work he might be getting paid for because he's spending the time helping me, then I try to pay him at least what he would have earned. A lot of people won't take it, but I offer anyway."

—"You should share your royalties with informants, but only after you've deducted your costs of fieldwork and preparation of whatever it is the royalties are being paid on."

—"Face it, we get rewards for successful fieldwork. That's why you and I are both full professors. The royalties from my books are nothing compared to the difference having published those books makes in my university salary. So if I publish a book that is primarily texts or if a record is released based on my field recordings, I give all the royalties to the informants. If I do something theoretical or general, that's mine."

The question must always be decided personally and specifically. If a collector is going out specifically to gather material for a money-making enterprise, some equitable arrangement for payment or for sharing the royalties with the performers should be worked out beforehand.

Few scholarly books make money, but that doesn't mean the collector won't make money because of the books. A scholar may spend four or five years researching and writing a study, it may be published by a university press which is delighted to find the book selling two-thirds of its first printing of 1,500 copies, and the author may get a royalty check of $1,000—which is not enough to cover field expenses, secretarial expenses, supplies, equipment, and so on, to say nothing of the time involved in doing the fieldwork, the necessary library research, and the writing. But a professor's pay for scholarly books isn't in the books' royalties, it's in what having published the books does for the professor's career: promotion, merit raises, access to grants, increased likelihood of job offers.

When I first started meeting folklorists in the early 1960s there was a sense of something vulgar about paying informants. The folklorists I met at Indiana saw themselves as dedicated scholars, little of their fieldwork was funded by grants, rarely did they make direct money from their publications, and many of them felt that paying for what people did anyway would somehow contaminate what was going on. That perhaps reflected attitudes of another time, back when folklore was a hobby, when folklore research was something one did among the backward and the primitive. Folklore now is serious business, and the research is done anywhere and among anyone. Just as any other kind of enterprise involving people performing services and taking time, the matter of payment should be determined on the basis of the relationships among the people involved, the money available, and the realities of the situation.

Releases

Many problems that come up in relation to folklorists not telling people their real roles or confusions over payments can be obviated by asking people to sign releases. A release is a simple contract in which an informant gives a fieldworker specific license regarding the material provided in the collecting session.

I don't know any folklorists who got written releases twenty years ago. Publishers required releases if you were including someone's photograph in a work, but there was little concern with a person's words. Two things have changed: one is the attitude of the collectors toward the material; the other is the litigiousness of the American public.

So far as I can tell, collectors didn't used to think much about the rights of people from whom they collected data. Perhaps the notion was "This is public domain stuff anyway, they don't own it anymore than anyone else does." That didn't stop folklorists from copyrighting the materials in their own names, however, which meant *they* were staking out some sort of claim. Most folklorists nowadays have far more respect for their informants' rights. They're far more likely to understand that their informants aren't passive conduits whose sole function is to deliver to a waiting tape or disc or roll of film information in which the folklorist happens to be interested.

The litigiousness is more troublesome. People now sue over the most trivial things. A young boy sued the manufacturers of Cracker Jacks a few years ago because he failed to find a toy in his box. *Sued!* Publishers are scared, sometimes with good reason.

I routinely get releases from everyone I photograph or tape—if I can. Even if I'm fairly certain I'll never use the material for anything commercial or scholarly, and even if I'm fairly certain I won't be turning the tape over to an archive, I try to get a release, to protect myself and anybody else later on. I don't ask students to get releases when they're doing fieldwork projects, but I caution them—especially graduate students whose work tends to be fairly high-level—that if they have any publication plans it's far easier to do the paperwork now than a few years hence.

Ives recommends as part of the interview a statement telling the informant what's going to happen to the tapes:

> You must tell the informant three basic things: that the tapes will be preserved, that people will be able to listen to them, and that he will be asked to sign a release at the end of the interview. I suggest some variation of the following, but try not to memorize it. Put it in your own words:
>
> "I just want to tell you what's going to happen to these tapes we'll be making. They will be kept permanently in the Northeast Archives at the University of Maine. Then anyone who wants to find out how river-driving was done here on the Penobscot can learn by hearing about it from someone who actually did it himself. After the interview, I'll be asking you to sign a release, which will simply say that you're willing to have us use the material in this way. Is that O.K.?"
>
> If the informant has any questions or hesitations, now is the time to get them settled. If he wants to restrict the material somehow, you can explain whatever your archive's policy is in this regard and try to work out something satisfactory. But do not suggest the possibility of restrictions; let it come from the informant, if it comes at all. (1980:51)

This may seem like a redundant practice that just asks for trouble—going through the request for a release twice. But, Ives explains, the " 'up front' bit is *not* a release in any way. It's simply a way of making sure the interviewee understands what is going on. Have you ever had it happen that when you ask for a release at the end that you are refused—largely because the interviewee didn't know what was coming? My little system is designed to get that all settled. Seems to work, too."

I don't know any cases of anyone suing an archive because someone was allowed to listen to a tape without the performer's authorization or prior general consent. Permission *is* needed if you're going to use the informant's name and likeness in any kind of publication or broadcast. Some collectors handle the problem by using false names for all informants in their books, which generally rids them of the need to provide a release. Unless there's a legal or professional reason for anonymity—say, the speakers are criminals who fear prosecution for what they reveal, or doctors talking about malpractice who feel other doctors will somehow take revenge on them for their violation of the code of brotherhood—most modern scholars would look upon this as being very close to plagiarism. And if a publication includes photographs or is about a community small enough for the speakers to be identified by the contents of their statements, then changing the names accomplishes nothing.

Documentary filmmaker Frederick Wiseman, who is also an attorney, for years has taken nothing but taped releases. He feels it's as binding as anything else and that what's most important about a release is the interviewee's awareness of what's going on. Few people who know they've said on tape "You can do what you want with this stuff" are willing to go to court to complain that you did something untoward with that stuff.

Killing Time contained over 100 photographs made in Cummins, the Arkansas prison for adult males. A few years after the book was published, my publisher received a letter from an Arkansas prisoner complaining that his picture had been included in the book without his permission. Letters like that cause anxiety at publishers' offices. I was informed about the anxiety. I looked through my releases and found the man was right—he hadn't signed any of the forms. Some 300 other men had, but not him. (I remembered very well the day I'd photographed him: I'd been working in one of the dormitories all afternoon, photographing and carrying on conversations.) I looked at the contacts sheets from that afternoon; everyone else on those contacts had signed the releases.

I wrote the man a letter in which I reminded him that he knew I was taking pictures (in the image published he's staring directly into the lens; it's one of three images of him on that contact sheet), that I'd asked his permission before making the photographs, that I'd sent him copies of the pictures, that he knew I was working on a book because by that time everyone in the prison knew me and knew what I was doing, and that I'd asked everyone in the dormitory that day to sign the release whether or not they'd been in a picture, just in case. He'd been standing there when I handed the clipboard with the release form to the man in the next bunk and he'd been there when I'd shouted out, "Anybody didn't sign this yet or doesn't want to sign it for some reason?" and he hadn't said anything. I apologized for including his picture and for any embarrassment that might have caused him, and

I said I had no intention of doing him harm and surely wouldn't have used the picture if I'd realized he hadn't signed the release.

He must have been satisfied with my letter because neither the publisher nor I ever heard from him again. If he hadn't been satisfied he could have gone to court and sued us, though he probably wouldn't have won—there were enough witnesses who could have testified that I tried to get releases from everyone and also that I tried to find out if anyone objected to having his image published. The affair would have cost the publisher and me a great deal of money, however, and the publisher probably would have agreed to take that picture out of any subsequent editions.

What's more important than how we might have fared in court is this: The man was right. It was *my* responsibility to be sure that no one objected to inclusion of the photographs in a book, and the fact that I missed someone speaks about the inefficiency of what I thought at the time was a pretty neat procedure. It's not just a matter of being sued and winning or losing; it's also a matter of possibly doing someone real harm. People shouldn't have their pictures published if they don't want their pictures published; we shouldn't want to publish someone's picture if it might cause harm. I'm more careful about permissions now.

Your own instincts may not be enough to let you know what's acceptable and safe and what's not. If you're in a culture not your own, ask what's permissible, what might do harm, and respect the responses. Polunin (1970:20) quotes Ishaq Qutub: "In our study of some Bedouin tribes in Jordan, we encountered difficulties in taking pictures. Bedouins don't like to have their women exposed to outsiders, and they consider that the taking of pictures of their wives or daughters impinges on the family honor *(sharaf)* in that the pictures might be seen by strange men. A young Bedouin may even refuse to be wed to a girl whose picture has been seen or taken or owned by a man from another Bedouin tribe or not a Bedouin."

The rich and famous don't have the same protections you and I and most ordinary people do. The courts have held that public figures can be photographed and quoted by name without authorization—so long as their images and words aren't used for commercial purposes. "Commercial" in this sense means things like an ad: you don't need Paul Newman's permission to quote him saying a certain tire is great if you're writing an article about Newman or about racing, but you can't quote him in an advertisement for that tire. It's all right to make a point using something said by public figures but not if the point is part of a sales pitch. Public officials acting in their public capacities are fair game: if Mayor Koch gives you an interview about his job or if he does a television interview about some action he took, those statements are in the public domain.

It's easy to get goofy over the matter of permissions and releases, but it's not usually worth it. Most people are happy to have their names and pictures in print, and most fieldwork doesn't make its way into print anyhow. Most people who don't want their names or faces used don't mind at all if you use things they say. Just be sure to ask how they feel about it and then be sure to honor their requests. As I said earlier, it's always good to remind yourself that there's nothing so important in folklore fieldwork that you have to deceive anyone in the process. Mistakes happen, but lies are unforgivable.

I recommend a variation on the Golden Rule: Think what use might be made of this material later, think how you'd feel if your words or image was used that way, decide whether you'd want the option of saying yes or no to such use, then act accordingly when it comes to a release. If you're doing a paper for a class and your teacher maintains an archive, you can always write on the first page, "This material may not be quoted or reproduced without permission of the author of this paper and the informants quoted herein." Then, if someone later culls those archives and wants to use your material, the burden is on that person to get the necessary permissions. If your paper includes things that might do people harm, then you perhaps shouldn't be depositing it in an archive over which you have no control.

I've seen releases that occupy an entire page, stuffed with so many whereases, therefores, and howevers that the page is gibberish. I've also seen releases that were a single sentence. I've asked lawyers about the relative merits of the two. One said: "If you're photographing someone who makes a living from her image, a high fashion model say, then a long release is a good idea, and you should think of it as part of the working contract. The release names the limits on what you can do with her property, her image. But if you're talking about someone you've talked to and photographed for a study of some kind, then I don't see any reason for going overboard. All you want is a record that proves the person knew you were taking the information and that the person knows it might be published and doesn't mind either."

When I'm documenting a lot of people in a place (e.g., the death row film, the Arkansas book) I have a lot of people sign the same release sheet. At the top I type the release statement; the rest of the page is for the signatures. If there are some people I'm worried might not sign, I see that the form gets to them last. It's far easier to say,

"No, I don't want to sign this" when the page is blank than it is when everyone else has signed. On death row, I think I gave the clipboard to the man in the first cell and asked him to sign and pass it on, then I went off and did some work. Later I picked the clipboard up at the last cell and did the same thing on the other two tiers. Curiously, even some men who for legal reasons had said they couldn't be in the film signed the release form. They were satisfied with our oral agreement and signed the release for reasons I've never fully understood. (But even though they appeared in some of our raw footage, we didn't include those shots in the film.)

The death row release went something like this: "I give Bruce Jackson, Diane Christian, Documentary Research Inc., their heirs and assigns permission to use my image and my voice in their film about Death Row in Texas, and to use my image and voice in any publications connected with their research here and in connection with any publicity they think appropriate." It was simple and direct, it said what we were doing, and their signatures said they understood what we were doing. That's all a release has to do.

Other Collectors

To whom do the informants "belong"?

This may strike you as a weird or silly question. The obvious answer is "Nobody. Slavery ended in this country a hundred years ago." The question might be put another way: "What kind of obligation do fieldworkers owe one another regarding sources of information?" I'll tell you about an experience I had that illustrates some of the problems that can occur in this area.

A woman called me at home one night and said that she and some colleagues—a group of filmmakers from UCLA—were assembling a series of films about American storytellers. "We want to include your fisherman," she said, "and I'm calling to find out how to get in touch with him."

"What fisherman are you talking about?"

"You know, the one you're making the film about."

I asked how she knew about the film, since the application was still being considered by NEA.

"Someone at Folk Arts told me about your project."

I said I didn't think it was a good idea for two folklore-oriented film companies to be pursuing this man at once. If nothing else, we'd be structuring each other's films.

"You don't have the right to keep us from him," the woman said. "What makes you think you have that right? You don't own him."

I said that was certainly true, and I wasn't going to do anything to keep him from them. But I wasn't going to make any introductions either.

"How can you do that to him?" she said.

"Do what?"

"If he's in two films he might get famous and he might make a lot of money."

I said something appropriately vulgar and hung up. The next day I called NEA to ask who there had been giving out specific information about grant applications still pending. The official denied any responsibility and said no one else in the office and no one on the panel had given out such information either. How did he know that? "We don't give out that kind of information, that's how I know that."

When you're really angry is often a good time to step back and check what you're getting angry about. I was angry that someone at a federal grants agency seemed to have been feeding other investigators information about a project still in the developmental stage. I was more angry about these people at UCLA who thought it reasonable to ride on work done by other people: if they wanted a fisherman, they should go out and find their own. What right did they have to screw up my project? None, so screw them.

When I cooled off, my feelings about them hadn't changed any, but my feelings about my own position did go through a little reshuffling. What rights did I have here? What rights did the informant have? What rights did strangers have? Would I have objected to them so strongly had they come upon the informant on their own? I didn't want them to start making a film while I was making a film because I knew their questions would contaminate the answers I was going to get, but what if the informant would have enjoyed being in two films or a dozen films? What right did I have to stand in the way?

I never did help them. I thought the impropriety of the way they got the information and the pushy way they demanded immediate access justified that denial. I decided that everything I knew about them said they were people with no professional decency and there was no reason they should get any help from me whatsoever. That's how it seemed to me at the time. Now, I think that from my point of view I was right, but I didn't have the right to make the decision for the informant. I don't know what his point of view was because I didn't ask him. I had a right to protect my project, but I didn't have the right to deny him a choice that should have been his.

I don't think it was professional for those other collectors to have put me in that position in the first place. Once they knew I thought their presence would disrupt my study, they should simply have said, "How about introducing us when you're finished?" or something of that order. I think that as researchers we have a responsibility to each other. Honor other people's sources. If you know someone has been getting good material in a certain place or from a certain person or group of persons, don't rush over there trying to score on their ground-work—at least not without their knowledge and permission. Sometimes the intrusion of another fieldworker will destroy the rapport the first fieldworker has been working to develop. Sometimes the questions asked by a second fieldworker will so accurately coordinate the field for the helpful informant that the value of subsequent conversations will be reduced. It's not a matter of one researcher *owning* rights to the informant; it's more a matter of common sense and common decency.

There was then and there is now no document outlining the ethics of folklore fieldwork. That's probably because most of us assume the Golden Rule is well enough known not to need reassertion. The assumption is sometimes invalid. So here is The Rule As It Relates to Other Fieldworkers: Don't rip off your colleagues and friends; don't screw up their work. If you have a good reason for visiting their grounds (it's not *theirs,* but the work they're doing is, and you know your presence will influence that), be up-front about it.

Kenneth Goldstein urges fieldworkers

> to get in touch with any collector who has worked in the area planned for a field trip. In most cases such a person will turn out to be the best possible source of information about the places and its inhabitants, especially if his field work was done in fairly recent years. Also, considerable information which never gets published is in his keeping, and may help the stranger to avoid making *faux pas* in the new society which he is entering, as well as informing him which collecting methods work best, which subjects are taboo, and which social classes are to be avoided on initial contacts, among other suggestions. Most important of all, he can usually supply names and addresses of potential informants or official contacts, and may be persuaded to write these people and assist in easing a collector's way into the community. (1964:39)

Goldstein recommends newcomers take the suggestion of the International Folk Music Council that collectors " 'should normally avoid working in the field in which another collector is still active.' " But if it's for some reason necessary, he advises that the incoming collector should contact the resident collector to obtain his approval and to make friends. There is more than courtesy involved here. If the resident collector has set up good relations with the inhabitants of the area, he can, if he has a mind to do so, make it literally impossible for the incoming collector to work effectively there. A friend in the field, on the other hand, can smooth the way, make field work easier and pleasanter, and considerably shorten the period of rapport establishment. And there is always the good possibility that the coordinated activities of the two collectors in the same area will so perfectly complement and supplement each other that the total achievement of the two will add up to more than simply the sum of their individual efforts. (1964:39–40)

For Goldstein's "resident collector" we should substitute anyone who was there first, with one exception: you wouldn't want to do that with the kind of parasitic collectors described on pp. 264–65. I don't have any good advice to offer here. If you're lucky you'll find out about the abuse before you go to work and know not to start a conversation with that particular person. By far the great majority of folklore field-workers in recent years have behaved decently and fairly toward their informants, so the odds are on your side.

Some areas have been mined by students—you may find their papers in university folklore archives. Rarely will these earlier collectors object to a later visit to one of their informants. But when one collector is in the process of doing work, it's usually a good idea to stay away unless you're invited in. A second collector can do great damage because the informant can infer, from your two sets of questions, what it is you people are after. The informant may or may not be right, but in any case the responses of the informant will be tilted, they'll locate themselves in the grid block named by those coordinates or the area of overlapping circles.

If another folklorist has worked in an area you're going to work, do whatever you can to find out what kind of work was done and what kind of impression was left. Being associated with some earlier collectors may do you more harm than good. You may not know what problems the other collector had or what difficulties resulted. There may have been the kinds of discovered deception I noted earlier, or social blunders, or kleptomania. An earlier collector may have found some splendid informants, all of whom love him or her and love the idea of being folklore informants because such a fine impression was made; or that person may have alienated everyone in sight. An earlier collector's questions may have taught everyone there what he or she thought folklore was and they, forever after, feed only a certain kind of information to folklorists who aren't able to push on through that limiting definition.

Sponsors

Much fieldwork is done on the fieldworker's own time and paid for out of the fieldworker's own pocket. Some fieldwork is funded by foundations, government agencies, schools, corporations, or organizations of various kinds. Whenever the work is paid for by someone else, all the ethical problems noted above are compounded.

I've discussed the problem of determining ownership of the folklore collected. When a sponsor is involved, there's the added question of who owns the physical materials themselves—the tapes, photographs, film, even the notebooks—and who controls the ultimate use of those materials. Some grantors provide funds and expect nothing in return except a report on the work done; others demand censorship rights over published results or ownership of all raw materials. Sociologist William Foote Whyte, author of the classic participant-observer study *Street Corner Society,* couldn't publish what would have been his second book because his contract with the organization that provided his research funds gave that organization approval rights and the organization decided to withhold the necessary permission (Whyte 1984:196).

What happens when you have a grant to conduct research into a certain topic but once you get into the field you find your access to that topic is blocked or a far more interesting topic presents itself? What are your responsibilities to the people paying the bills? You should be aware of those responsibilities before you spend their money.

Sometimes a fieldworker receives from an institution supplies and loaned equipment in exchange for a promise to deposit all original materials in that institution's library or archives when the fieldwork is done. What if the collector decides some of that material should be kept secret to protect the informants' privacy? Destroying or holding back some of the field material violates the agreement with the sponsoring agency; depositing it may violate the informants' trust.

Money rarely comes free. A good rule of thumb is: Before you take someone else's money for work you want to do, know exactly what that money is buying and decide if you're really willing to pay the price.

The Golden Rule One Last Time

When you're in doubt about whether an action on your part is ethical or not, a good starting place is to put yourself in the subject's position and consider how you would feel if you learned what that friendly person was really up to. If you'd be annoyed and offended that you were made a sample in a study you didn't want to be part of or were recorded or photographed without your knowledge or permission, don't do those things to others. If you'd feel betrayed because things you said in confidence were made part of a public report, then don't betray confidences—or at least tell people who think they can trust you that you can't keep secrets. Hemingway once defined the good as "what you feel good after." Think about how you'll feel later—perhaps how you'll feel if you ever see that person again. If the answer is "not so good," then don't do it.

FIELDWORK IS NOT EVERYDAY LIFE.

Appendix/Death Row

Documenting the Row

I avoided death row for a long time. The opportunity was always there, I just didn't want to take it. During my first field trip to a prison (Indiana State Prison, in 1961) the assistant warden offered to show me the electric chair and let me talk to condemned prisoners. I refused. I thought it would be voyeuristic. My concern was with folklore and I felt those men had problems enough without having to deal with the idly curious.

During the years I did research in Texas prisons I could have visited the row anytime. The authorities there let me go anywhere I wanted, talk with anyone I wished. I thought it reasonable to talk to people about their lives in crime and their adjustments to the world of prison, useful enough to let them talk about the old days and for me to collect songs and stories and technologies. But the situation of the men on the row was so precarious and painful that my own academic curiosities seemed trivial in comparison. I could justify to myself a conversation with a long-term convict about the technology of safecracking or the folklife of prison, but I couldn't justify such a conversation with someone waiting for the state of Texas to run several thousand volts of electricity through his body.

Except for the work in Arkansas that resulted in *Killing Time,* I didn't do much prison research in the 1970s. I wrote several books based on fieldwork I had done in the mid- and late-1960s, but my active work for most of the 1970s was political. In 1978 I was invited to lecture on criminal justice at Sam Houston State University in Huntsville, Texas. While there, I met for the first time James Estelle, who had replaced George Beto as director of the Texas Department of Corrections. Estelle said that if I ever wanted to take up my prison research again the place was still open to me. I thanked him but had no intention of taking him up on the offer.

Before I left Huntsville I visited Billy Macmillan, now an assistant director of the prison. When I'd last seen him he'd been a field major on Ellis. When I first met Macmillan he was a field sergeant and had maneuvered me so I wandered through a patch of high grass infested with redbug. I learned about the redbug the next day when the itching started, but I hadn't learned about the joke for fifteen years. People in the Southwest are content to hang back about their jokes.

Macmillan said TDC was presently going through a massive lawsuit. He asked if I would be willing to testify in court about changes I'd seen in the prison system since I first did research there in 1964 and about how TDC compared to other prisons I'd visited.

"Sure," I said, "but I'll say what I think is wrong with the place too."

"As long as you say what you've seen," Macmillan said, "I don't care what else you say." I said I'd do it if I could visit all the prisons again so I wasn't talking in the abstract. Macmillan said arrangements would be made.

And so I began visiting TDC again. I had long thought TDC was the most repressive and the safest of American prisons: prisoners there had the least freedom and the greatest chance of serving their sentences without physical harm. The system had one more unit in operation than it had when I'd done my research in the 1960s—fifteen rather than fourteen separate prisons; it also had more than twice the convict population—25,000 rather than 12,000. The plaintiff in the pending court case, *Ruiz* v. *Estelle,* argued that those repressive measures and the increasing overcrowding were so extreme as to be unconstitutional.

One of my visits was to death row. I saw how the row differed from the rest of the prison. For one thing, none of the usual prison counters of behavior mattered there because the row was the single place where the rhetoric of rehabilitation was meaningless (one was there waiting to die, not trying to be improved) and where the rhetoric of punishment was inappropriate (the punishment was not time served on the row but execution). The row was a prison within a prison, a place not covered in any of the usual sets of rules. Men lived there for years while the legal system decided whether they'd be killed or resentenced to a prison term or set free. Death row was a special city with a life all its own, one outsiders knew nothing about. I thought someone should do a study of life on the row: How did the men survive? What were the ways in which they made existence meaningful? What were the unique relationships between the condemned men and their guards? How did the prison officials justify this set of prison conditions that differed so radically from the conditions in the regular cellblock directly across the hall? Someone should do it, but not me.

That July we had a conversation in Ketchum, Idaho, with Carey McWilliams, who as editor of *The Nation* had published some of my articles about prison problems. I told him about the row and that I thought someone should document it.

"Right," Carey said. "When are you going to do it?"

"No," I said. "It's too depressing. And I don't want to be a voyeur."

"Don't be silly," Carey said. "For one thing, it ought to be done. For another, you've got the access. So go do it."

"I don't *want* to do it," I said. Carey scowled. So we went and did it.

Diane and I knew from the beginning that we wanted to do a film and a book—the film would show what the rhythm of the place was like and what the people who lived there were like; the book would provide the space for discourse film can't afford.

We'd never made a film before, but we'd been marginally involved with another film that same year, so we had an idea what things cost and how film budgets looked. At the time (1978) the accepted rough guideline for 16mm color documentary film production was $1,500 per minute. We decided to do a thirty-minute black-and-white film. On the basis of the death row project description and some sample video footage I'd shot with a Portapak in the Arkansas penitentiary a few years earlier, I was awarded an Independent Filmmaker's grant from the American Film Institute. Diane and I received a grant for the book portion of the work from the Fund for Investigative Journalism. We asked one New York foundation interested in criminal justice matters for $65,000 for the film; they said no. It was a nice no, so I wrote again and asked for $25,000; they said no and said how much the rejection pained them. I wrote back and said it pained us far more, so how about $8,500; I threatened that if they didn't give us the money we wouldn't ask anymore. They gave it to us, but made us promise we wouldn't use their name in the credits (which we didn't). Polaroid gave us two cases of SX-70 film so we could give everyone on the row snapshots to send home; the SX-70s would be useful to us because we could use a set to keep the names straight. Levi Strauss contributed a few thousand dollars and so did the Playboy Foundation.

We had about $25,000, so we decided to make a sixty-minute color film. We were $65,000 short of the accepted production minimum, but we had enough to do the location work and get the film processed.

We figured the rest of the money would come in later. Anyway, those $1,500 budgets were based on films with lots of people, all of whom got paid. No one except the cameraman got paid for working on *Death Row;* and Diane and I would do all the other work ourselves. In retrospect, knowing what we know now about the costs of film production and the complexity of film editing, it was quite crazy.

We wrote to everyone on the row explaining our purpose and saying we thought the work would give them an opportunity to tell the outside world what they thought about where they were. If the row was the place most isolated from outside eyes, it was also the place insiders were most cut off from outside conversations. Three men responded saying they'd be happy to help out however they could. That seemed enough for a start.

Jerry Puglia (our camerman), a volunteer grip from the media services department at Sam Houston State University, and I arrived at Ellis early on a Tuesday morning. Diane was to arrive the next afternoon. Our plan at first was that the three of us would work on the filming while Diane did long interviews elsewhere in the prison. She would feed us suggestions. As it turned out, her interviews not only suggested things we should cover and people we should film but became the major part of our book about the row.

We decided that Diane would do her interviews in another room for two reasons. Even if the prison authorities had agreed to let us film with her there, they would've insisted on having guards around while we were working, and that would've ruined the interviews and changed the mood. We couldn't have worked in the cells. More important, there are toilets in each cell and the cell doors are the traditional steel bars. There's never any privacy on the row. Had Diane been there all day long, new and uncomfortable constraints would've been placed on the residents.

The first day didn't work out as planned. It was a disaster. The reception was frozen and hostile. Hostility on death row is like hostility in few other places. Someone on one-row (the ground-floor line of cells) said, "We hear you're a witness against the convicts in *Ruiz*." Death row is a noisy place in the day—toilets flush, eight television sets are on constantly, radios blare, people call back and forth to each other. I had the feeling that men all the way up to three-row heard the question and were listening for the answer.

"I'm testifying about what I've seen here over the years. I'd say the same thing if I was testifying for the plaintiffs."

(During a dinner in Houston several months later, one of the plaintiff's attorneys asked me, "With what you're saying, why aren't you testifying for our side?" "You never asked," I said. I wished there were some way I could just go in and say what I knew without belonging to one side or the other, but the gamesmanship and structure of the court trial doesn't permit that. A Justice Department attorney at that dinner asked me what I thought was the biggest change in TDC. I told him it was the overcrowding and that I thought some of the most severe problems resulted from that. "I hope you guys give me a chance to testify about that. Ask me some questions about it when you cross-examine tomorrow." He said he certainly would. As it turned out, not one of the three lawyers asking questions asked me about overcrowding: the defense didn't because it wasn't their job to put information detrimental to their case in the record; the plaintiffs didn't because, I suppose, they were afraid I was setting them up for some kind of fall. Lawyers think that way, perhaps with good cause since most of their time is spent dealing with other lawyers. It didn't matter: the plaintiffs won anyway, and won big. Judge William Wayne Justice accepted nearly every aspect of the plaintiffs' complaint; his order was the most sweeping of any judicial prison reform orders. TDC now has some 35,000 prisoners, but the cells are no longer crowded; the management system that used convict trusties as intermediaries between convicts and authorities was abolished, and TDC is now one of the nation's most violent and dangerous prison systems.)

"My lawyer wrote me that I could be in the film," another said, "but he told me I shouldn't do it unless he's here while you're doing it."

"Where is he?"

"He lives in New York."

The lawyer's name was Joel Berger. He had written the same letter to many other inmates on the row. The next week one of the prisoners told me that Berger was in the visiting room. I found Berger there and asked why he hadn't at least let me know he was writing that letter, since he knew we were coming down from New York with a film crew. "I'm a lawyer," Berger said, "I'm a very busy person. I don't have time to be writing letters to people." "But if you had shown me the letter we could have worked something out." "I told you: I'm a lawyer. I'm too busy for that."

One man on the row showed me Berger's letter and said, "I want to be in the movie. I don't like somebody in New York thinking I'm too stupid to know what I can say and what I can't say in a movie." We filmed him. We filmed Thomas Andrew Barefoot (who was executed in October 1984) getting a haircut and shaving in his cell and talking about rules. But the mood on the row was still palpably cold and hostile. I was in despair: after all those years of *not* doing anything about the row and after all those months of scuffling for the money to get started, it looked like we might as well pack up, cut our losses, and go home.

While Jerry and the grip were packing up the gear for the day (we had one shot set up for the next morning; if things didn't pick up after that we were through) I walked along the tiers talking to anyone who wanted to talk. There weren't many who did. On the third tier was one of the men who'd written us an enthusiastic letter; he'd said in the morning that he'd be happy to give us advice, but he certainly couldn't be in the film. "You may think I misled you," he'd said, "and you'd be right. But I happened to change my mind, you see." I suppressed several things I thought would be fine responses, nodded, and started to move on. He called me back. Now, in the early evening of that first Monday, he wanted to chat. He asked what kind of books I wrote. I said it was difficult to describe them. He asked to see one.

I don't like showing people my books. Except for close friends, I almost never give them as presents unless someone asks specifically for them or has helped in the making of one. Diane had urged me to bring a few of my prison books along on this trip. "What's the point of that?" I'd said. "They'll just add weight and take up space." "Bring them anyway," she said, "you never know."

I went down to the first level and took from one of the bags copies of *Killing Time* and *In the Life*. I left them with the fellow on the third tier and went to the motel. Jerry and I didn't talk about the state of things in the car on the drive back to Huntsville. I don't think he understood how precarious the situation was; he was still getting over the shock of realizing where this film was being made and who was taking part in it. His previous experience had mostly been with commercials.

When we got back to the row at 6:30 the next morning the books were on the far end of one-row—fifty-seven cells from where I'd left them. People said hello to us cheerily. People chatted. The man on three-row said, "I read them books. You don't tell the convicts' side and you don't tell the man's side. You just tell your side."

"I told you," I said. "I try to write about what I see."

"Can't ask for more than that," the man said. "I'll be in your movie."

"Me too," said the man in the adjacent cell.

We set to work and the day was a good one. Some men on the row were still distant, but there seemed to be none of the hostility or coldness of the previous day.

About 11:00 A.M., while we were filming on one-row, a man called down from two-row and said he wanted to be interviewed. I had enough shots set up for the rest of the day, so I said I'd interview him right after lunch on Thursday. About every hour for the rest of the day and two or three times Thursday morning he called down and reminded me about the interview. I finally told him that if he asked one more time we wouldn't do it. Actually, I didn't mind at all having him call down like that because I thought it would stimulate others to take part more enthusiastically.

As it turned out, I had things exactly backward. The interview with him Thursday nearly brought everything to a dead stop.

We began the interview a little after noon. We spent perhaps an hour filming and taping. He told about being gang-banged in the county jail and told how he'd been an informer there and here on the row. In Texas, and many other states as well, men who are catamites and fellators in prison only are called "punks"; those who do it in the free world as well are called "queens." Queens have much higher status than punks because, as one convict put it, "At least they're man enough to admit what they are." Punks are seen as doing it out of weakness, and prison is a place where strength and weakness (or the appearance of either) count for a great deal. Being an informer in prison is worse than being a punk, though there are probably far more informers than punks at any one time. Being an informer isn't nearly so bad as being *known* as one. There are many times a regular convict decides informing is moral—to prevent a killing that will result in tighter restrictions on everyone, for example, or to cut out new competition in one of the prison hustles. Being a punk is always bad, being an informer is bad if done for the wrong reasons; being known as a punk and a snitch is terrible.

The man told us he didn't look forward to having his sentence commuted to life because if he were ever returned to population—the general prison community—he'd be killed. "They'd all like to get me if they could," he said. Jerry thought it was a shocking statement of fact; I rather thought it was bragging. We finished the interview, he returned to his cell, and we moved the camera back out to one-row to film the afternoon's commissary run.

While Jerry and the grip were setting the lights, I went to see someone on two-row. As I walked along the tier someone said in a low voice, "You lousy cocksucker, I'd like to cut your fucken throat."

"Me too," the man in the adjacent cell said.

Under the best of circumstances that would be unnerving to hear. On death row, where murder isn't a theoretical matter to anyone, it's far more unnerving.

"Group Two, recreation!" the building tender shouted from the end of the row. Group Two included everyone in the last five cells on one-row and the first ten cells on two-row. Recreation consisted of ninety minutes in the cellblock's dayroom for whichever inmates wanted to be out of their cells for a while. The cell doors opened and those men who wanted to go to recreation filed along the narrow iron corridor and down the tier of iron stairs to the small room off the one-row corridor. I knew that if I didn't get this present hostility—whatever its cause—cleared up, we were finished working on death row, so I followed the group in there.

"Knock when you want to come out," the guard said as he closed the door and locked it from the other side.

On death row the guard stays out of the recreation room. Recreation is the only time more than one death row prisoner is allowed out of his cell at the same time. The guards avoid risk by locking them in the rec room and watching through a window. If there's trouble, they call other guards from other wings before venturing inside. When the steel door slammed and I heard it locked behind me, it occurred to me that what I was doing wasn't very intelligent. But by that point there was nothing to do but carry through on it.

I walked directly to the man who'd made the threat. He was standing with four or five other men near the window. "Why did you talk to me like that?" I said. "I haven't done anything to you."

He scowled at me for a minute; the men around him stared at me in silence. I heard the dull murmur of conversation from the far side of the room. The conversation was slow, too slow. No one else was looking at us but I knew everyone else in that room was paying careful attention to what was going on. You don't have to look at someone to watch him.

The man said, "You know what you did? You *know* what you did?"

"What did I do?"

"You filmed ——!" He named the man on two-row.

"I'm aware of that. So what?"

"Do you know what he *is?* Have you any idea what he *is?*"

"Yeah," someone else said, "do you know what he is?"

"He's a punk and a snitch," I said. "So what?"

"So what!!" the first man yelled, his face very close to mine. "What kind of image is *that* to give the world of death row?"

My first impulse was to laugh, but fortunately I was able to repress it. Instead, I let myself get as angry as he was. "You know what *you* did?" I shouted. "Do you know what *you* did?" He backed up a step.

Now the entire room was silent and the other groups weren't pretending not to watch. "I'll *tell* you what you did. You listened for two days while he yelled to me and yelled to me about filming this interview and you never said one word. I walked by your house a dozen times and you never said one word about it. You waited until I had used up a thousand dollars' worth of film and processing and wasted two hours and then afterward you got me convicted and sentenced. You did the same thing to me you probably say the cops did to you: you set me up. You're not a reasonable person and I don't want to talk to you anymore."

"Now wait a minute," he said, in a voice very different from the voice earlier.

"No," I said. "I don't want to talk to you. Anyway, what do you think people out there would think of a film about death row if it showed everyone as nice and sweet and gentle? They'd think it was just a bullshit film, that's what they'd think."

"Wait a minute," he said.

"No. You're not a rational person."

I knocked on the door and signaled the guard. I waited there for what was probably only a few seconds but seemed an eternity while the guard found the key and fumbled with it in the lock. My back was to the room.

Jerry and I went back to filming on one-row. After a while, the group in recreation came out and went back to their cells. I could see, at the periphery of my vision, the man who had threatened me earlier standing close to the bars of his cell on two-row. I didn't look up. After a while, one of the porters brought me a note. "From —— on two-row," he said. I saw the man watching the porter hand me the note. I put the note into my shirt pocket and went on with the shot. I could've read it then, but I didn't want to. I was really angry by this time. Being angry was probably my way of coping with the understanding that I shouldn't have gone into the rec room after the threat. Fieldwork isn't worth getting killed for.

After a while I went under the tier of the walkway, out of sight of two-row, and I read the note. It said, "It is important that I talk to you immediately. Please come to my cell." There was a signature and a cell number. I put the note back in my pocket and went about my business. A few minutes later, where the man could see me, I took the note out, read it, then looked up and nodded. He was still standing at the bars. When we finished the shot I went up to his cell.

"Look" he said, "about what I said before. I was wrong, okay? We talked about it after you left. If we want this movie to tell people what death row is like we've got to work on it with you. You guys can't do it by yourselves." I nodded. "So can I be in the movie?" he said.

"Me too," said the man in the next cell.

That was it. After that incident the only people who weren't in the movie were men who for specific reasons couldn't afford to have themselves seen on television. One was Candyman, convicted of poisoning his own son's Halloween candy for the insurance; he felt he'd had too much publicity already and had hopes of a new trial (he didn't get it; he was executed in 1984). Another said his seventy-five-year-old mother thought he worked in another part of the country; his brother remailed his letters to her so she wouldn't know where he was. "If she found out I was down here," he said, "it would kill her. But I'll be happy to talk to Diane about anything you two like." A third was a former college teacher on the row for a contract killing. I don't know what his reasons were because he never talked to us at all except to comment on the weather. He spent a lot of time doing exercises in his cell. I think there was only one other resident of the row who still hung back.

Once the death row community decided we were reasonable people and that the work was worthwhile and participation was in their interest, we had a new problem: it was impossible to film everyone who wanted to be filmed or to tape everyone who wanted to be taped. How do you say to someone, "Sorry, not you?" without hurting his feelings or without insulting him or without announcing a decision you've already made about content? We didn't ever find a satisfactory solution to that one.

Diane had another problem during her interviews down the hall. Some men she talked with were, for our purposes, splendid informants. They spoke well, they were conscious of detail, they had a lot of information. Others weren't very good informants. Some were just inarticulate. The problem was, a status system seemed to be developing: if someone came back to the row after only thirty minutes, he felt embarrassed when he knew someone else had been there for two hours. Several times Diane extended conversations long past their reasonable ending points so as not to embarrass the man. She asked me to be more careful in my preselection of who went down. Even so, some men who weren't asked to be interviewed told others they had been asked and had refused.

It wasn't just rapport with the death row prisoners that was necessary. We also had to seem reasonable and the project useful to the building tenders—the convict trusties who worked on the row—and to the prison personnel—the guards and the medical attendant. That happened, too.

What I've just written tells you how I remember having gotten around an impediment to conversation and filming on the row, but it doesn't tell you why those men talked to us. What if there had been no problem about my status? Why would they have bothered talking to us then?

Some men on the row would've talked to us because there was always a chance we might have helped them in their cases. They didn't know how and they didn't know if, but death row is a place where almost every other avenue of help has failed or been exhausted. Why *not* talk to us? Once they decided we weren't harmful, there was nothing to lose by hoping we might be helpful.

Some men talked because they wanted people to know what the place was like. Some talked because we gave them a chance to vent their grievances against the criminal justice system or the prison administration or other residents of the row. Some talked because they thought the film might do some real good.

And the final reason, one I think of major importance for many of the men who took part in the film and who talked to Diane in connection with the book, was discussed by Rosalie Wax in reference to her research in Nesei Relocation Centers during World War II. "While I would like to think that the data I obtained there bear some relationship to my personal skill," Wax wrote, "it would be gross self-deception not to admit that many informants talked to me week after week partly because there was nothing more interesting to do" (1960a:92).

Truth and Voice

Jean Malaurie, the distinguished anthropologist and editor and publisher of the Terre Humaine series, asked me to write for the French edition of *Death Row* a preface dealing with the long-standing argument about the relative values of the qualitative and quantitative methods in the social sciences. "Sure," I told him. "No problem. I'll get it done as soon as I get back to Buffalo."

Talking was easier than writing. Malaurie didn't get his introduction for nearly two years. Every time I tried to write it, I produced either a boring pedantic argument or ad hominem remarks, neither of which seemed to serve the purpose Malaurie had in mind when he asked for the essay. He was after pages that would specify why those ordered transcriptions of field interviews were meaningful. I think I secretly hoped that one day the translated book would arrive and I wouldn't have to think about the problem anymore. Malaurie, always the tactful gentleman, sent Christmas cards and occasional notes and clippings about the second printing of the Terre Humaine translation of another of my books but said nothing about the preface or about the progress of the translation of *Death Row*. He was waiting me out.

One evening in mid-April 1984 John Coetzee visited for dinner and we got into a conversation about voice and purpose. A Dutch film-maker had not long before optioned his novel *In the Heart of the Country*, and a Canadian filmmaker had optioned my novel *The Programmer*. Mine is external and easily translatable to the language of film; *In the Heart of the Country* takes place in the mind of a lonely woman and the reader never knows what portions are fact and what portions are fantasy or dream. We talked about the differences in the ways readers of books and watchers of films deal with the voices presented to them by the makers of either. Then Coetzee asked me the question quoted below and I made some sort of answer. Later that night, after Coetzee had left, I asked Diane what she thought about what I'd said. "You're right," she said, "but it's something you've said before. Look at the end of *A Thief's Primer*." I hadn't read the pages she referred to in a decade, but I remembered the point of them well enough. They had to do with personality, the presentation of self, and the legitimacy of presentation. Diane was right, but not totally right: there was something additional in what I'd tried to say in the conversation at dinner. A few days later I woke at five A.M. (I'm not an early riser), listened to the mourning doves in the bushes outside, and continued in my head the conversation with Coetzee and Diane. Then I got up and typed the preface to the French edition of *Death Row*.

The problem is important for folklorists now that most folklorists believe their subject is found in context rather than items. The brief essay I wrote for Terre Humaine provides what I think is both a useful and a necessary perspective on the substance of this book. So here, in closing, is an English version of that French preface.

* * * * *

Since *Death Row* was first published, the number of condemned men in Texas has nearly doubled, three Texas prisoners have been executed by lethal injection, and the murder rate in Texas has remained almost exactly the same. Both sides have the empty satisfaction of seeing their point confirmed: the liberals can say, "See, your killing hasn't made any difference," and the conservatives can say, "These three killers got what we think they deserved." Justice remains an abstraction, and expediency and publicity continue to rule.

The South African novelist John Coetzee asked me what I suppose is a crucial question in regard to this book and the kind of work upon which it is based: "Those men you and Diane interviewed and filmed on death row, how can you know when they were being self-serving and how can you know what truth is in what they say?" The answer has to do not only with the words of these condemned men in their extreme situation; it has to do with all such words uttered by people to other people who can never know the final truth or falsity of what is being said.

There is the truth of the utterance itself. The utterance, the statement, is a fact, a social fact, one as valid as any other. This man at this time and in this place chose to offer this narration about himself/This car was parked on this street on this day at this hour/The amount of tar in this brand of cigarettes is this many milligrams. The *whys* of these facts are other matters entirely, but none of them is simple to determine: we may never know why this man presents himself this way, but neither may we ever know why Jacques parked the car here rather than there or why the manufacturers of Galoises decided this level of tar was more acceptable or more preferable than that level of tar. We make our conclusions about those things when they happen to enter our consciousness, but most of the time we do not pay attention to the why of facts at all; we simply deal with the whether of them.

I don't know anyone who perceives himself or herself as achieved, as a completed person, as a person for whom all things really do make sense, as a person who has yet to become the person who can be understood by others. Most people sense themselves in process. But most people I know *present* themselves as being achieved; they present themselves as if they made sense at this moment in time. The reason the examining magistrate found Camus's Meursault a monster was not because he killed the Arab on the beach; rather, it was because Meursault could not or would not offer the expected narrative explication of the event. Meursault suggested he fired the superfluous bullets because of the brilliant sun that afternoon. The sun was a fact of Meursault in process, a fact the magistrate found unacceptable in what society insists be a statement of a person achieved.

Whether the condemned men who speak to you on these pages *believe* their presentations or not is interesting, but not finally important; what is important is first that they feel the need to organize their verbal presentations of themselves so they are rational, and second that they know how to do it.

I say "they know how to do it," but I do not say "they know how to do it successfully." I think very often the disjunction between the self in process and the idealized achieved self can be discerned by the careful listener or the careful reader. We read autobiographies to learn not just facts about a certain famous person (facts are usually better learned in biographies) but to learn how that person chose to redesign the reality we remember.

The truth of the statement has only partly to do with the truth or accuracy of the facts in the statement. There is the fact of the presentation: a version of a self is asserted here. Is it "true"? What does "true" mean in such a context? That those facts happened exactly that way? Of course they didn't. The stories most people give of themselves and the explanations they have for themselves are always narrative and always after the fact; life is never narrative and the moment in which things happen is never after the fact. The imposition of narrative requires the luxury of retrospection, a sense of what things seem to have meant, a willingness to discard as unimportant or irrelevant facts not consonant with the retrospective sense of meaning. All reconstructive discourse—a statement by a murderer waiting in a tiny cell in Texas, the autobiography of Henry Kissinger, the letter of a lover to a lover who is presently angry—is craft.

There is no such a thing as a neutral observer. We chose our subjects, our instruments of measurement, our questions. The social scientists who elect to work with questionnaires that can be evaluated by computers have already decided to ask the kinds of questions that produce the kinds of information computers can evaluate, which means they have found it reasonable to exclude from consideration enormous masses of other information. They have next decided what questions would go on those questionnaires and what kinds of people would be asked those questions and what people would pose the questions and what kinds of operations the computer would perform upon the answers to the questions. They have decided that quantifiable information is valid in ways other information is not. The process, once determined and put into action, may be something like "pure science," but nothing leading up to the process is or can be pure, hence neither is nor can be the product. A sociological fact or conclusion that is statistical may look more true than a sociological fact or conclusion that is verbal, but appearance and truth are not the same thing in sociology any more than they are anywhere else. The truth of numbers depends on the truth of the vision of the person ordering the accounting, just as the truth of words depends on the truth of the vision of the person uttering the words.

The reader of a quantitative sociological or anthropological study is insulated from the world of original information by several layers of personality: the person designing the project (who may or may not be the person gathering and encoding and analyzing the information), the persons providing the information, the abilities of the machines analyzing the information. That is not to say the information from quantitative studies is any the less true because of those several layers; it is only to remind you that it is not any the more true because the results seem to be unambiguous. Numbers in themselves are absolute and unambiguous, but the meaning of numbers is rarely absolute and more rarely unambiguous.

In a qualitative study such as this one you are also insulated from the world of information—but only by two layers of personality. The world of information is how people on death row perceive their experience and how they present it: two sets of information, one contained within the other. You, as reader, have to decide whether the voices they offer present a real vision of that world of the condemned; you cannot argue the presentations of self they offer, for those are no more or less authentic or fictional than any autobiography, and they are facts as is any autobiography. You are further insulated from the immediate information by the woman and man who offer it to you— by Diane Christian and Bruce Jackson, who conducted interviews, who watched and listened, who selected from a great mass of words a smaller mass of words, and who ordered those words in a way that made sense to them. We ask you, as does every author of every work, to trust us, to believe we got it right.

There is no reason you should trust us, and there is no need for you to trust us. Just as the statements of the condemned are themselves facts, this statement by us is itself a fact. It is a carefully scored orchestra of voices, presented to you in a coherent and contained and limited form. For you, it makes sense or doesn't makes sense, elicits passion or moves you not at all, seems valid or doesn't seem valid, exactly as a film or novel or government report or symphony is or is not coherent and sensible and true and moving. You evaluate the statements of the condemned men and our organization of those statements on the basis of whatever information you have available, information that is necessarily limited. But we never have *all* the information about anything; we always judge and understand on the basis of partial information.

It is possible for some quantitative studies to have all the information about some things. That is because quantitative studies can be so limited, so narrow, so trivial, their questions admit no complication, no ambiguity, and finally no meaning. The author's hand disappears in quantitative studies, but it moves the strings nonetheless.

Diane Christian and I several times speak to you in our own voices in *Death Row,* and we ask you to consider voices spoken to us, voices spoken for you. If, as we believe, those voices give you a vision of that spare world achievable in no other way, and if those voices help you understand aspects of the human experience you did not understand so well before, then we will have achieved all any scientist—social or otherwise—might wish.

Bibliography

James H. Johnson's *Doing Field Research* (1975) is a perceptive and sometimes passionate interrogation of the problematic ethical and conspiratorial character of much social science fieldwork. His book deals with field research from the perspective of a sociologist, but his questions can be asked with equal justification of a folklorist, anthropologist, or oral historian undertaking similar inquiries. Equally useful is William Foote Whyte's autobiographical reflection on fieldwork technique and ethics, *Learning from the Field* (1984). Hortense Powdermaker's *Stranger and Friend* (1966) is a fascinating and sensitive autobiographical account by an important anthropologist. The only autobiographical account of fieldwork by an American folklorist is John A. Lomax's *Confessions of a Ballad Hunter* (1947); the Lomax book doesn't provide much detail about the work itself and glosses over a number of real problems. In *Mules and Men* (1935), Zora Neale Hurston offers interesting fictionalized collecting narratives, some of which were based on actual events.

For discussions of ethical and personal questions as they relate to the works of certain well-known fieldworkers, see Robert A. Georges and Michael Owen Jones's *People Studying People* (1980). Edward D. Ives's *Tape-Recorded Interview: A Manual for Field Workers in Folklore and Oral History* (1980) is a readable and useful guide to what is probably the most common fieldwork strategy. It helped me threen years ago when it was a mimeographed pamphlet. I took some practical counsel and several bibliographic leads from it and I recommend it highly.

Adams, Ansel. 1966. *The Negative: Exposure and Development.* Hastings-on-Hudson, N.Y.: Morgan and Morgan.

Adams, Richard N., and Jack J. Preiss, eds. 1960. *Human Organization Research: Field Relations and Techniques.* Homewood, Ill.: Dorsey Press.

Agee, James, and Walker Evans. 1960. *Let Us Now Praise Famous Men.* Boston: Houghton-Mifflin.

297

Allen, Barbara, and William L. Montell. 1981. *From Memory to History: Using Oral Sources in Local Historical Research.* Nashville: American Association for State and Local History.

Almendros, Nestor. 1984. *A Man with a Camera.* Trans. Rachel Phillips Belash. New York: Farrar, Straus, and Giroux.

Baddeley, W. Hugh. 1975. *The Technique of Documentary Film Production.* Rev. ed. London and New York: Focal Press.

Bartis, Peter. 1979. *Folklife and Fieldwork: A Layman's Introduction to Field Techniques.* Washington, D.C.: Publications of the American Folklife Center.

"Batteries." *Consumer Reports* 48, no. 11 (November 1983): 588–92.

Bauman, Richard, and Joel Sherzer, eds. 1974. *Explorations in the Ethnography of Speaking.* London: Cambridge University Press.

Becker, Howard S. 1958. "Problems of Inference and Proof in Participant Observation." *American Sociological Review* 23:652–60.

———. 1968. "Introduction." In *The Jack-Roller,* by Clifford R. Shaw, pp. v–xviii. Chicago: University of Chicago Press.

———, and Blanche Geer. 1957. "Participant Observation and Interviewing: A Comparison." *Human Organization* 16 (3): 28–32.

———, and Blanche Geer. 1960. "Participant Observation: The Analysis of Qualitative Field Data." In Adams and Preiss, 1960, pp. 267–89.

———, Blanche Geer, David Riesman, and Robert S. Weiss, eds. 1968. *Institutions and the Person.* Chicago: Aldine.

Bell, Michael J. 1983. *The World from Brown's Lounge: An Ethnography of Black Middle-Class Play.* Urbana: University of Illinois Press.

Botkin, B. A. 1938. *Supplementary Instructions to the American Guide Manual: Manual for Folklore Studies.* Mimeograph. 18 pp. Washington, D.C.

Bowen, Elenore Smith [Laura Bohannan]. 1964(1954). *Return to Laughter.* New York: Doubleday.

Brewer, J. Mason. 1965. *Worser Days and Better Times.* Chicago: Quadrangle.

Brunvand, Jan Harold. 1971. *A Guide for Collectors of Folklore in Utah.* Salt Lake City: University of Utah Press.

———. 1978. *The Study of American Folklore: An Introduction.* 2d ed. New York: W. W. Norton.

Byington, Robert H. 1978. "Strategies for Collecting Occupational Folklife in Contemporary Urban/Industrial Contexts." In *Working Americans: Contemporary Approaches to Occupational Folklife,* ed. Robert H. Byington, pp. 43–56. Smithsonian Folklore Studies no. 3. Washington, D.C.: Smithsonian Institution. Reprinted from *Western Folklore* 37, no. 3 (1978).

Cage, John. 1961. *Silence: Lectures and Writings.* Cambridge: MIT Press.

Carey, George G. 1970. *Maryland Folklore and Folklife.* Cambridge, Md.: Tidewater Publishers.

Carpenter, Inta Gale, ed. 1978. *Folklorists in the City: The Urban Field Experience. Folklore Forum* 11 (3).

Casagrande, Joseph B. 1960. *In the Company of Man: Twenty Portraits by an Anthropologist.* New York: Harper.

Catlin, George. 1973(1841) *Letters and Notes on the Manners, Customs, and Conditions of the North American Indians.* 2 vols. New York: Dover.

Cavell, Stanley. 1983. "Politics as Opposed to What?" In *The Politics of Interpretation,* ed. W. J. T. Mitchell, pp. 181–202. Chicago: University of Chicago Press.

Charters, Samuel B. 1962. "Some Do's and Don'ts of Field Recording." *Sing Out!* 12 (3): 49–53.

Christian, Diane, and Bruce Jackson. 1982. *Robert Creeley: Willy's Reading.* Buffalo: Documentary Research.

Clarke, Charles G., comp. and ed. 1980. *American Cinematographer Manual.* 5th ed. Hollywood: American Society of Cinematographers.

Clifford, Martin. 1977. *Microphones—How They Work & How to Use Them.* Blue Ridge Summit, Pa.: TAB Books.

Collier, John, Jr. 1967. *Visual Anthropology: Photography As a Research Method.* New York: Holt, Rinehart and Winston.

Cronk, Caspar. 1964. *Songs and Dances of Nepal.* FE 4101. New York: Ethnic Folkways Library.

Darnell, Regna. 1974. "Correlates of Cree Narrative Performance." In Bauman and Sherzer, 1974, pp. 315–36.

Dorson, Richard M. 1957. "Standards for Collecting and Publishing American Folktales." *Journal of American Folklore* 70:53–57.

———. 1964. "Collecting Oral Folklore in the United States." In *Buying the Wind: Regional Folklore in the United States,* pp. 1–20. Chicago: University of Chicago Press.

———. 1967. *American Negro Folktales.* Greenwich, Conn.: Fawcett.

———. 1972. *Folklore and Folklife.* Chicago: University of Chicago Press.

———. 1981. *Land of the Millrats.* Bloomington: Indiana University Press.

———, ed. 1983. *Handbook of American Folklore.* Bloomington: Indiana University Press.

Dundes, Alan. 1981a. *Analytic Essays in Folklore.* The Hague: Mouton.

———. 1981b. "Life Is Like a Chicken Coop Ladder: A Study of German National Character Through Folklore." *Journal of Psychoanalytic Anthropology* 4:265–364.

Edgerton, Robert B., and L. L. Langness. 1974. *Methods and Styles in the Study of Culture.* San Francisco: Chandler and Sharp.

Evans, Walker. 1982. *Walker Evans at Work.* New York: Harper and Row.

Fenton, Alexander. 1967. "An Approach to Folk Life Studies." *Keystone Folklore Quarterly* 12:5–21.

Fischer, Miles Mark. 1963. *Negro Slave Songs in the United States.* New York: Citadel Press.

Fleischhauer, Carl. 1983. "Sound Recording and Still Photography in the Field." In Dorson, 1983, pp. 384–90.

———, and Charles K. Wolfe. 1981. *The Process of Field Research: Final Report on the Blue Ridge Parkway Folklife Project.* Washington, D.C.: American Folklife Center, Library of Congress.

Foster, George M., and Robert V. Kemper, eds. 1974. *Anthropologists in Cities.* Boston: Little, Brown.

Freeman, Derek. 1983. *Margaret Mead and Samoa: The Making and Unmaking of an Anthropological Myth.* Cambridge: Harvard University Press. (*See also* the several articles in Ivan Brady, ed., "Speaking in the Name of the Real: Freeman and Mead on Samoa." *American Anthropologist* 85 [1983]: 908–47.)

Freilich, Morris, ed. 1970. *Marginal Natives: Anthropologists at Work.* New York: Harper and Row

———, ed. 1977. *Marginal Natives at Work: Anthropologists in the Field.* Cambridge, Mass.: Schenkman.

Gans, Herbert. 1968. "The Participant Observer as a Human Being." In Becker et al., 1968, pp. 300–317.

Geertz, Clifford. 1973. *The Interpretation of Cultures.* New York: Basic Books.

Georges, Robert A., and Michael O. Jones. 1980. *People Studying People: The Human Element in Fieldwork.* Berkeley and Los Angeles: University of California Press.

Giarelli, Andrew L. 1984. "Cheyenne Narrative." Ph.D dissertation, State University of New York at Buffalo.

Gifford, F. 1977. *Tape: A Radio News Handbook.* New York: Hastings House.

Golde, Peggy, ed. 1970. *Women in the Field.* Chicago: Aldine.

Goldstein, Kenneth S. 1964. *A Guide for Field Workers in Folklore.* Hatboro, Pa.: Folklore Associates.

Gorden, Raymond. 1975. *Interviewing: Strategy, Techniques and Tactics.* Rev. ed. Homewood, Ill.: Dorsey Press.

Grele, Ronald J., ed. 1975. *Envelopes of Sound: Six Practitioners Discuss the Method, Theory, and Practice of Oral History and Oral Testimony.* Chicago: Precedent.

Grierson, John. 1966. *Grierson on Film.* Berkeley and Los Angeles: University of California Press.

Harris, Joel Chandler. 1886. "An Accidental Author." *Lippincott's Magazine* 37:417–20. Reprinted in Jackson, 1967, pp. 243–46.

Heider, Karl. 1976. *Ethnographic Film.* Austin: University of Texas Press.

Henige, David. 1982. *Oral Historiography.* New York: Longman.

Honoré, Paul M. 1980. *A Handbook of Sound Recording: A Text for Motion Picture and General Sound Recording.* South Brunswick and New York: A. S. Barnes.

Hoopes, James. 1979. *Oral History.* Chapel Hill: University of North Carolina Press.

Horowitz, Irving Louis. 1978(1965). "The Life and Death of Project Camelot." In *Sociological Methods: A Sourcebook.* 2d ed. Norman K. Denzin, ed., pp. 406–21. New York: McGraw-Hill.

Hughes, Everett C. 1960. "Introduction: The Place of Field Work in Social Science." In Junker, 1960, pp. x–xv.

Hurston, Zora Neale. 1935. *Mules and Men.* New York: Lippincott.

Hyatt, Harry Middleton. 1970–78. *Hoodoo, Conjuration, Witchcraft, Rootwork.* 5 vols. Quincy, Ill.: Memoirs of the Alma Egan Hyatt Foundation.

Hymes, Dell. 1981. *"In vain I tried to tell you": Essays in Native American Ethnopoetics.* Philadelphia: University of Pennsylvania Press.

Ives, Edward D. 1964. *Larry Gorman: The Man Who Made the Songs.* Bloomington: Indiana University Press.

———. 1971. *Lawrence Doyle, the Farmer-Poet of Prince Edward Island.* Maine Studies, no. 92. Orono: University Press of Maine.

———. 1978. *Joe Scott, the Woodsman-Songmaker.* Urbana: University of Illinois Press.

———. 1980. *The Tape-Recorded Interview: A Manual for Field Workers in Folklore and Oral History.* Knoxville: University of Tennessee Press.

Jackson, Bruce. 1967. *The Negro and His Folklore in Nineteenth Century Periodicals.* Austin: University of Texas Press.

———. 1969. *A Thief's Primer.* New York Macmillan.

———. 1971. "In the Valley of the Shadows: Kentucky." *TransAction* 8, no. 8 (June): 28–38.

———. 1972a. *Wake Up Dead Man: Afro-American Worksongs from Texas Prisons.* Cambridge: Harvard University Press.

———. 1972b. *In the Life: Versions of the Criminal Experience.* New York: Holt, Rinehart and Winston.

———. 1974. *"Get Your Ass in the Water and Swim Like Me": Narrative Poetry from Black Oral Tradition.* Cambridge: Harvard University Press.

———. 1977. *Killing Time: Life in the Arkansas Penitentiary.* Ithaca: Cornell University Press.

———, dir. 1979. *Death Row.* 16mm film. Buffalo: Documentary Research.

———, ed. 1984. *Teaching Folklore.* Buffalo: Documentary Research.

———. 1985. "Things That From a Long Way Off Look Like Flies." *Journal of American Folklore* 98:131–47.

———, and Diane Christian. 1980. *Death Row.* Boston: Beacon Press.

———, and Michael Jackson. 1983. *Doing Drugs.* New York: St. Martin's.

Jacobs, Louis. 1979. *The Documentary Tradition.* 2d ed. New York: Norton.

Johnson, John M. 1975. *Doing Field Research.* New York: Free Press.

Jones, Michael Owen. 1975. *The Hand Made Object and Its Maker.* Berkeley and Los Angeles: University of California Press.

Junker, Buford H., with introduction by Everett C. Hughes. 1960. *Field Work: An Introduction to the Social Sciences.* Chicago: University of Chicago Press.

Kaplan, Abraham. 1964. *The Conduct of Inquiry.* New York: Chandler.

Keil, Charles. 1979. *Tiv Song: The Sociology of Art in a Classless Society.* Chicago: University of Chicago Press.

Kenworthy, Mary Anne, and Eleanor M. King, Mary Elizabeth Ruwell, and Trudy Van Housten. 1985. *Preserving Field Records: Archival Techniques for Archaeologists and Anthropologists.* Philadelphia: The University Museum, University of Pennsylvania.

Köngäs-Maranda, Elli Kaija. (n.d.) "How the Collector Creates the Artificial Audience." In *Travaux et inédits de Elli Kaija Kongas-Maranda*, pp. 196–205. Cahiers du Celat 1. [Quebec: University of Laval?]

Kotkin, Amy J., and Steven J. Zeitlin. 1983. "In the Family Tradition." In Dorson 1983, pp. 90–99.

Kroeber, A. L. 1900. "Cheyenne Tales." *Journal of American Folklore* 13:161–90.

Kroeber, Karl, and H. David Brumble III. 1983. "Reasoning Together." In Swann, 1983, pp. 344–64.

Kuhn, Thomas. 1970(1962). *The Structure of Scientific Revolutions.* Rev. ed. Chicago: University of Chicago Press.

Langois, William J. 1976. *A Guide to Aural History Research.* Victoria: Aural History Programme, Provincial Archives of British Columbia.

Leach, MacEdward. 1962. "Problems of Collecting Oral Literature." *PMLA* 77:335–40.

———, and Henry Glassie. 1968. *A Guide for Collectors of Oral Traditions and Folk Cultural Material in Pennsylvania.* Harrisburg: Pennsylvania Historical Museum Commission.

Lindahl, Carl, J. Sanford Rikoon, and Elaine J. Lawless. 1979. *A Basic Guide to Fieldwork for Beginning Folklore Students: Techniques of Selection, Collection, Analysis, and Presentation.* 2d ed. Folklore Publications Group Monographs, vol. 7. Bloomington, Ind.: Folklore Institute.

List George. 1960. "Documenting Field Recordings." *Folklore and Folk Music Archivist* 3(3): 2–3.

Lomax, John A. 1947. *Adventures of a Ballad Hunter.* New York: Macmillan.

———, and Alan Lomax. 1936. *Negro Folk Songs as Sung by Lead-Belly.* New York: Macmillan.

MacDonald, Donald A. 1972. "Fieldwork: Collecting Oral Literature." In Dorson, 1972, pp. 407–30.

Malaurie, Jean. 1982. *The Last Kings of Thule.* Trans. Adrienne Foulke. New York: Dutton.

Malinowski, Bronislaw. 1929. *The Sexual Life of Savages in Northwestern Melanesia.* London: Routledge and Kegan Paul.

———. 1935. *Coral Gardens and Their Magic.* 2 vols. New York: American Book Co.

———. 1950(1922). *Argonauts of the Western Pacific.* New York: Dutton.

———. 1954. *Magic, Science, and Religion, and Other Essays.* New York: Doubleday.

———. 1967. *A Diary in the Strict Sense of the Word.* New York: Harcourt.

Mamber, Stephen. 1974. *Cinema Verité in America: Studies in Uncontrolled Documentary.* Cambridge: MIT Press.

Mascelli, Joseph V. 1965. *The Five C's of Cinematography.* Hollywood: Cine/Grafic Publications.

Mead, Margaret. 1933. "More Comprehensive Field Methods." *American Anthropologist* 35:1–15.

——. 1972. *Blackberry Winter: My Earlier Years*. New York: William Morrow.

Merriam, Alan P. 1977. "Musical Change in a Basongye Village (Zaire)." *Anthropos* 72:806–46.

Mills, C. Wright. 1942. "The Professional Ideology of Social Pathologists." *American Journal of Sociology* 49 (September): 165–80.

Moss, William W. 1974. *Oral History Program Manual*. New York: Praeger.

Murdock, G. P. 1950. *Outline of Cultural Materials*. New Haven, Conn.: Human Relations Area Files.

Naroll, Raoul, and Ronald Cohen, ed. 1970. *A Handbook of Method in Cultural Anthropology*. Garden City, N.Y.: Natural History Press.

Nettl, Bruno. 1983. *The Study of Ethnomusicology: Twenty-nine Issues and Concepts*. Urbana: University of Illinois Press.

Nickerson, Bruce E. 1975. "Industrial Lore: A Study of an Urban Factory." Ph.D. dissertation. Indiana University, Bloomington.

——. 1983. "Factory Folklore." In Dorson, 1983, pp. 121–27.

Pelto, P. J. 1970. *Anthropological Research: The Structure of Inquiry*. New York: Harper.

Pincus, Edward, and Steven Ascher. 1984. *The Filmmaker's Handbook*. New York: New American Library.

Polunin, Ivan. 1965. "Stereophonic Magnetic Tape Recorders and the Collection of Ethnographic Field Data." *Current Anthropology* 6:227–30.

——. 1970. "Visual and Sound Recording Apparatus in Ethographic Fieldwork." *Current Anthropology* 11:3–22.

Powdermaker, Hortense. 1966. *Stranger and Friend: The Way of an Anthropologist*. New York: Norton.

Prigogine, Ilya, and Isabelle Stengers. 1984. *Order Out of Chaos*. New York: Bantam.

Radin, Paul. 1933. *The Method and Theory of Ethnology*. New York: McGraw-Hill.

Randolph, Vance. 1982. *Ozark Folksongs*. Norm Cohen, ed. Urbana: University of Illinois Press.

Ritsko, Alan J. 1979. *Lighting for Location Motion Pictures*. New York: Van Nostrand Rheinhold.

Roberts, Leonard. 1983. "A Family's Repertoire." In Dorson, 1983, pp. 100–105.

Rosenberg, Neil. 1976. "Studying Country Music and Contemporary Folk Music Traditions in the Maritimes: Theory, Techniques and the Archivist." *Phonographic Bulletin* 14 (May): 18–21.

——, ed. 1978. *Folklore and Oral History*. Folklore and Language Publication Series, Bibliographical and Special Series no. 3. St. John's: Memorial University of Newfoundland.

Royal Anthropological Institute of Great Britain and Ireland. 1951. *Notes and Queries on Anthropology*. 6th ed. London: Routledge and Kegan Paul.

Rynkiewich, Michael, and James P. Spradley, eds. 1976. *Ethics and Anthropology: Dilemmas in Fieldwork*. New York: Wiley.

Spindler, G. D., ed. 1970. *Being an Anthropologist: Fieldwork in Eleven Cultures.* New York: Holt, Rinehart and Winston.

Spradley, James P. 1979. *The Ethnographic Interview.* New York: Holt, Rinehart and Winston.

———. 1980. *Participant Observation.* New York: Holt, Rinehart and Winston.

———, and David W. McCurdy. 1972. *The Cultural Experience: Ethnography in a Complex Society.* Chicago: Science Research Associates.

Stekert, Ellen C. 1965. "Two Voices of Tradition: The Influence of Personality and Collecting Environment upon the Song of Two Traditional Folksingers." Ph.D. dissertation, University of Pennsylvania.

———, with Mary Dunnewold and Deb Dale Jones. 1985. "A Critique of 'The Crowing Hen and the Easter Bunny: Male Chauvinism in American Folklore,' by Alan Dundes." *Folklore Women's Communications* 37:13–18.

Sturtevant, William C. 1977. *Guide to Collecting Ethnographic Specimens.* 2d ed. Smithsonian Institution Leaflet 503. Washington, D.C.: Smithsonian Institution Press.

Súilleabháin, Seán Ó. (1963). *A Handbook of Irish Folklore.* Reprint. Hatboro, Pa.: Folklore Associates.

Sussman, Aaron. 1973. *The Amateur Photographer's Handbook.* 8th ed. New York: Thomas Y. Crowell.

Swann, Brian, ed. 1983. *Smoothing the Ground: Essays on Native American Oral Literature.* Berkeley and Los Angeles: University of California Press.

Tedlock, Dennis. 1983. *The Spoken Word and the Work of Interpretation.* Philadelphia: University of Pennsylvania Press.

Thomas, Elizabeth Marshall. 1959. *The Harmless People.* New York: Knopf.

Titon, Jeff Todd, gen. ed. 1984. *Worlds of Music: An Introduction to the Music of the World's Peoples.* New York: Schirmer Books.

Tremaine, Howard M. 1982. *The Audio Cyclopedia.* Indianapolis: Howard W. Sams and Co.

Turner, Victor W., and Edward M. Bruner, eds. 1986. *The Anthropology of Experience.* Urbana: University of Illinois Press.

Waserman, Manfred J. 1975. *Bibliography on Oral History.* Rev. ed. Denton, Tex.: Oral History Association.

Wax, Rosalie Hankey. 1960a. "Reciprocity in Field Work." In Adams and Preiss 1960, pp. 90–98. Originally published as "Reciprocity as a Field Technique," *Human Organization* 11, no. 3 (1952): 34–41.

———. 1960b. "Twelve Years Later: An Analysis of Field Experience." In Adams and Preiss, 1960, pp. 166–78.

———. 1971. *Doing Fieldwork: Warnings and Advice.* Chicago: University of Chicago Press.

Webb, Eugene J., Donald T. Campbell, Richard D. Schwartz, and Lee Sechrest. 1966. *Unobtrusive Measures: Nonreactive Research in the Social Sciences.* Chicago: Rand McNally.

Whitehead, Tony Larry, and Mary Ellen Conaway, eds. 1986. *Self, Sex, and Gender in Cross-Cultural Fieldwork.* Urbana: University of Illinois Press.

Whyte, William Foote. 1955(1943). *Street Corner Society: The Social Structure of an Italian Slum.* 2d ed. Chicago: University of Chicago Press.

———. 1960. "Interviewing in Field Research." In Adams and Preiss, 1960, pp. 352–74.

———. 1984. *Learning from the Field: A Guide from Experience.* Beverly Hills: Sage.

Wiggins, William H., Jr. 1983. "The Black Folk Church." In Dorson, 1983, pp. 145–54.

Wilgus, D. K. 1959. *Anglo-American Folksong Scholarship Since 1898.* New Brunswick: Rutgers University Press.

———. 1983. "Collecting Musical Folklore and Folksong." In Dorson, 1983, pp. 369–75.

Williams, Thomas R. 1967. *Field Methods in the Study of Culture.* New York: Holt, Rinehart and Winston.

Worth, Sol, and John Adair. 1973. *Through Navajo Eyes: An Exploration in Film Communication and Anthropology.* Bloomington: Indiana University Press.

Zeitlin, Steven J., Amy J. Kotkin, and Holly Cutting Baker. 1982. *A Celebration of American Family Folklore: Tales and Traditions from the Smithsonian Collection.* New York: Pantheon.

Index